The Leader's Ladder

5 steps to Braver Leadership with Structure and Tough Care

Bengt Savén

BraveShip
wisdom into action

The Leader's Ladder
5 steps to Braver Leadership with Structure and Tough Care

Bengt Savén

ISBN: 978-91-639-1068-5

First English edition, print 2017:1

Original's title: LedarStegen: 5 Steg till Modigare Ledarskap med Struktur och Tuff Omsorg, 2014

Author: **Bengt Savén**

Cover and layout: **Uno Ullvén**

Cover photos: **iStock**

Illustrations: **Martin Gradén**

Publisher: **BraveShip AB, Linköping, Sweden**
www.braveship.com

Printed in cooperation with Bulls Graphics, Halmstad, Sweden

BraveShip
wisdom into action

Foreword by Etsko Schuitema

The Leader's Ladder is one of those unique texts that transcend the distinction between the theoretical and the practical. Based on the extensive experience Bengt Savén has had both of the Lean methodology and of the Care and Growth leadership model, the book provides immensely helpful tools for leaders to produce genuinely and practically enabling environments for their people.

In my consulting experience, I have repeatedly seen that a synthesis of a leadership excellence approach and an operational excellence methodology provides the drivers for an authentic transformation process that delivers engaged employees. In weaving the requirements of the Care and Growth model and the Lean methodology, Bengt has achieved just such a synthesis.

The added advantage that Bengt has is that he developed his insights not only as a consultant, but also as a line leader who was responsible for delivering a business outcome. It is also important to remember that the practical application that Bengt has done has been within the context of aircraft manufacture, which is probably as exacting an environment as it is possible to get. What you have in this text is a methodology which works because it has been tested by its author in a very challenging environment.

It is also important to recognize that this book does not only represent a practical application of a pre-existing theoretical framework. In applying the ideas of the Care and Growth model, for example, Bengt has reworked them into a form which fits his context and hence contributes a unique richness to his handling of the material. This book is therefore not merely a 'how to' investigation. It represents a serious contribution to our thinking about organizations and the human being at work.

Foreword by Bengt Savén

To ...

... you who strive to become a better leader, not just for yourself, but also for the sake of others.

I hope this book will help you to improve your leadership by giving you new insights and tools – so that you can choose to do less of certain things, and more of others.

The idea ...

... I wish to convey is that, by taking small steps, you can develop a better, more sustainable and braver leadership style based on reflection, structure and *Tough Care.*

The steps of the *Leader's Ladder* are designed to support your development as a leader so that, in the end, everyone benefits – you and your subordinates, as well as your customers, business owners and society as a whole.

The gratitude ...

... I wish to express is great. The Leader's Ladder is my synthesis of experiences and insights gathered from many people. Two of them stand out. One is my friend and mentor Etsko Schuitema, whose wisdom and unique leadership model (the Care and Growth Model) have inspired many parts of this book. The other is my friend Tor Berggrund, who has been my sparring partner during the years of writing. A heartfelt thank you to both of you for your friendship and for sharing your insights.

I also want to thank all colleagues, from all corners of the world, with whom I have had the pleasure of discussing leadership, especially those who read and commented on the first manuscript, like my former boss in Australia, David Cleland (then CEO for ABB Motors' plant in Melbourne).

Furthermore, my sincerest gratitude goes to Signe Savén (coordinator), Esma Anderson (editing), Uno Ullvén (layout) and Martin Gradén (illustrations) who helped me to make a book out of my text and sketches. And last but not least, to my wife Marie: Thanks for all your support!

My thoughts ...

... also go to my own fumbling leadership as a 28-year-old manager of a small team, most of whom were more than twice my age and, to a year later, when I took over the lead of a larger team, which included their former boss who wanted to keep his old position. I wish I could then have had a clearer understanding of how to be a good leader.

Despite my many opportunities to practice, complemented by various leadership courses, it took me a long time to formulate a holistic understanding of what leadership really is about – the model that I have tried to convey in this book. At times I came very close to giving up the writing. My biggest motivation to continue was my desire to share my many years of privileged experience, from different settings around the world, with you who now facc thc samc challenges I once did.

Your leadership may be more important than you realize. It provokes thoughts and emotions in the people around you. It has the potential to create team spirit, joy, motivation and growth. Therefore, I sincerely hope that this book, with its three fundamental models (the Leader Contribution Model, the Collaboration Tree and the Leader's Ladder), can become your handbook, in developing a leadership style that goes beyond ordinary management – to benefit not only you, but all the people affected by your way of leading.

Content in brief

Content in detail

Introduction

Leadership

A common definition of leadership is: "Leadership is to create good results through other people." However, this definition might lead us in the wrong direction. The phrase "through other people" creates the impression that we will exploit the other.

If we want to use other people, we can do it by buying, intimidating or manipulating them. None of these three strategies actually have anything to do with leadership. They are neither good for your leadership, nor for the long term result of the collaboration you aim to lead. Bought people lack the willingness to put in any extra effort (without extra pay); intimidated people don't dare to do the extra; and manipulated people will eventually notice it and resist by doing as little as possible.

It is much better to base one's leadership on caring for others. If you demonstrate an unselfish desire to create good collaboration, and expect the same from others, you will create an energy and attitude that will radiate to the people around you.

Leadership is important. Just look at the difference that Nelson Mandela made in South Africa. When I read how he described his childhood in his book, *Long Walk to Freedom*, and how he was guided and inspired by adult role models, it reinforced my belief that we all have the potential to become good leaders.

Very few people are born as good leaders, nor do they become so by merely doing a course. You can, however, develop your leadership abilities by taking several small steps.

Great leaders are not only to be found in politics; they are also present in our everyday lives. For example, we all know how important the leadership of parents and teachers are. And let's not forget the manager at work! A lousy boss can destroy everyone's day. A good leader, however, can lead others to great achievements and growth.

While management is defined top-down, leadership is determined bottom-up. People are assigned to managers, but leaders earn their followers.

You are appointed to be a manager by your manager. That position gives you formal decision-making power over others within a certain framework. If you are chosen as a leader by individuals, they voluntarily give you the power to guide them and make decisions about important issues that affect them. Without followers who have given up some of their own decision-making power, there are no leaders.

In this context, power means having the ability to take decisions that will be executed. As a manager, you have been given the formal power to influence people's behavior. As a trusted leader, you complement that assigned power with legitimate power, which is based on the trust that your followers have placed in you. The combination of the two gives you great power, and great responsibility, to influence people's lives and shape your organization's future.

Brave and unselfish leaders dare to do what they deem, in the long term, to be for the greater good of everyone, even when it may not be in their own immediate best interest. In the short term, it's often more pleasant to be a coward – it often requires less work and comes with fewer risks, for example possibly losing face or one's position.

However, in the long term, the braver and more unselfish leader is rewarded with higher self-esteem, more respect and better results. Managers who solely focus on the next financial report might be appreciated by some impatient investors, but they will never become great leaders.

Professor Oren Lyons, stresses this when he quotes the leadership teachings of his ancient ancestor, known as The Peacemaker:[1]

"When you sit and you counsel for the welfare of the people, think neither of yourself, nor of your family, nor even your generation. Make your decisions on behalf of the seventh generation coming. Those faces looking up from the earth; layer upon layer, waiting their time. Defend them, protect them, they're helpless; they're in your hands. That's your duty, your responsibility. You do that, you yourself will have peace."

1. Professor Oren Lyons is Chief and Faithkeeper of the Onondaga Native American Nation. His ancestor, The Peacemaker, united and founded the Six Nations in North America.

It is challenging to always wear the "big hat" (taking the holistic and sustainable long-term perspective) that Lyons is talking about. However, we all have that big hat in our wardrobe that we can take out and wear more often. But that requires some unselfishness, and often a bit of courage. The *braver leader* will be prepared to sacrifice narrow, short-term goals for more important holistic, long-term ones.

My sources of inspiration

Many years in managerial positions, on different levels and in different organizations, have given me personal experience of what is important in leadership. Teaching and researching leadership has also given me the opportunity to learn from others' experiences and research findings. The two sources that have inspired me the most are the Care and Growth Model and the leadership in organizations that have really succeeded with Lean and Agile ways of working.

The Care and Growth Model is a leadership model developed by Etsko Schuitema. It is inspired by the findings from a research study of the mining industry in South Africa. The researchers were studying 37 different mine shafts over a period of eight years and conducted close to 10 000 interviews. To their surprise, they found very big differences both in the financial results and the level of trust the miners had in their managers. The researchers tested many hypotheses for the causes of these differences. One after the other suggested explanation had to be dismissed, for example, the effects of the working environment, salary levels, and support from HR or the unions. In the end, there was only one hypothesis left, namely the quality of the miner's relationship with his boss.

The most important factor in this regard was shown to be how the boss handled complaints and suggestions for improvements. The researchers also found that there was a clear connection between the financial results of the mines, and the perception of how much management cared for the miners.

The study led to the development of the Care and Growth Model that highlights the importance of caring for subordinates, as well as expecting them to be accountable and grow. The model rests on four axioms. The first one states that leadership is about legitimate relationships of power, rather than the buying of labor. According to the second axiom, a relationship of power is legitimate if the aim is to empower the subordinate. The third axiom stresses that a leader must be prepared to incrementally suspend their level of control, and the fourth says that maturity is about being here to give, acting with generosity and courage.

The Care and Growth Model focuses on how the leader relates to each individual. It stresses both the need for authentic care for each subordinate, and for holding them accountable when both means and ability are present.

During the years that I served as the deputy CEO of a South African company, I engaged Etsko's support in my task of developing the leadership of more than 70 managers. It was a privilege to take on that challenge together with him, and we had many rewarding discussions ranging from the core of leadership to appropriate actions in everyday situations. These dialogues have given me several new insights that have inspired important concepts in this book, for example what I call *contribution management* in chapter 3, and the leadership values presented in chapter 10.

My other major source of inspiration was Lean – a label assigned to a combination of values, principles, methods and tools with the combined purpose to efficiently deliver, improve and learn. The main characteristics of Lean are the strive to work-flow effectiveness through process and systematic improvement.

Process improvement is about reducing waste in value-creation flows. Process improvement focuses on the objects, that is, what absorbs the value (e.g. cars, patients, errands or tasks), rather than on the resources that create the value added (e.g. workers, clerks, machines or tools). It is about creating customer value, in time and with minimal waste.

It has been shown that a process (or flow) perspective offers several advantages over the traditional resource perspective. Contrary to what most people believe, it was shown possible to combine a fast and reliable flow with the efficient use of resources. This is achieved by avoiding unnecessary handovers and restarts, as well as by systematically making improvements of the process.

Systematic improvement is about creating supporting structures and abilities, so that everyone continuously is involved in detecting problems early and solving their root cause. However, systematic improvement is not only about solving today's problems; it is also about challenging yourself to close knowledge gaps in order to reach new levels of collaboration.

Organizations that have been successful based on Lean strategies are also characterized by long-term responsibility to both society and customers, as well as by a systems view of its operations – where all parts of the system cooperate to reach common goals.

One frequent mistake is to limit Lean to only highly repetitive mass production.[2] However, not all Lean endeavors are successful. The most typical reason why Lean ventures fail is the combination of overemphasizing the tools and underemphasizing the leadership.

Successful Lean is heavily dependent on good leadership. Senior managers have the tendency to delegate Lean efforts – very often under the misconception that it is a time-limited project, and that it requires better behavior solely from their subordinates and not also from themselves. The major benefits of Lean are therefore not realized, meaning they will miss the opportunity of getting the whole organization to cooperate based upon common values, principles and ways of working.

Without good leadership a Lean endeavor can easily become an afterthought, with only very limited and localized improvements. Combining true Lean with skilled leadership, however, develops outstanding organizations, not only in terms of financial results, but also when it comes to the creation of better customer value and more meaningful jobs.[3]

A successful Lean strategy is not only dependent on good leadership – it can also become the drive for leadership development. I have seen how managers, as they develop a deeper understanding of Lean principles and the use of Lean tools, have become increasingly better leaders.

Jim Collins' book, *Good to Great*, was another source inspiration. His book is based on thorough research of successful companies in an effort to understand how outstanding companies managed to make the transformation from good to great, and stay there.[4] Unexpectedly, and almost reluctantly, the researchers found that the crucial ingredient all the great companies had in common was a certain type of leaders, which they called "level 5 leaders". Collins states:

2. Repetitive short work cycles require predictable, and somewhat stable, demand. The ability to adapt to the environment, sometimes labeled "Agile", is viewed by some as the opposite of Lean. My view on Lean (in line with what is sometimes called true or real Lean – e.g. see *Real Lean* by Bob Emiliani) is, however, that it incorporates the ability to adapt and respond quickly to outside changes, to a great extent through teamwork, a focus on learning from experiments, and tools used with a high frequency (pulse). Thus a Lean strategy makes good use of Agile thinking and tools. Nevertheless, it is often a good strategy to try to make the working environment as stable as possible, e.g. by trying to smooth customer demand and reducing disturbances as far as possible. After all, it is always beneficial to increase *both* the ability to create a stable predictability *and* the ability to deal efficiently with variations.

3. One example of what can be achieved with the combination of Lean practices and good leadership comes from the DeLaval industry outside Stockholm. During their first five-year period devoted to Lean they reduced injuries by 75%, quality costs by 70%, and inventory by 65% in their Tumba operations. At the same time they increased delivery performance from 80 to 99% and total productivity by 60%. Similar examples can be found in a wide range of industries, but also in health care, municipalities and other service organizations.

4. Jim Collin's research team studied companies that managed to create outstanding results over long periods of time (only 11 out of 1 435 organizations managed to reach the criteria of more than three times a profitability index during a minimum of 15 years). They compared each of these eleven great companies with a similar company in the same line of business – companies that had not been able to reach equally good, lasting results.

"Good-to-great transformations don't happen without level 5 leaders at the helm. They just don't." He continues to conclude that this type of leader has managed to combine contradictory features: "Level 5 leaders are a study in duality: modest and willful, humble and fearless."

This combination of great leadership qualities can be found in other outstanding leaders, for example Nelson Mandela, and their importance is also evident in both Lean and the Care and Growth Model. What makes the similarities even more interesting is the fact that the qualities were found in different countries and on different continents of the globe (North America, Japan and South Africa), without any direct influence on each other.

These similarities indicate that there is a common core of good leadership, irrespective of place and culture. I summarize this core in three statements:

- **A good leader is a *humble* person who respects other people.**
- **A good leader is a *willful* person with a passion to achieve a vision through collaboration.**
- **A good leader is an *unselfish* person who cares about their subordinates and supports their growth.**

The retired manager Sumida Toshinobu, whom I had the pleasure of meeting during one of my visits to Japan, expressed this in another way: "The leader's task is to support society, create enthusiasm and deliver something good. It is also important to give back as much as possible to the subordinates. Companies with managers who only think of themselves do not last long."

The messages from my main sources of inspiration are remarkably similar, but yet with some differences. For example, the Care and Growth Model emphasizes the individual working contribution before the result, while in Lean it is the common working standard, the method, which is in focus. Both of these messages can be provoking to the manager who was taught that pure financial control is the core of leadership.

While some messages in this book might be provoking as they break away from what we have been taught, others might be regarded as mere common sense. However, common sense is often worth highlighting – so that is not forgotten. The 18th century French philosopher Voltaire famously said: "Common sense is not so common."

Thus, stop once in a while – both to learn from new experiences and to allow your own common sense (what you already know deep inside) to surface.

1. A great leader

“To lead and motivate people is the most differentiating, and hard to copy, trait for creating competitive advantage.”
– Unknown

Great leadership is not easy – but it is important, and possible to learn. This book contains concepts and tools for developing such leadership. Its purpose is to give you a clearer vision, as well as a new structure, for your future leadership. It also provides you with a set of powerful tools to step by step practice and improve your leadership.

Allow the process to take its time. There is a lot of truth in the words of the former German Chancellor Helmut Schmidt: “To reach a distant goal you have to take many small steps.”

This first chapter highlights the core of great leadership and presents the terminology that will form the golden thread that runs through the rest of the book. The chapter contains:

- **Leadership for collaboration**
- **A great leader**
  - Shows Tough Care with Courage
  - Builds structure
  - Looks for contribution before results
  - Makes the three leader contributions
- **Keywords**

1.1 Leadership for collaboration

Leadership in working life is about creating collaboration. When collaboration is really good, no-one stagnates – on the contrary, every individual will grow and contribute more, and in better ways, to the common good. Great leadership is about, little by little, creating such collaboration.

My starting point is that the aim of leadership is to facilitate better cooperation, with the aim to *deliver, improve* and *learn*. In this context, "deliver" means to produce results for the organization and value for its stakeholders, not least for its customers. "Improve" means to develop the *organization's ability* to create value in an effective way. "Learn" means the growth of each *individual's ability* – both as a coworker and, in more general terms, as a human being. I chose to illustrate this type of good collaboration as a tree, see figure 1.

The crown of the tree

The Collaboration Tree describes how we cooperate to create value for ourselves and for others. The value we create is illustrated by the crown of the tree – with four fruits, each apple representing the value for each main stakeholder group of the organization: customers, employees, owners and broader society.

The branches of the tree

The three goals of collaboration are to deliver value to the stakeholders, to improve the effectiveness of the organization and to guide each individual's growth. This is symbolized by the three branches of the tree.

The trunk of the tree

The three necessary conditions for good collaboration are *means, ability* and *attitude* – *MAA* in short. Having the ability to perform the required tasks is not enough. One also needs the means, for example equipment, tools, structures and information. In addition, everyone's attitude, especially the willingness to contribute, is essential to succeed.

The roots of the tree

A tree needs good roots if it is to grow big and sturdy. In an organization this corresponds to a strong set of common values that underpin and inform goals and behavior. Respect for people and the environment, as well as everybody's intent to contribute, are good starting points for a value base for successful collaboration.

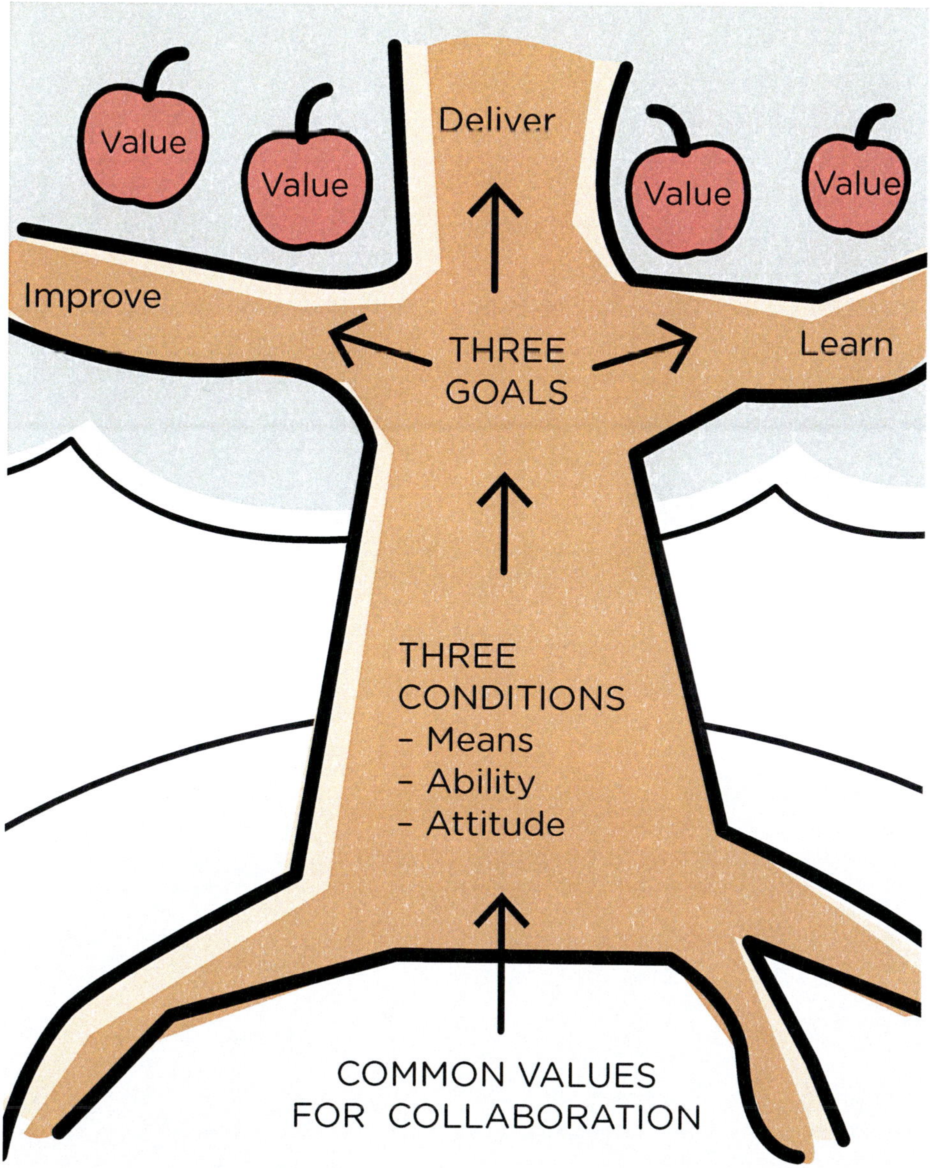

Figure 1 The Collaboration Tree
... a metaphor for good collaboration.

1.2 A great leader…

From the Collaboration Tree, combined with my own experiences and sources of inspiration, I deduce four pillars for great leadership:

- **A great leader shows *Tough Care with Courage.***
- **A great leader builds *structure.***
- **A great leader looks for *contribution* before results.**
- **A great leader makes *the three leader contributions.***

Even if leadership behavior has to be adapted to both the situation and the person, these pillars are the foundation for good leadership. The rest of this chapter explains the pillars and the terms that will be used as the backbone of this book.

…shows Tough Care with Courage

A great leader possess a strong, and largely unselfish, will to create excellent results while, at the same time, caring for the people involved. They succeed in transmitting that will to their followers.

This drive can be translated to legitimate hard expressions, for example, uncompromising demands. I summarize it with the term *Tough*. High expectations and demands are positive for collaboration – if they are realistic and combined with a helpful spirit of cooperation and the opportunity to influence the work situation.

The soft side of leadership is about caring for each individual with holistic and individual considerations and support. This is summarized with the term *Care*.

A leader who acts with *Tough Care* strives for the greater good of all coworkers. This includes challenging them to grow and to be accountable for their own contributions.

Tough Care means a balance of hard and soft expressions, adapted to each individual. Coworkers who already have the desire to contribute their best seldom need hard demands from the leader, but rather challenging tasks with the guidance needed to be able to take the next step.

Lastly, the leader must dare to translate Tough Care into action. This means doing and expressing what is holistically and sustainably the most advantageous for the common good of all, even when it is unpleasant or risky. I summarize this with the term *Courage*.

Combined as *Tough Care with Courage*, it is a shorthand version of a value base for great leadership.

... builds structure

A great leader coordinates the work of creating a structure for the team in order for them to *deliver*, *improve* and *learn*. The structure provides support for connecting the parts and coordinating everyone's contribution to the working whole – a complete system for excellent collaboration. Targets, rules, workflow standards, methods and tools are all examples of essential parts forming the structure.

Good structure does not negate flexibility. On the contrary, a proper structure can support the combination of stability and agility. It provides the base for effective operational control built around target-setting and work-standard improvement. It can also be used to guide market analysis, strategy formulation, root-cause analysis, experimenting with new ideas and many, many more tasks.

Furthermore, structure can be used for leadership support. The tools described in appendices A-C are examples of elements of such a structure. By improving your structure you can avoid the jerky, reactive kind of management style that happens when your actions are mainly based on reacting to events that have already occurred.

However, a prerequisite is, of course, that the structure is used. As a leader, you should not only take the lead in creating a suitable structure, but also ensure that it is followed and improved with appropriate discipline.

... looks for contribution before results

A great leader is interested in the work itself. They look more at the process and the contributions than at the results.

It is not uncommon for managers to direct more of their interest upwards, to the boss's opinion, rather than downwards, to the needs of their subordinates. A real leader focuses on helping every coworker to deliver and grow by, for example, challenging, supporting and removing obstacles.

After all, the result depends on the sum of all contributions. Better and better contribution from everyone is the only sustainable way to get better results.

A great leader is very interested in *how* the work is carried out, without interfering with too much control. They give freedom within a certain framework, and expect their subordinates to take on more and more accountability for effective, stable and constantly improving ways of working.

Excellent collaboration occurs when you replace control from the top with framework management – that means providing the framework and structures needed. It calls for trust, and it calls for support.

The individuals' contributions, supported by the agreed common ways of working, determine the results. Better ways of working (how) create better output (what) with higher customer value. This is valid irrespective of the type of work done, for example, whether it is in product development (specifying the output) or in production (delivering the specified goods or services to customers).

The crucial combination of *what* and *how* can be remembered by the phrase: *The right output the right way.* You implement that phrase by having the team focus on customer value, while you focus your leadership on each subordinate's work contribution. It is by jointly improving both the *what* and the *how* that you create the best value.

... makes the three leader contributions

A great leader makes three types of contributions, one for each of the necessary conditions for good collaboration, that is, means, ability and attitude – MAA. The three types of *leader contributions* are made to subordinates to enable them to succeed in their daily work.

As the leader you cannot do all the work needed to secure good conditions, but you have the responsibility to lead the work to strengthen all three of them. You need to make your best possible leader contributions to help your subordinates to give their best work contributions, meeting today's and tomorrow's demand. The best way to do that is captured by the five leader steps of *the Leader's Ladder.*

1.3 Keywords

Listed below are short definitions of the central terms used throughout this book:

The three conditions for good collaboration are *means, ability* and *attitude*. These conditions, abbreviated as MAA, are essential for a working whole – that is, for a well-functioning system of collaboration.

Means are the common resources and the structure needed for the collaboration to work efficiently, that is everything needed for the value creation, except what the individuals bring with them to work in the form of ability and attitude.

Ability is the individual's proficiency at converting their knowledge and experience into action in a specific context, such as to perform a certain task or to cooperate with colleagues.

Attitude is a person's intent to contribute to the collaboration. An individual's attitude mirrors their willingness to be held accountable for their work contributions (to deliver, improve and learn). Note that there is a risk of misinterpreting a subordinate's attitude, for instance when there are hidden circumstances which might affect their behavior.

A *leader contribution* is a leader action – what you do, say or in another way express – that strengthens at least one of the three collaboration conditions of means, ability or attitude (MAA).

A *work contribution* is a coworker action – what they do, say or in another way express – that favors the three goals of collaboration, namely to deliver, to improve or to learn. Work contributions are always dependent on, and have often an effect on, means, abilities and attitudes (MAA).

Contribution management is a management style in which the leader concentrates on the individual's work contribution in order improve means, abilities and attitudes (MAA).

The base level is the expectation of *what* should be accomplished through the work (e.g. expressed as requirements of products or performance indicators) and *how* it should be accomplished (e.g. expressed as a working standard) that you can compare your work effort to.

Tough Care summarizes both the soft and hard aspects of the leader's care for their subordinates. The hard side is typically expressed as clear expectations of work contributions or as clear and honest feedback, including confrontation if there is a possible lack of attitude. The soft side is typically expressed as real listening, compassion and support.

Braver leadership is to have the courage to make the appropriate leader contribution that the situation requires, and to do more of it, more often. As a braver leader, you dare to more often challenge your boss, your colleagues and your subordinates when it is for the greater good of the long-term collaboration. This, however, requires you to have founded your own leader values well enough so that you can act based on them even when you potentially put yourself at risk.

To anchor means to clarify, understand and internalize the mission, tasks and goals through reflection and good discussions.

A *good discussion* is characterized by everyone involved being fully engaged in listening, talking and trying to understand an important subject, in order to better deliver, improve and learn. Good discussions can actively be designed to be short and with the required frequency, or *pulse*, needed for a specific subject. This can be secured with the support of a proper *structure*.

2. The Leader's Ladder:
an overview

"Begin with the end in mind."
– Stephen Covey

The Leader's Ladder is a model of great leadership, with the purpose of supporting your growth as a leader. In line with the Stephen Covey quotation above, the model starts out with the end in mind, that is, to create personal growth and excellent collaboration – improving stakeholder value as depicted by the crown of the Collaboration Tree.

The Leader's Ladder highlights the things that a great leader needs to prioritize. It does so by distinguishing five crucial steps of leadership behavior. The chapter starts with a short description of the ladder and ends with an explanation of the connections between the steps. It contains the sections:

- **Five steps to leader contributions**
- **Five steps that complement each other**

2.1 Five steps to leader contributions

Great leadership rests on the ability to create the three conditions for collaboration – to build *means*, *ability* and *attitude* – MAA. But, *how* do you do it? The simple answer is: Through climbing the five steps of the Leader's Ladder.

1. ***Anchor*** **both own and common tasks and goals.**
2. ***Visualize*** **the system, the expectations and the gaps.**
3. ***See*** **the person, the game and the root cause.**
4. ***Challenge the individual*** **to grow and be accountable.**
5. ***Build team, flow and structure*** **– with pulse.**

Figure 2 illustrates the five steps of the Leader's Ladder. These steps answer the question of how you can become a great leader. All five the steps contribute to build means, ability and attitude. This connects all the five MAA contributions steps in figure 2 directly to the trunk of the Collaboration Tree from figure 1.

Furthermore, there are other links between the Leader's Ladder and the Collaboration Tree. The bottom step of the ladder links to the value base represented by the roots of the tree. And all the steps relate to the three branches of the tree, as they all contribute to *deliver* value to all stakeholders of the organization, to *improve* the collaboration, and to make it possible for all involved to *learn* and grow as individuals.

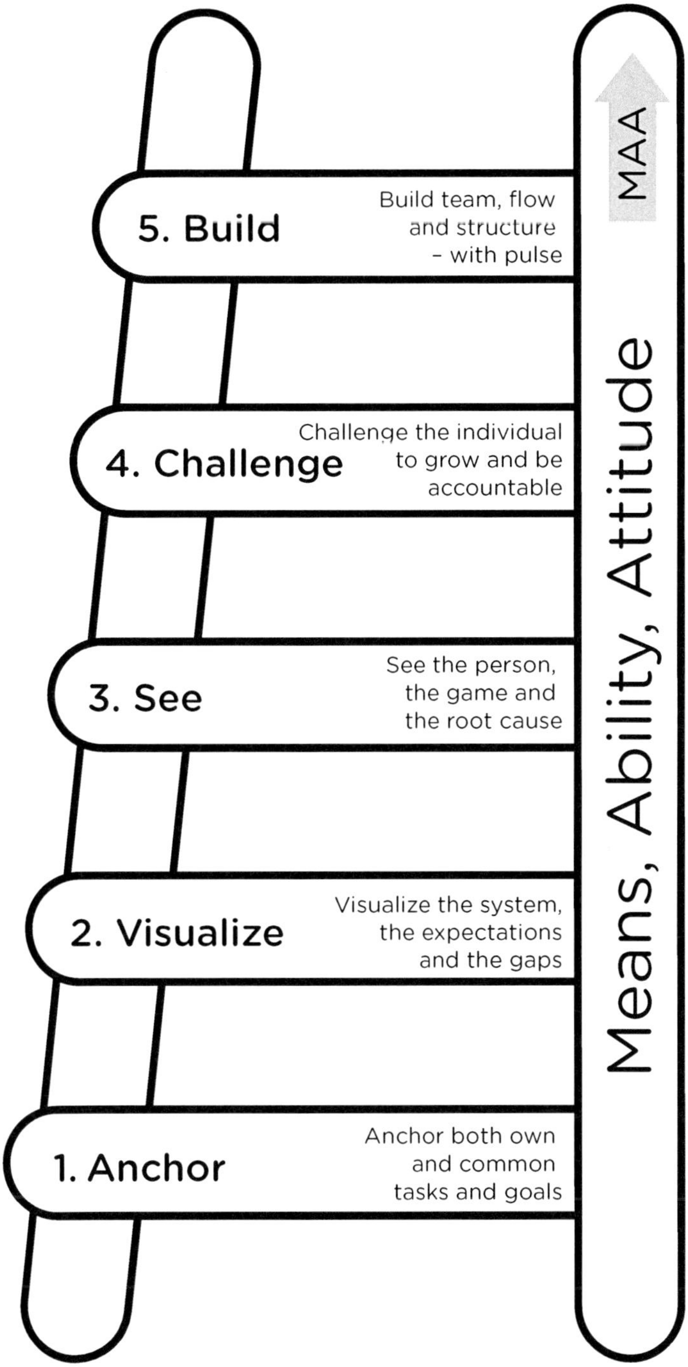

Figure 2 The Leader's Ladder
... with the five steps to better leader contributions.

Step 1: Anchor

To *anchor* means to increase the understanding of the fundamentals of the collaboration, especially the main tasks and goals. Anchoring is primarily achieved through good discussions and inner reflection. An understanding of the tasks and goals forms the base for securing an attitude of willingness to contribute – both for yourself and your subordinates. Anchoring is also the base for knowing which means and abilities are needed for future value creation. When anchoring both yourself and your team, you need facts, openness and time for reflection.

Step 2: Visualize

To *visualize* means making the most important information clear to everyone involved. That includes facts on the present situation, as well as the expectations for the future. The difference between the expectation and the actual situation, that is, the deviation or gap, can be utilized both for daily control of delivery, and for the long-term improvement work. If everyone can see today's position relative to the expected, the attitude of willingness to contribute is strengthened. However, in order for what is visualized to be translated into appropriate action, only the most important information must he highlighted, constantly updated and used for good discussions.

Step 3: See

To *see* includes seeing the real root causes of successes and problems. However, to see is especially about taking time to really notice each coworker and their work contributions. It is important for every human being to be seen; it increases our feeling of belonging and our willingness to contribute. To see a subordinate's work also increases the leader's ability to understand how means and abilities can be strengthened. This, however, requires the leader's presence – both physically and mentally.

Step 4: Challenge the individual

To *challenge the individual* means expecting every individual to contribute and be accountable. It also includes giving them both clear feedback and the support they require. The expectations usually have to be adopted individually and need to result in firm commitments in terms of accountability. Such a commitment manifests the intent to contribute – for example to expedite delivery to a customer on time, improve a part in the system or learn something new. Both clear expectations and clear feedback about work contributions are fundamental in challenging a subordinate in a balanced and fair way.

Step 5: Build team, flow and structure

To *build team, flow and structure* means creating team spirit, efficient work processes and a supporting structure of methods and tools. When a work group starts to function as a team, you can start to challenge the team itself – not only each individual. A team spirit expressed as "one for all and all for one" has a huge impact on the attitude of collaboration. It enables a shared commitment from the team to deliver, improve and learn. A supporting structure that gives stability as well as freedom is essential both for building team spirit and creating efficient work flows. Such a structure should be adhered to in a disciplined way, but at the same time, be open to easily be improved upon by the people involved.

2.2 Five steps that complement each other

The Leader's Ladder is a model for leadership development, and is meant to be an everyday support – not a symbol of something you just climb once. The five steps must be climbed repeatedly, and often in parallel. There is, however, a logical sequence that should prevent you from skipping one of the steps.

Step 1 → 2: from anchoring to visualizing

Without a good understanding of tasks and goals, it is impossible to visualize the right information.

Step 2 → 3: from visualizing to seeing

Without clear expectations, it is difficult to see and evaluate work contributions, and without visible deviations, there is no point of reference for the detection of problems and their root causes.

Step 3 → 4: from seeing to challenging

Without seeing each individual and their contribution, it is very hard to give relevant feedback and to challenge them to the next level of growth.

Step 4 → 5: from challenging to building

Without everyone being accountable to contribute to the common good, it is unlikely that a good team spirit, effective flows and supporting structures can be successfully improved and maintained.

Step 5 → 1: from building and back to anchoring

With good team spirit, effective flows and supporting structures come the opportunity to raise the bar and take on new tasks and goals.

The five steps together aim at providing you with the ladder's handrail (illustrated as the right part of the ladder) to improve the three necessary collaboration conditions (MAA) – that is, to strengthen the common means of your system, as well as the ability and attitude of every individual.

3. **Anchor** both own and common tasks and goals

> *“If you don’t know where you are going, you will probably end up somewhere else.”*
> *– Laurence Peter*

If you do not know why you want to lead, it is impossible to decide what to do as a leader and, even more so, how to do it. Anchoring here means the work of thoroughly discussing, understanding and internalizing the most important tasks and goals. It is important for everyone in the organization. Hence, the first step of the Leader’s Ladder, to *anchor*, is about both anchoring tasks and goals yourself and doing it together with your subordinates. The chapter includes the following parts:

- **Anchor your own drive and leadership goals**
- **Anchor in the Leader Contribution Model**
- **Anchor in mission, vision and targets**

3.1 Anchor your own drive and leadership goals

“It is amazing what you can accomplish if you do not care who gets the credit.”
–Harry S Truman

To be generous with whom gets the credit, as Truman suggests, is just one example of how important generosity is for great leadership. It is only when we are prepared to give more than we are assured to get back that really good collaboration can happen. Such unselfish generosity is an important characteristic that the majority of us require from the person we want to follow. But what other qualities are we looking for in a leader?

The dream boss

Put the two following questions to yourself: “Who do I admire the most?” and “What character traits should the person have that I really want to work for?”

Your honest answers will form the base for your own development as a leader. Meditate over your response. Are there any similarities between the person you admire the most and the person you would like to follow? If that's the case, which characteristics or behavior do they have in common?

Is it partly about humility, respect, care and generous support? Does it also include honesty, clarity and the drive to reach meaningful goals? In that case, you are not alone. The answers to what characterizes a person you are really prepared to follow typically include the above qualities, and more. The wish list can roughly be divided into two groups: soft and hard characteristics.[5] A great leader has the courage and the ability to find the right balance between the soft and hard in all the situations they face. I call this balance Tough Care.

Most hard expressions of Tough Care are driven by the need to balance the best interests of many stakeholders, that is, customers, colleagues, owners and the broader society, including the environment. However, remember that being legitimately tough with an individual is also about caring for them, giving them the chance to grow.

5. Etsko Schuitema's consultants have put the second question to many people in different countries. Their answers show that the typical list of soft qualities (designated by Schuitema as “care”) includes: being approachable, listens, being understanding, being trustworthy, having a sense of humor, being supportive and having your best interests at heart. A typical list of hard qualities (designated as “growth”) includes: being honest, being fair, having a vision, giving direction, being knowledgeable, having integrity, being decisive and giving feedback.

Tough leader actions are characterized by firm standpoints on for example targets, the choice of the way forward or the need to confront a lack of attitude. To be able to do that properly, you need to not only have the required knowledge, but you also need to be steadily anchored in your value base. In addition, you often need courage to act according to those values.

The term Tough Care summarizes the answer to the question of who most of us would really like to follow. Tough Care stresses the leader's ability to be "both ... and ...", for example being both person and task oriented; being both understanding and firm on demands; being both straightforward and the custodian of a good atmosphere; of creating both security and challenges; of both giving freedom and demanding discipline.

Is this in line with the type of leader you want to be?

Four stakeholders and your motives to lead

Now, ask yourself another question: "Why do I want to be the boss?"

Is your answer more about yourself than about others? If so, you are still more of a manager and less of a leader. Is your answer about creating value for other people? If so, you have a good base for your leadership.

"Respect for people" is often put forward as the most important element of a value base for collaboration. In its widest sense, it means to respect all the stakeholders' legitimate interests in the organization.[6] It implies that, as a leader, you cannot only prioritize the goals of the owners, but should also work to increase value (given cost limitations) for your customers and make it possible for your subordinates to earn a living, enjoy a secure working environment and grow their abilities. Furthermore, you have a responsibility to society – not only to follow the law, but also to devise value-creating opportunities, to contribute to the common good through taxes (both directly and indirectly), as well ensuring ecological sustainability.

While there are managers who seem to care solely about their own careers and deliver in line with the latest wishes of their superiors, there are others who only seem to care about being liked by their subordinates. You become less of a leader not only if you are too egoistical, but also by placing too much focus on just one stakeholder. Read the following quotes and consider which stakeholder group(s) the people involved seem to have forgotten.

6. The four key stakeholder groups are the people within your organization, your customers, the business owners and broader society. In the public sector, the term "owner" corresponds to the principal authority. The term "broader society", or just "society", includes the rest of the environment that is affected by your organization.

Employee at a care home:

"I quickly learnt that doing a good job was all about following routines and making it easier for my colleagues. I would put one of the old ladies in bed early, regardless of whether she wanted to see her favorite TV show, just to make it easier for my colleagues on the night shift."

Site manager of a bus company (after solving the so-called problem of too many passengers, by devising an alternate route with fewer stops and fewer passengers):

"It was the only way we could speed up that line. We had to stick to the turn-around times."

Radio reporter:

"Having people feeling good is not a goal in itself in a profit-driven organization."

Company executive:

"It is profitable to invest in employees' health and working environment."

Yet another example comes from a big corporation that was caught paying large amounts of money to corrupt officials through questionable agents in order to gain entry into a new market. When first questioned by journalists, the CEO justified it by saying that the investment will pay off. The next time their behavior was questioned, he told the media that the deal was not illegal.

People also use similar motivations for why we should not discriminate against people based on gender, race, disability, age, etcetera. Some would say diversity is more profitable, while others maintain that it's illegal to discriminate. I say: Not to discriminate, bribe or exploit people is not primarily a question about economy or law – it is primarily a question of ethics, of being human.

If, as the leader, you give exaggerated attention to one of the stakeholders while neglecting some others, you are limiting the organization's ability to create long-term value. So don't forget any of the four major stakeholder groups. Without satisfying the interests of the business *owners* and the *customers*, the organization will cease to exist. Without working towards the greater good for *society* as a whole, you will risk not only breaking the laws, but also lose the meaning of contributing to something larger. In addition, if you don't care for the *people* in your organization, you will lose both their granted legitimacy to lead and the foundation to motivate everyone to improved contributions. You will create both meaningfulness and broad legitimacy to lead by working for the long-term common good of all four stakeholder groups. A great leader respects all stakeholders' legitimate needs and dares to stress the long-term and ethical arguments along with the economical and legal requirements. That is motivating.

Two rules of thumb

Even if you decide to lead with all four stakeholders' best interests at heart, two of them should receive special attention in your everyday leadership. The business owners, however, are not one of them. In one sense they are, of course, the most important stakeholder – they have the ultimate power over your employment and the organization's future. That's one reason the owners have to get their share of the value created. When the owners' primary goal is profit, they must receive an acceptable return on their investment, including a risk premium. That's buying a "ticket for a continued ride".

Nevertheless, from an everyday perspective, two other stakeholder groups are more important for your leadership – because in the end, they will benefit the value creation for everyone. These are your customers and your employees. My two simple rules of thumb read:

- **In dialogues with your team: Keep the focus on *how* the team most effectively creates value for *the customers* – both internal and external!**
- **In dialogues with each team member: Keep the focus on the well-being, work contributions and growth of *the individual*!**

Richard Branson has put this in another way: "Put your staff first, your customers second and your shareholders third – then all three will benefit."

A great leader can swiftly and naturally shift from customer focus to coworker focus, and back again.

Having *customer focus* when you develop team collaboration is natural from several angles. Firstly, to deliver value to the organization's external customers is the very reason for the organization's existence.[7] It is the fulfillment of customers' needs that determines the organization's income. The long-term ability to meet, or even exceed, customers' expectations will benefit all the other stakeholders. Thus, this becomes the most important driving force for running and improving an organization. Understanding this is easy for

7. I do not consider maximizing shareholder value as the great purpose of an enterprise, even if some owners might disagree. I rather agree with Richard Ellsworth when, in his book *Leading with Purpose*, he claims customer satisfaction as the real purpose. He argues that the other stakeholders are necessary, but that they do not decide the purpose. What makes the customer unique, is that only what is good for the customer combines economic value with social value. To create customer value with effectiveness (the right product the right way), rather than with just efficiency, is the best way to ensure the fulfillment of all stakeholders' different needs.

everyone, irrespective of the type of organization you work in. As the leader, you should therefore gather your team around the question: "How do we, with minimal waste, create better customer value together?"

Having coworker focus is as important when dealing with individuals as customer focus is in leading team work. Having coworker focus means frequently and respectfully interacting with each person based on their well-being and work contributions. It also means providing the means required for them to do a good job, not wasting their time, and it means giving opportunities, security and support for their growth. Finally, it means holding them accountable for contributing their best to the collaboration, returning to the question: "How do you take the next step in your growth and make even better work contributions?"

Conflicts of interest will occur between stakeholders. Important deliveries to customers and tasks really vital for the profitability of the organization must, of course, take high priority. However, nothing should be allowed to lead to the abuse or exploitation of people. Do not take decisions that cause irrevocable damage to someone – whether it is a subordinate, you yourself or anybody else.

I want to stress the importance of anchoring yourself in what your long-term internal motivations as a leader really are. The reason for this is that your leadership starts with you and your example. Remember that you can change and develop what motivates you, or as James Allen poetically put it: "A man sooner or later discovers that he is the master-gardener of his soul, the director of his life."

3.2 Anchor in the Leader Contribution Model

> *"I do not focus on winning, just on the perfect run."*
> *–Ingemar Stenmark*

Stenmark's approach explains why he completely dominated the world's ski racing for so many years. However, his view is as relevant for excellence in leadership as it is for excellence in sports.

A great leader focuses on "the perfect run" that each individual needs to contribute, are able to contribute and *how* they really contribute. The key word is contribution, or more specific in this context, work contribution. This section is about anchoring your drive to lead in what I call *the Leader Contribution Model.*

Work contribution

The work contributions of a coworker consist of their input to the three goals of collaboration: to deliver, to improve and to learn. A contribution is built up by actions – what they do, say or in any other way express. A contribution mirrors both the ability and the attitude of the individual.

The result of collaboration is built up by all individuals' work contributions. In turn, every contribution depends on the common *means* available, as well as the *ability* and *attitude* of each individual. Thus, an organization's results rest fully on the availability of the three collaboration conditions, MAA. Figure 3 highlights the need to work with all three conditions in order to support the individual to make better work contributions.

Figure 3 The Work Contribution Model
The work contribution of an individual depends on the means, the ability and the attitude (MAA). The sum of all work contributions constitutes the organization's result.

The value creation of the whole system is manifested through work contributions – all of them resting on MAA. The means form the common parts of the working system. In addition, everybody brings their own abilities and attitudes to work.[8]

In other words, the common means together with everyone's individual abilities and attitudes, that is, the sum of all MAAs, forms a collaboration system for value creation.

Contribution management

Figure 3 illustrates that the result, the best value creation, will come about when all the three MAA conditions are in place. This is a crucial insight for your ability to lead effectively. You can use it for prioritizing what you do and how much emphasis you place on *how* everyone contributes compared to how much your emphasis is on results.

8. In an organization that has to compete in a market, some conditions are more important than others – especially the ones that are hard to copy or difficult to buy. This applies, for instance, to some of the ways of working, some of the abilities (e.g. leadership abilities) and all of the attitudes.

Bosses who solely *manage by results* are often only interested in the financial report and the related key indicators. They do not feel responsible for improving MAA (either they believe that all MAAs are already good enough or that their subordinates are the ones responsible to fix what is missing). Such bosses concentrate their interactions with employees around communicating and following up tougher new targets.

A leader who *manages by methods* is primarily interested in *how* the common ways of working affect the result. This interest manifests itself by the leader, together with coworkers, spending time to improve their common ways of working. They will start out with the questions: "Why did the work result turn out better or worse than expected?" and "How can we create an even better result next time?"

A leader who *manages by contributions* has enhanced this way of method management by looking at *how* every individual contributes to the team's collaboration. The method management's focus on common ways of working is also the foundation for contribution management, because common work standards (to an appropriate level of detail) often form the basis for individual contributions (e.g. needed as a support for newcomers and as a standard for improvements). However, in contributions management an individual perspective complements this general perspective on ways of working. In other words, you concentrate on improving both the common means (including common methods) and the individuals' abilities and attitudes.

Working with the way tasks are performed is fundamental to leadership. Despite that, ways of working and contributions are seldom core interests for managers.

It is different in sport. Imagine the coach of a sport team gathering the players and yelling: "This is terrible! You really have to get your act together and win the next game! I don't care how you do it, as long as you win with at least 5 points!"

Is that constructive? Hardly. Is it common among sports coaches? No. A coach who does not care about *how* the results are achieved will not stay long.

Such a one-sided results orientation is, however, quite common in business organizations, especially among high-level managers. Such managers are totally focused on results, probably because their superiors expect it and their compliance brings greater career opportunities. In the long run it can result in the entire top management consisting of people with a very narrow view of this vital aspect of good leadership. Many top managers need to understand the power of contribution management better – both to adjust their own behavior and to recruit the right managers to the levels below them.

Of course results are important! Contribution management, however, leads to the best long-term results possible, precisely because it is about using the results to create better ways of working and better individual contributions from people who are learning and growing. Leaders who use results in this way are genuinely interested in understanding the details of the work, but without the need to personally micromanage them – instead, they empower people to improve them. This is the best way to improve long-term results.

It might initially be difficult to make the switch from today's results being a goal in itself to it becoming the means to achieve greater goals. However, it is necessary in order to build systematic improvement and a learning environment. In such an environment, the results from yesterday are used to improve your work contributions today – to get better results tomorrow.

It is from this perspective that Stenmark's quote should be read. It claims that the individual contribution, here and now,[9] is more important than the result. This is surely a provocative perspective for the person whose immediate counter reaction is: "We are here to produce results!" Maybe even followed by: "How hard can it be to give me those results? – I don't care how, just do it!"

Again, results are important, especially when measured in terms of long-term value creation. Nevertheless, it is just the result of something – that is, the result of *how* we cooperate. And, with good collaboration being the prerequisite for good value creation, it is what a great leader must concentrate on.

Leader contributions

It is not only all the members of the team who should contribute to the whole, but also their leaders, and they do it by making *leader contributions*. It means contributing to the collaboration by supporting their people to succeed by strengthening the three MAA conditions as shown in figure 4.[10]

9. There is a direct connection between being focused on a work contribution and being present in the now. The poet Karin Boye has expressed this as, "Yes, there is goal and meaning in our path – but it's the way that makes it worth our while." Eckhart Tolle suggests something similar when, in *Practicing the Power of Now*, he writes: "Do not be concerned with the fruit of your action – just give attention to the action itself. The fruit will come of its own accord."

10. My main inspiration in defining contribution management, including the base for the Leader Contribution Model as illustrated in the figures 4, 13 and 22, comes from *Leadership: The Care and Growth Model* by Etsko Schuitema.

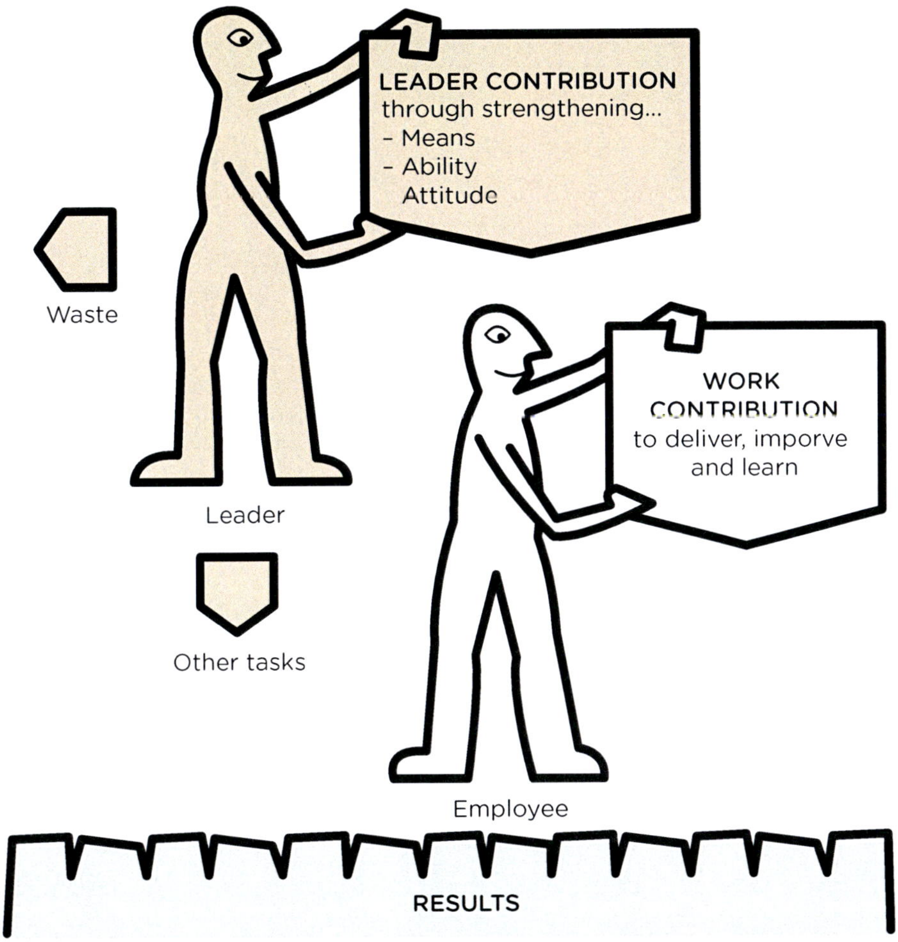

Figure 4 The Leader Contribution Model
The work contributions from all team members (including your "other tasks") will affect the results directly, while your leader contributions will affect it indirectly.

Your leader contributions are directed at the people you lead. The other things you do during a normal working day are referred to as "other tasks" and "waste" in figure 4. These two arrows in the illustration represent the things you do that are not aimed at your subordinates – for example administration and tasks aimed directly towards achieving the results. Examples of other tasks are placing orders, approving invoices, making slides for a customer presentation or reporting to upper management. These tasks create direct value, while other things managers do are waste of time. But even the tasks that create direct value are secondary to a leader compared to the importance of making their leader contributions.

At first glance it might look impossible to, by oneself, take responsibility for MAA – that is all the means in the system as well as everyone's ability and attitude. However, as the leader, that is exactly what you have to do in order to lead the joint effort to improve them.

You cannot create all the means required on your own, but you can lead the effort of strengthening both resources and structure. Neither can you develop another person's abilities by yourself. You can, however, provide tasks and challenges, together with the training and support needed to handle them, for the individual to grow.

You also cannot, by yourself, improve the attitude of another person. However, you can show them Tough Care, cultivating their best by giving them expectations and feedback, as well as holding them accountable for their contributions.

Hence, the three types of leader contributions are:

Leader contribution I – Strengthen the *means*
By making suitable resources and structures available, you contribute to developing and maintaining the common means for an adequate and well-functioning system.

Leader contribution II – Strengthen the *ability*
By arranging tasks and challenges, together with training opportunities and support, you help to develop each person's ability to be *able* to contribute both individually and as a team member.

Leader contribution III – Strengthen the *attitude*
By showing Tough Care you facilitate everyone's attitude of *wanting* to contribute and grow.

The need for different means and abilities vary between organizations. It is, for example, obvious that different types of equipment and skills are required in hospitals, municipal offices, schools and industries. Even within different branches of one industry the means and abilities needed can vary substantially. However, there are some that, to a great extent, are similar, such as the methods, tools and abilities to perform systematic improvements. In addition, the desired attitude of wanting to contribute is very similar for all types of organizations. In the following section I will concentrate on these MAA areas where the leader contributions are similar, irrespective of where one works.

Leader contribution I – Strengthen the means

As a leader, you are responsible for providing the means necessary to build a well-functioning system to support your subordinates' efforts to contribute. The term means here includes resources and structures. The resources needed for the work is often obvious, for example appropriate facilities and equipment enabling the different tasks. However, the structures needed to support delivery, improvement and learning are often less obvious. The means in a well-functioning system often include the following structures:

- **Descriptions of the mission, vision, principles, strategies and targets.**
- **Product information that specifies the end result of the operational work.**
- **Work process descriptions and standards outlining the best way of working down to the appropriate level of detail.**
- **Methods and tools supporting both individual and collaborative tasks in order to deliver, to improve and/or to learn.**

Also the cultural habits (e.g. of respectful communication), based on common values and ways of working, form part of the means.

Leaders cannot develop and maintain all the means necessary on their own, but they have the responsibility to ensure that it is done – and that it becomes better and better. In the three appendices you will find examples of methods and tools that will support your own leadership development.

Leader contribution II – Strengthen the ability

Every working day we bring our ability to work. But how do we develop it? The key is to understand the abilities we will need tomorrow – and then to create corresponding training opportunities. However, like athletes, we also need coaches who can help us to understand how to adapt to an ever-changing field, and teachers who can show us how to do new things.

A leader needs to have a good understanding of each coworker's present abilities, as well as which abilities will be needed tomorrow. You can provide the appropriate training opportunities based on these two considerations. There are several ways to support training, for example a training course and/or, not the least, on-the-job-training, where tasks are described and demonstrated, and feedback is given by an experienced coworker, or even by you yourself if you have the time and ability. In any case, you are responsible for all subordinates getting the training opportunities they require and deserve.

Sometimes training courses are needed, sometimes not. Most often a clear task, coupled with practical training and collegial support, is the best way to strengthen ability.

Leader contribution III – Strengthen the attitude

A great leader genuinely cares for what's best for each individual.[11] This requires both hard and soft actions, including what you do, say or in other ways express. You show this type of Tough Care in different ways:

- **You *look after* the basic security of each individual and offer them a place where they can feel the harmony of belonging to a group with team spirit.**
- **You *see* each individual and their contributions, making them feel significant in contributing to a purpose larger than their own self-interest of receiving a salary.**
- **You *challenge*, support and give straight feedback so that each individual can grow.**

Your Tough Care affects the attitude of every single one of your subordinates. What you look for in a person's attitude is the reflection of their intent to contribute. Hence, to evaluate the attitude in a situation is to gauge if the intent behind the behavior displayed is predominantly unselfish or not. Sometimes that is difficult. Part of the reason why it is so perplexing is that you cannot see the intent on the outside – you have to deduce it from the actions shown.

Two people can do or say exactly the same thing, but with completely different intent. For example, someone can do something wrong because they did not understand the work description, while another can make exactly the same mistake in order to get extra overtime pay.

Security is an important aspect of strengthening attitude. If people feel secure, their willingness to act unselfishly increases – simply because they do not have to worry about themselves when helping others.

11. Your *real care* for another person is linked to their *real needs*. Many thinkers have tried to define our needs. Abraham Maslow is one of the most influential of them, however questioned. He divided human needs into five levels in his hierarchy of needs: physiological, safety, love and belonging, esteem, self-actualization. Esteem is based on the desire to be accepted and valued by others. Building self-esteem, however, requires accepting who you are internally. Self-actualization refers to a person's full potential and the realization thereof, e.g. maturing in line with figure 28. It is easy to picture that we want to fulfill our needs in a strict order from the basic physiological needs and upwards. Nevertheless, all of them exist simultaneously and are prioritized by the individual at any given time (and not necessarily in strict hierarchical order), such as making braver leadership possible through risking safety in order to do what is right.

Such security partly stems from being able to count on the support of the leader. This in turn provides the platform for trying new improvement ideas and the courage to challenge one's own limits in order to learn and grow.

However, the most important way you can strengthen attitude is to set a good example, combined with frequently praising good attitude and confronting bad. Thus, you have to start with your own attitude before trying to affect that of others.

Leadership waste

Now ask yourself: "How much of my working time do I devote to leader contributions?"

If your answer is "too little", you should try to create more time for leader contributions and examine the rest of what you do during a normal working day. It is common for managers to spend too much time on administration, participating in too many long meetings or doing "other tasks" that a subordinate could do just as well, such as reporting results. Consider this when you examine your present non-leadership tasks:

- **If it is not important – remove it.**
- **If it is partly a waste of time – make it more efficient.**
- **If it is something someone else can do – delegate it.**
- **If it involves repeated acute problem-solving – solve the root cause.**

In other words, you have to choose what not to do in order to make room for more important tasks. Once you have created space in your calendar, you can choose to take on other things. This way you can devote more of your time to make more, and better, leadership contributions. Sometimes this means taking them over from someone else.

Surrogate managers

If managers choose, because of lack of time or something else, not to make the most important leader contributions themselves, someone else has to do it for them. That person can be called a surrogate manager.[12] Surrogate management can possibly be done by:

12. Peter Block defines a surrogate manager as a person who "acts on behalf of, or in place of, a manager". Etsko Schuitema defines the term a bit narrower when he ironically states: "By surrogate management we understand the employing of a specialist, secondary or proxy function to deal with the human problem in order to leave leadership free to pursue the business of maximizing profit."

- **An HR department (or a union) that has been given the main authority of deciding on remuneration and the handling of conflicts.**
- **A staff function that has been assigned the full responsibility for quality improvements, management system development and/or change management.**
- **A communication expert who has been given the task to convey important messages from top management to "the people".**

However, by relying too much on these surrogates, management can risk abdicating vital leadership tasks such as rewarding and censuring, resolving conflicts, securing structures for systematic improvement and involving everyone in open dialogues.

The negative effects of abdicating important leadership tasks are made permanent if the corresponding authority is taken away from managers at lower levels.

Do not get me wrong. In large organizations there is definitely room for HR, change management and communication experts – but only as support to leaders, not taking over vital leadership responsibilities such as giving frequent feedback, being the custodian of improving work standards or strengthening good discussions.

Your most important *leader contributions* are related to the caring for, and growing of, your subordinates. If lack of time prevents you from doing that, you must change your priorities. Etsko Schuitema's research shows how important this is. People want their leaders to care for them and, ultimately, the results of the organization depend on it.[13]

13. Etsko Schuitema concludes: "The role of HR in the business is absolutely critical. During my research, I looked at the highest performing mines in Africa. [...] The best performing mines were those with the best line managers who communicated directly with their employees and team members. Where HR takes away some of that responsibility and communicates directly with employees, for example on issues of pay or performance review, this undermines the role of the line manager. Interestingly, mines that behaved in this way tended to be poor performing mines."

3.3 Anchor in mission, vision and targets

It is vital for you as the leader, together with your subordinates, to anchor yourselves in the knowledge of where you are heading and why. This section highlights three important aspects of this:

- **Your *mission* is the purpose of the collaboration – a summary of the value that the organization strives to create for customers and other stakeholders.**
- **Your *vision* is a "barrier-breaking image" of your future collaboration.**
- **Your *targets* are the milestone conditions that you have determined to reach by certain points in time – to better perform the mission and to reach the vision.**

All three of these anchor points are important for your leadership. They help you to maintain both motivation and direction – and help your subordinates to do the same.

It is necessary to make sense of these aspects to clarify the direction of your collaboration. They all distinguish what is more important from what is less important. Both you and your team need this for your everyday decision making.

The mission, vision and targets can be defined both for the whole organization and for smaller departments. In the case of the latter, they can show the department's role as part of the whole value-creation effort of the total organization, or even of the entire value chain passing through several organizations.

Good collaboration in your team depends on everyone in the team pulling in the same direction. To do that it is not enough to have a nicely formulated mission and vision on a paper or poster. It is the image of the mission, vision and targets in everybody's minds that counts.

Leading by Objectives

Management by Objectives (MBO) is a term widely used for a management style based on decentralization, by giving targets rather than giving instructions. Here I will describe a work process for *Leading by Objectives* (LBO)[14] in which the targets are set jointly by an interactive and iterative approach, involving the people on all hierarchical levels, instead of through a purely top-down hierarchical process.[15] Such an LBO method can be described as a process of seven main activities:

1. **Analyze current position performance and trends by scanning the environment.**
2. **Update the mission and vision statements if needed.**
3. **Agree on long-term goals and strategies on the upper level.**
4. **Agree on short-term targets on the upper level.**
5. **Break down the output (from phase 1-4) in dialogue with each team at the next lower level – coordinating and agreeing on new targets. Do this level by level until the whole organization is involved.**
6. **Plan and do the actions that bridge the gaps for each target (in every team on every level).**
7. **Check the outcome and act to secure improvements. Adjust targets and continue.**

Environmental scanning (activity 1) is important for a successful LBO process. The purpose is to gather strategic intelligence about ongoing or possible changes in the market, for example in customer expectations, in competitor behavior or new technology that can impact on how you create customer value. The environmental factors are then analyzed together with the internal factors in order to decide on updated strategic goals and new short-term targets.

In a large organization, activity 5 must be repeated until the breaking down of targets has reached the working level. Each repetition of this is like a handshake between the manager of the upper level with those who directly report to them. This iteration is sometimes called *target sharing*.[16]

14. LBO is inspired by a Lean approach to policy deployment called Hoshin Kanri. Note that the word "objective" here refers to both longer term and broadly stated goals, and shorter term and very specific targets.

15. Many organizations perform their process only once a year. However, it is desirable (inspired by Agile principles and tools) to make the LBO process flexible enough so that it can continuously handle changes in targets, priorities and actions as soon as new facts are known or after unexpected events have occurred.

16. It is sometimes also referred to as "catchball" due to the way that the need for improvements and the corresponding targets are discussed up and down the hierarchy in several iterations.

Target sharing aims at creating understood, coordinated and committed targets in all parts of the organization. It is partly about logically breaking down higher goals to lower-level goals. However, it is also about giving everybody the chance to understand what each target really means and to internalize the target. The latter implies that everyone should get the opportunity to turn each goal into an important part of their own personal set of goals.

Activity 6 and 7 are about the *planning*, *doing* and *checking* of improvement activities and then *acting* to secure the improvements made.[17] These iterations need to be done in short cycles – in every team on every level. Sometimes it includes experimenting with small steps to overcome knowledge gaps, as well as adjusting target levels to make them more challenging, or more realistic.

Target sharing calls for good discussions in and between teams on all levels within the organization. The discussions should be focused on the reason for a particular target, how targets depend on one another, how everyone can contribute to achieve the target and how the target fulfillment will be measured.

As the leader, your role is to facilitate these discussions. Remember to listen carefully – both for misunderstandings and for ideas about how targets can be set, and for ideas for solutions. If you do this well, the LBO process can become an important leadership tool for systematic improvement as well as for creating and maintaining meaning.

In many organizations a similar process as the one described above is carried out once a year, often just before determining the budget for the coming year. However, exactly as with the financial budget, there are big advantages if the process can be repeated more regularly, for example based on frequent adjustments when important new facts are found in the environment, or in the internal performance. Especially activities 6 and 7 need to be repeated in short cycles, as will be described in chapter 7 and in appendix B.

17. This is summarized as the PDCA wheel that is described in chapter 7.

Anchor together in your common mission

Meaning is important. Researchers have found that the greater meaning of your work – the meaning that comes from contributing to something larger than yourself – is often considered more motivating than salaries or bonuses.

In some work places, for instance in hospitals and schools, the greater meaning is more obvious. In some other organizations, however, it might require some effort to make the meaning clear to everyone. Looking at figure 5, it is clear that the person defining their job as "I am cutting rocks" finds less meaning than the person saying "I'm building a bridge for other people". The rock cutters do not see their work in a broader context. The bridge builders, however, see their jobs as contributing to a bigger cause.

Figure 5 Creating meaning
From a rock cutter to a bridge builder by deriving meaning from a task.

The global furniture retailer IKEA, known for its value-driven leadership, has formulated its mission as: "To create a better everyday life for the many people." It is just one example of how a common motivating aim can energize individuals to improve collaboration.

However, the formulation of a mission is not limited to the top node of an organization. Done the right way, the mission formulated at a lower level can explain how the people in that department can contribute to the bigger mission of the whole organization.

Do not underestimate the power of a common mission. The lack of it limits your collaboration potential. If we do not agree on where we are heading we will find it very hard to agree on what needs to be done. Differences in intent can create serious conflicts.

Thus, spend time on anchoring together in a common purpose as this is the starting point for building a clear direction and a motivating team spirit.

Anchor together in your common vision

It is impossible to lead successfully without a vision. The reason is simple; if you do not have an image in your head of what your future collaboration should look like, you have no stable direction for your leadership.

A manager with no vision will make contradicting decisions, resulting in fuzzy leadership. Most people have some kind of vision of what good collaboration is about, or have at least experienced its opposite. Thus, probably both you and your subordinates can present images of what your working days ought to look like in the future. If, in dialogue with your team, you put all your individual images on the table, you will be able to make them more concrete, share them, improve upon them and hopefully turn them into "a common vision".

Reaching a common vision is an essential foundation for great collaboration. Try to put it into simple words or, even better, into a picture, to make it easy to remember.

A vision should be a barrier-breaking image in the sense that it clearly shows the challenging differences from the present state. These differences might be about the need for new abilities, new ways of working or learning, new quality levels, faster responses or new ways of treating colleagues or customers.

Formulate the vision together in order to make the words and/or picture understandable for everyone. Put it up on a wall where everyone can see it and be reminded to return to its meaning. Then it might become a meaningful foundation for everyday decisions, both small and big.

Not having a good vision will hinder your efforts to move in the right direction. But doing the vision formulation without involving the people, or without returning to it regularly, is a waste of time. Henry Ford once put this warning into a catchy slogan: "Vision without execution is hallucination."

Direction, targets and action

A target is a condition that should be met by a certain time. Targets can be set both for the short and long term.[18] Important long-term targets are called strategic goals. The chosen way of reaching such a target is called a strategy.

Both short-term and long-term targets can be seen as stations en route to the vision. If it is not obvious that the stations are along the same route, you must take the time to anchor the logic between the different targets and the vision – both by yourself and with the team. Ideally, the route from sub-targets through the strategic target to the vision should be clear to everyone, as shown in figure 6.

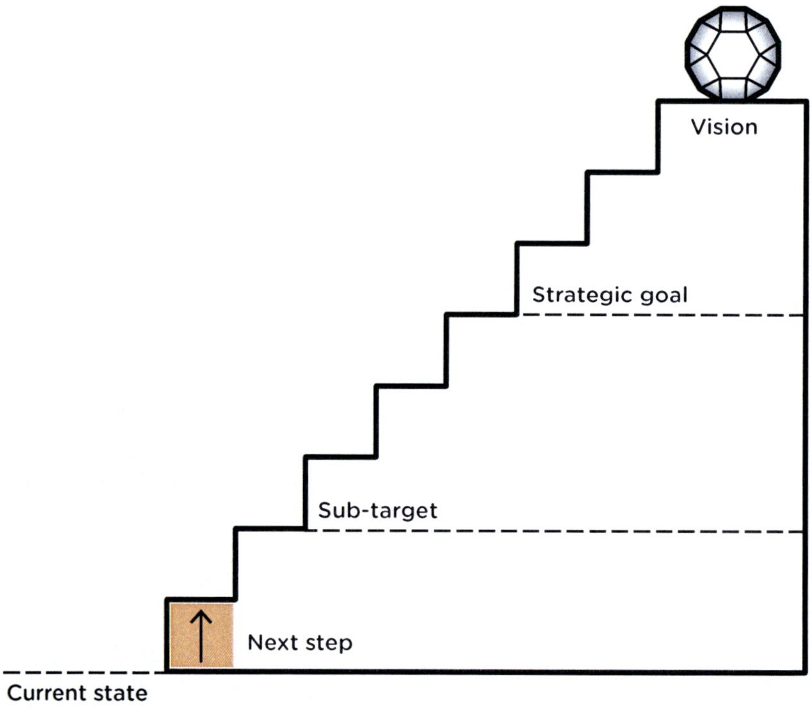

Figure 6 The next step in the right direction

The route from the current state, through sub-targets and strategic goals, towards the vision.

18. The terms "objectives", "goals" and "targets" are used synonymously here to express a wanted future condition, independent of hierarchical level. However, "targets" usually refer to very specific, and often more short-term, future states, while "goals" usually refer to wanted conditions further away in the future.

The strategic goals, together with the vision, are very important as they point out the course to take. If they are shared, it makes it possible for everyone to align their energy and efforts in the same direction as their colleagues. It also underpins decisions about what to concentrate on, and not least, what not to do. Jan Carlzon, the former CEO of SAS, emphasizes this in his best-selling management book, *Moments of Truth*, where he writes about the manager's responsibility to make and communicate the overall direction and long-term goals in order for all employees to be able to make the countless number of decisions that the organization depends upon every day.

John F Kennedy's target formulation from 1961 about moon landing[19] is a classic example of how a clear long-term goal can become the energizing base for great collaboration. A more recent, and down to earth, example comes from the Swedish municipality of Södertälje. In their effort to use Lean principles for giving the citizens better service for their tax payments, they formulated the slogan "Twice as good". The different teams subsequently translated it into goals formulated to ensure that every hour of waste they could get rid of was used for quality and efficiency improvements, as well as for employee development.

The long-term targets are very important, but so are the sub-targets. A sub-target is a well-defined future state that, given a true understanding about the current state, determines what needs to be done next.

The next step is in one sense the most important. It is the start of the journey that begins here and now. Sometimes it is frightening to take it, but it needs to be taken. Often it is better to experiment and learn instead of being passive, or as Jan Carlzon puts it: "Mistakes can usually be corrected later; the time that is lost in not making a decision can never be retrieved."

Good targets

The purpose of targets is to motivate both good individual work contributions and good collaboration. A motivating set of targets are:

- **Few and balanced.**
- **Meaningful.**
- **Understood and shared – preferable locally formulated.**
- **Challenging but realistic.**
- **Possible to follow up through set conditions and time.**

19. "First, I believe that this nation should commit itself to achieving the goal, before this decade is out, of landing a man on the moon and returning him safely to the earth. No single space project in this period will be more impressive to mankind, or more important for the long-range exploration of space; and none will be so difficult or expensive to accomplish."

The list is important for your leadership as it helps you to motivate both yourself and others through a smarter set of targets. Use it as a checklist when you use the LBO process. Let us go through the list to look at some critical issues when setting targets.

To decide on *few and balanced* targets means striking the balance to set important targets that are few enough to have focus on, but many enough to balance different stakeholders' perspectives (e.g. through +QTE as described in the next section).

A *meaningful* target motivates people by appealing to their emotions, ethics and logical reasoning. Visualize the strain of logic that connects short-term targets to the more long-term goals and the vision (see figures 6, 39 and 40 for examples) in order for everyone to be able to understand its importance and the logic behind every target.

A target is *understood and shared* when every one of your subordinates understand both what it means and how it is measured, and share the desire to contribute their best in order to reach it. It is usually preferable to let each team formulate their own targets.

A target is *challenging but realistic* if it is possible to reach on time at the same time as it demands some extra effort in order to do it.

Finally, the wanted future condition has to be specified in a way that makes it possible to *follow it up in relation to a set time*. The target condition is often specified by the level (a numeric value) of a measure (a Key Performance Indicator, KPI). However, this is not always possible. Sometimes the desired future state needs to be described in words. If this is the case, it should be done in such a concrete way that it is possible to follow up if the condition has been reached or not at the specified time.

It is preferable to describe the target condition in words rather than choosing a less relevant numeric target just because it is easy to measure. Resist people who argue that a target must be measurable with hard facts. This view of targets is particularly dangerous because it might lead you to forget important areas. Thus, it is better to talk about target conditions instead of targets. The word condition implies that a target level can be described in words just as well as it can be described by a KPI numeric.

Balance with +QTE

The need for balancing financial KPIs with other perspective KPIs was highlighted by Robert Kaplan and Thomas Norton in their book *Relevance Lost*. They turned away from the short-sighted view of performance management and introduced the widely spread concept of a *balanced scorecard*. The first iteration of the concept suggested four perspectives of KPIs, namely: Financial, Customer, Internal Business Processes, and Learning and Growth. A variant of this balanced view on target setting is called +QTE. It is based on stakeholders' interests and is also divided into four perspectives:

- **+ stands for the Human perspective – i.e. to secure SHE (safety, health and environment), team spirit and learning.**
- **Q stands for the Quality perspective – to deliver without defects and meet both spoken and unspoken needs.**
- **T stands for the Time perspective – to respond quickly, have short lead times and stick to promised delivery times.**
- **E stands for the Efficiency perspective – to deliver high value without wasting resources.**

Each of the above perspectives holds a set of possible KPIs directed at a specific stakeholder group. Working to improve safety, health, environment, team spirit and learning (+) will obviously benefit the people working for the organization. Quality (Q) and delivery performance (T) will mainly favor the customers, while efficiency (E) is especially advantageous to the owners.

However, even if the value creation in each of the four perspectives has a prime stakeholder, all four will have direct and indirect effects on all the other stakeholders as well, not least on society. In other words, +QTE is important for everyone. After all, without one of the four stakeholder groups, there is no future for the organization.

Some organizations use +QTE not only to guide the balance of its improvement work, but also for a strict order of prioritizing. The "+" is the prime priority and the "E" the last. That is an unusual way of thinking for profit-driven organizations. However, the logic behind this prioritization order is not only ethical, but also perfectly logical even for those with a pure profit focus, especially if they have a long-term perspective on their earnings.

Let us look at the logic, starting from the back. Without delivering we cannot make a profit, without quality it's better not to deliver and without healthy and skilled people we cannot over time produce the usable goods or services that the customer requires.

Leif Östling, the former CEO for the global truck company Scania, stressed the importance of the +QTE prioritizing rule as the number one factor for Scania's successful development during the first decade of this millennium. More recently, I have also heard lower level managers at Scania praise the importance of the +QTE sequence, for example by a shop manager saying: "If I control my operations based on the healthy attendance of my people and on the quality we produce, all the other KPIs will follow."

The importance of getting a good balance between different KPIs is as important in the boardroom as it is on "the floor". The maturity of any management team is partly defined by the ability to manage based on a wide range of KPIs. The +QTE grouping is an excellent way to achieve a good balance between them. In the long term, it will benefit all stakeholders, not the least the owners.

Locally set targets

There is definitely some truth behind the expression "what gets measured gets done". The right KPIs with the right target levels can energize an organization to improve and perform better. However, if done the wrong way, it can do more harm than good.

Pushing KPIs and target levels from the top down to the bottom of an organization might have an advantage from a standardization point of view, but it comes with several risks. One obvious risk is that the targets are seen as a control mechanism, replacing trust.

Another is that centralized KPIs are sometimes picked because they are easy to measure, not because they are important. Moreover, even if a KPI is important and adequate at the top level, it might not be the case on lower hierarchical levels. A performance measure decided at the top might therefore be irrelevant or too abstract to understand on a lower level, which can be very demotivating.

Enforcing bad targets from the top might not only lead to waste of time, both in administration and on the value creation level, but it can even lead the efforts in the wrong direction.[20]

Yet another risk of enforcing target levels top-down is that they can easily be set too high or be too easy to reach. Both are demoralizing. You risk even more if you want to combine top-down targets with bonuses. It might lead to individuals with lack of attitude trying to cheat a poorly executed performance management system.

20. Take as an example the chief of police who set a target on the number of alcohol tests that should be performed during one week. It resulted in police officers performing a lot of tests, but at times and places that they expected few lawbreakers, in order to save time and meet the target.

Leading by Objectives must be based on a genuine, honest and shared will to reach targets. Thus, the target levels should not only be set in iterative dialogue. The measures should also, as far as possible, be *locally formulated* by each team – as long as the targets are aligned with those of the rest of the organization.

The members in a mature team are able to translate the organization's goals to targets that are valid for their own team. This process gives the team the opportunity to engage in *good discussions* about the requirements, obstacles, measures and levels. Such a process increases both understanding and motivation.

Localized target formulation also makes it easier to adapt targets to local customer needs as well as to actual problems or opportunities the team is faced with at that time. Often the local targets can be made simpler, based on manually gathered daily data, such as immediate feedback from internal or external customers.

Localized target formulation makes it possible to adjust the target level as soon as a performance level is reached. It also makes it easier to change from one measure to another if the first target is reached or if new facts or challenges have been found.

In other words, localized target setting in mature teams is often both more motivating and more dynamic – resulting in more challenging targets.

Anchor in values and principles

Besides to anchor everyone in your common tasks and targets, you also need to get a collective understanding of *how* you will take on your tasks and reach your targets. Organizations that have been successful based on a Lean strategy often use common values and principles for this process.

Just as there must be a golden thread from the mission and vision to strategic goals and short-term targets, there must also be a golden thread from values, through principles, methods and tools, to actions. This is illustrated in figure 7 as a chain starting from the values of a person to finishing with their work contributions.

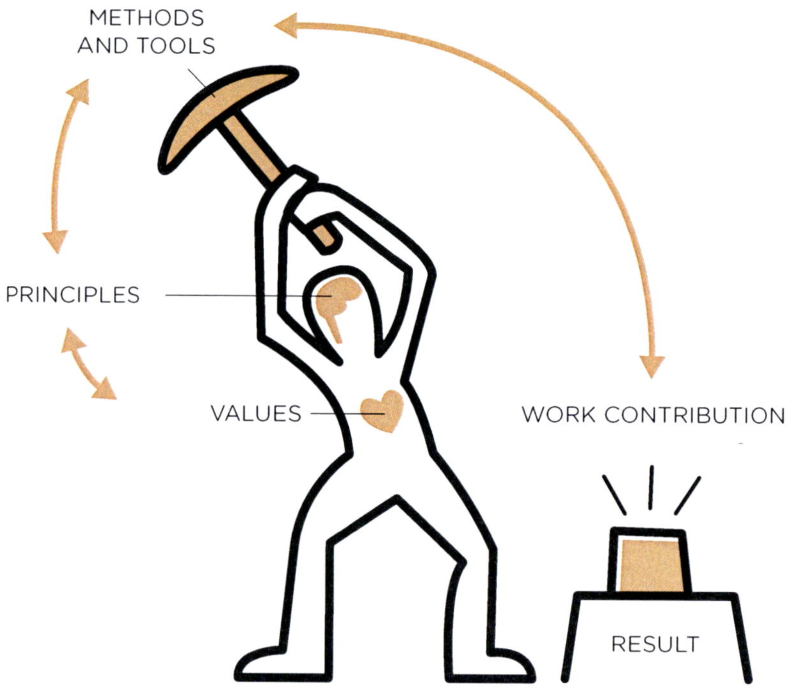

Figure 7 Linking values to work contribution
The relationship between values and work contribution.

Common values form the base for working principles. The principles in turn underpin everyday decisions on how to run the collaboration, including the methods and tools needed. These in turn uphold all the work contributions that together build to form the result. Note that the arrows in figure 7 are double pointed to illustrate that learning goes the opposite way; deviations from expected results can make us change the way we do things, the methods and tools we employ, and sometimes even the working principles we rely on.[21]

Many organizations that have been successful with Lean have formulated shared values, many times centered on respect for people. They also have agreed-on common principles on how to run their businesses. The principles normally stress the importance of holistic work flows as well as the continuous improvement and learning, for example based on work standards and solving root causes to problems. Most often these organizations visualize their principles, typically in the form of a house or a temple. Figure 8 shows an example of such an illustration.

21. Figure 7 is normally viewed from a common perspective, i.e. highlighting the common means in the form of common values, principles, methods and tools. However, it may also be viewed from an individual's perspective, with internalized values and principles (connected to attitude) as well as with the individual's skills to handle methods and tools (connected to ability).

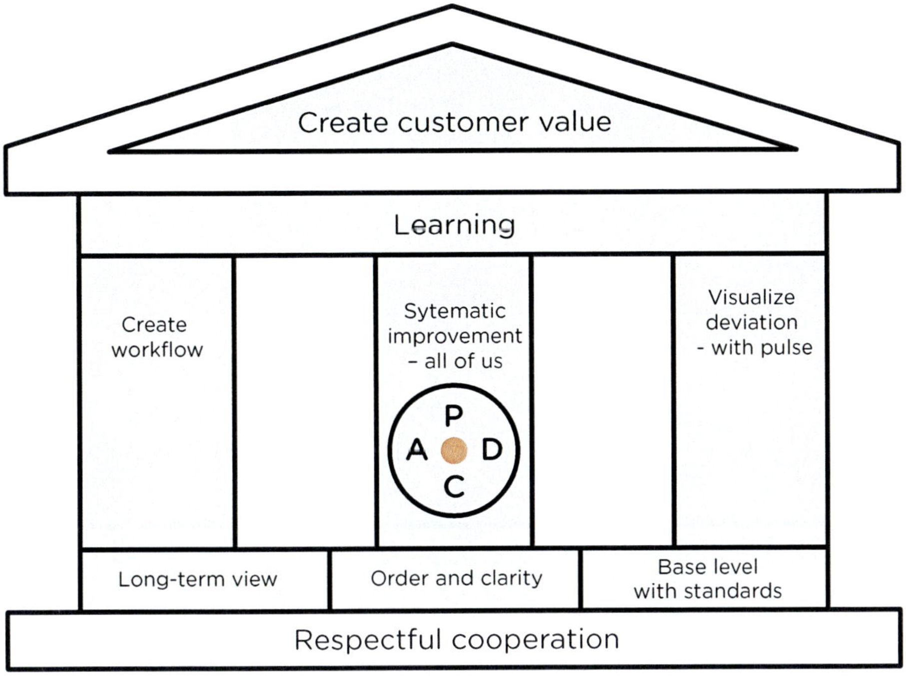

Figure 8 The house of principles
One example of an illustration showing the value base and work principles.

Make an effort to become anchored in your common values and principles so that they form a stable foundation for your collaboration. Visualize your conclusions in a place where it helps your team members to remind each other about them – to create better daily decision making. As their leader, you can make good use of that investment, not only for decision making but also as a frame of reference when you give daily feedback to your subordinates.

In summary, the first step of the Leader's Ladder, anchoring, is the base for the next four steps. Anchoring requires you and your team to be open to new ideas, being willing to listen, to understand, and when needed, being prepared to change both direction and behavior. It is very easy to get stuck in old "truths", or as someone put it: "If you have been lost for a long time, it will start to feel like home."

However, anchoring is not enough to create great collaboration. The second step of the Leader's Ladder highlights another important priority for your leadership, namely to visualize facts and relationships.

4. **Visualize** the system, expectations and deviations

> ***"What I hear, I forget.***
> ***What I see, I remember.***
> ***What I do, I understand."***
> ***–Confucius***

There is a lot of wisdom in the 2500-year-old quote above. And, it has a clear bearing on your leadership. Let your people see, and let them try.

However, to be able to see important things, they must first be visible. By visualizing facts and relationships in an understandable format, you provide a base for understanding and action. The logic is: What is visible can be seen. What is seen can be discussed. What is discussed can be understood. Moreover, what is understood can be properly acted upon.

There are many reasons why we do not visualize and share information enough. One of the reasons is that we tend to assume that what is clear to us, and what we see as self-explanatory, is as true and obvious to others. This is rarely the case.

Therefore, after *anchoring* in what is most important, you have to *visualize* what is needed for better collaboration. This chapter includes the following parts:

- **Visualize yourself**
- **Visualize the system**
- **Visualize expectations and deviations**

4.1 Visualize yourself

> *"Honesty is about more than avoiding lying.*
> *It is also about being open."*
> *– Scriptor*[22]

Your openness might be more important than you think. There are three vital aspects to what you should dare to do as a transparent leader:

- **Dare to show who you are and what you stand for.**
- **Dare to share information and knowledge.**
- **Dare to be open with what you do not know or understand, and with your mistakes.**

If you lead by example in this, your subordinates will likely follow. If you don't, they will also definitely not do it. And that would be a great opportunity lost. A group of people where everybody is open to share their opinions, their knowledge and their need for knowledge, has the potential to develop into a great team.

Let me use the *Johari window* to explain why openness is so important to your leadership. It is a graphical model dividing the knowledge about a human being into four parts, as is shown in figure 9.

The top left quadrant symbolizes what is known about you by both yourself and by others. It is the so-called *arena*, the part of you that you see and others see. The top right is the *blind spot*, the aspects of yourself that others see, but that you are not aware of. The bottom left, the *hidden area* (or *façade*), is your private space, which you know yourself, but keep hidden from others. The last quadrant on the bottom right, *the unknown*, represents the things about yourself that are seen by neither you nor others.

22. The author, Bengt Savén.

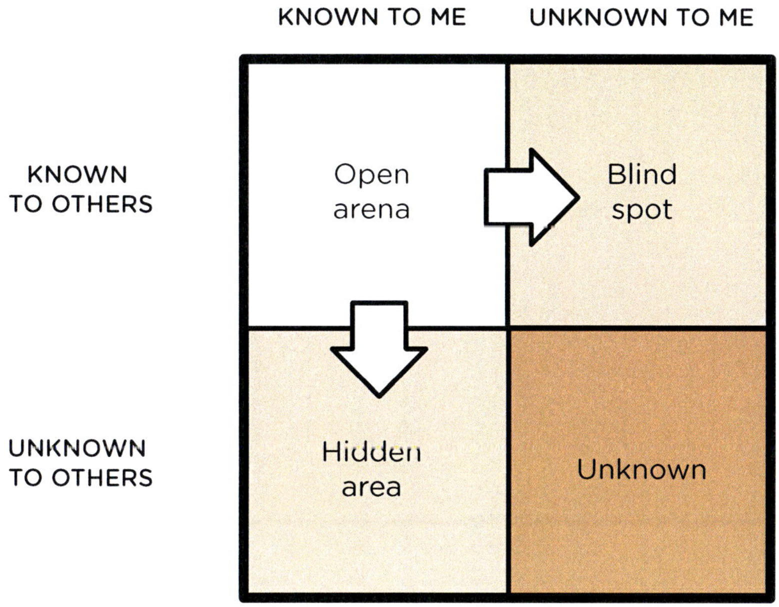

Figure 9 The Johari window
An illustration of the knowledge about oneself (based on Luft and Ingham, 1955).

You can increase the arena by making the blind spot smaller, that is, understand more about yourself. You can also do it by decreasing the hidden area, by letting other people know more about you.

To become a great leader, you should try to make your arena bigger. You can do it by showing your values and sharing your mistakes. This takes courage. That's why you have to set the example. If others follow your example of openness, you should give them credit for their courage. And, by the same measure, confront subordinates who hide information or problems even though they know that it will harm the collaboration.

When you create a more open atmosphere together, the discussion can be more constructive, with more perspectives and facts available. In this way, you collectively increase the problem-solving ability of the team, as well as the learning. In addition, you will learn more about yourself – for example your strengths and weaknesses, the support you need, and what makes you feel good.

If you chose to lead towards more open communication, the content will be more important than the form. Avoid buzz words and information campaigns. Talk with people, not to them. Talk simply and honestly from your own convictions. Listen and be prepared to change your opinion. In other words, visualize yourself, for the sake of team openness and better collaboration.

4.2 Visualize the system

Motivation is strengthened when people have the opportunity to understand and influence their work situation. It is therefore your task as the leader to contribute in such a way that the system you work in is transparent and can be improved. Thus, one important leader contribution is to make the facts, processes and cause-and-effect relationships visible – preferably in a place where people meet regularly, in order to encourage good discussions.

The system

A system is a number of parts that work together to achieve a goal. Every organization is a system.[23] The more facts and understanding you have about the parts and how they relate to each other, the more you can affect the results and the improvement of the system.

In the context of collaboration, the system consists of the people with their respective abilities and attitudes, as well as the common means of resources and structures needed to achieve the goals. The means are in turn built up by both hardware (e.g. workplace, equipment, tools and consumables) and information (e.g. target statements, process and method descriptions, instructions, customer and supplier data, etc.). Seeing the people and the means as parts within a system provides you with a holistic view of all the parts and how they relate to each other. This helps you and your team to connect the parts better – and to see and strengthen the weaker links.

You should strive to make the system not only meaningful to your subordinates, but also possible to understand and influence.[24] If it is possible to influence the system, it is also possible to improve it. As the leader you can help to improve the system in two ways. You can empower and support your subordinates to improve their own parts of the system, and you can secure better cooperation between different parts within the bigger system.

Both of these leader tasks require the system to be transparent and simple enough so one can understand how the parts work together. Making it more transparent and simple will aid both effectiveness and well-being.

---

23. You are free to define what is included within the system and what is excluded, i.e. the environment. A machine, a computer program, a small department or a complete organization – these are all systems. The parts within a system may be anything from physical components and information to human beings. Thus, the cooperation between the system parts varies from physical connections and automated information sharing to human interactions.

24. Aaron Antonovsky, an Israeli American sociologist and academic, highlighted this in his research concerning the relationship between stress, health and well-being. He pointed out that people cope better, and stay healthy, when provided with a "sense of coherence" about life and its challenges.

Parts to visualize

Below are some examples of system parts that often need to be visualized:

- ***Direction and targets*, i.e. the mission, vision and objectives, as well as the principles that should be used to reach them.**
- ***Cause-and-effect relationships*, i.e. the known logic between a source and its wanted or unwanted effects.[25]**
- ***Tasks and responsibilities* for departments and individuals so that unnecessary overlaps or blank spots can be avoided.**
- ***Work descriptions* and the corresponding abilities required to get the work done in the best way – from a macro-level process map down to work standards, with the level of detail needed.**

The last bullet point is not the least important. By visualizing the presently best-known ways of working, you form the base from which continuous improvements can take place. Without improving how you do the work, you will never get lasting improvements. Thus, ways of working need to be made visible, and the people doing the work should have the opportunity to improve it.

This holds true for ways of working all the way from the top level (overall process map), through the intermediate level (process descriptions) to the detailed level (e.g. method, operations and workplace descriptions).[26] How you describe your ways of working is less important than actually doing it.

Important information needed to run an organization is often gathered in what is called a management or quality system. Such a system normally has several purposes, for example to create order for easier access to information, provide guidelines for securing quality and form the basis for follow-ups. Documents are the core of such a system. Some of these are controlling documents, which direct what must be done, while others are supporting documents that combine guidelines with freedom. Many controlling documents are based on external authority regulations, while others are developed internally in order to control what should be done, and how.

25. The knowledge might be documented as checklists of activities needed to be performed or avoided, or as charts with interdependencies of goals or problems.

26. The most detailed descriptions of best ways of working have different names in different organizations, e.g. element sheets or standard operation procedures. The need to document details vary with the type of work done as well as with the maturity of the work team.

A good management system will provide everyday support to both your leadership and the work of your team. For a system like that to function optimally, it should never be too big, too complicated or too centralized. It must remain vibrant in the sense that it stays useful and can constantly be upgraded by the people doing the work.

Details should be controlled centrally only when it is motivated by safety, legal or quality reasons, or when there are overarching advantages to common centralized standards. Otherwise, the authority to adjust the system should reside with the individuals who are doing the work every day, and seeing the outcome of it. This is a prerequisite for continuous improvement.

Thus, instead of letting a staff team from a distance decide how things should be done – maybe because the abilities or attitudes of the persons doing the job are questioned – you should build a decentralized management system based on trust and learning, secured by good leadership.

Transparent decisions

A decision is a choice between alternatives. Lack of decisions, unclear decisions or decisions that are not implemented can be paralyzing for an organization. Decisions that are not understood can be equally destructive. It is important to understand the cause-and-effect relationships that a particular decision is based on – not only for the person(s) making the decision. Subordinates who do not understand why an important decision was taken might lose part of their motivation to contribute. Try to help them to understand.

A *transparent decision* is a choice that is visible and understandable for everyone, even if everybody does not like it. The decision-making process itself should also be transparent.[27]

Making transparent decisions is an important aspect of leadership. Let it form part of your work to visualize the system – for the sake of understanding, motivation and strengthening attitude.

27. Sometimes it is not possible to be completely open about the decision-making process, e.g. if sensitive or secret information requires a decision to be taken by a restricted group. When a decision is taken and communicated under such circumstances, it might evoke surprise, anger and resistance. It is then very important to explain, as far as possible, the reasons behind the choice, even if it has to be done after the decision has been taken.

4.3 Visualize expectations and deviations

> *“Learn to love every difficult situation as an opportunity in disguise.”*
> *– Scriptor*

It is said that without darkness there is no light, without silence no sound and without prejudice no enlightenment. I would like to add: Without goals there are no problems, and without problems there are no improvements.[28]

The logic to this is simple. A problem is a negative deviation between the actual position and a wanted position. If you do not have a desired position (a goal), it is impossible to experience a problem. And if you do not experience a problem, that is, a gap between where you are and where you want to be, you cannot create the drive needed to make improvements.

Thus, to put it more bluntly, an organization with competitors will go under if it never experiences any problems. However, I should add that the word “problem” here ought to be replaced by “deviation” to stress that gaps can be both negative and positive. Note that even a negative deviation can, and should, be looked at as an opportunity.

Negative deviations, when the actual state is not as good as the desired or expected situation, should be responded to by addressing the root causes that are preventing you from reaching the wanted position – and to learn from it.[29]

Positive deviations, when you perform better than expected, should be celebrated – and also learnt from. Cherishing both positive and negative deviations is an important part of great leadership.

28. Alternatively, if you replace “problems” with “opportunities”: Without a vision, it is hard to see the opportunities, and without seeing opportunities, it is difficult to summon the energy for continuous improvements.

29. A deviation can, for instance, be that the quality is not up to the promised standard, the costs are higher than estimated, the schedule is not met, or that somebody is not following the agreed working standard.

Two types of deviations, two types of control

To control here means to adjust input in order to reach a goal. It requires more than just the ability to adjust the course. It requires that you know both where you are going and where you are.

Controlling the direction of an organization can be compared with an orienteering competition.[30] Not only do you have to know where you need to go (the next control point) and where you started, but also how to regularly compare your *real position* with the *expected position*, learn from any deviation, and adjust the direction accordingly.

To be able to steer in the right direction – a vital part of any leadership role – you need these kinds of reference points with which to compare the real situation.

However, in order to be able to steer wisely, it is important to understand that there are two types of references; one for operational use (the base level) and one for improvement use (the target level). Both types of references are expressions of expectations. Moreover, both can be stated in roughly the same way, for example by using different levels of the same KPI. Yet there is a fundamental difference between a base level and a target level.

The base level expresses an expectation of what needs to be reached today – based on existing *means*, *abilities* and *attitudes* (MAA).[31]

The target level expresses an expectation of what needs to be reached at a certain future point in time. To reach this level, you need to improve at least one of the MAA conditions.

The difference between the two levels lies in how high you put the bar. Either you put the expectations on today's level or on a future higher level. That gives two types of control; *operational control* in reference to the base level, with the purpose to *deliver* in line with today's standards, and *challenge-driven control* in reference to the target level, with the purpose to *improve* the collaboration performance. This is illustrated in figure 10.

30. In orienteering, each contestant has to navigate in unfamiliar terrain, using a map and a compass, from the starting point, through different control points, to the goal.

31. In very repetitive operations, e.g. in the automotive industry, the base level is often very detailed and visible. In a high-volume car assembly, the base levels are very obvious, e.g. shown by the pace (takt) of the moving line with marks on the floor where certain assembly operations must be finished, visible work descriptions and exact positions for needed components. The aim is to scan constantly for deviations (from base levels in pace or quality) in order to quickly fix every deviation as soon as it becomes apparent. Such a repetitive system will, over time, become very refined and predictable. The opposite type of system, where today's work is completely different from yesterday's, will require other types of base levels. When the working days are full of unique tasks never done before, it is hard to predict both the times needed and the expected quality outcome. However, one still needs to express these expectations as base levels. Such base levels will not be as stable as in repetitive operations, but even if they need constant updating, they are still required. To visualize base levels in a project environment you can use the answers to the following questions: "Which activities need to be done today, next week, ...?", "Can the activities be performed to a known standard?", "Who should do which activity today, next week, ...?" and "How and when should each sub-result be tested and documented?" See appendix A for tools supporting this.

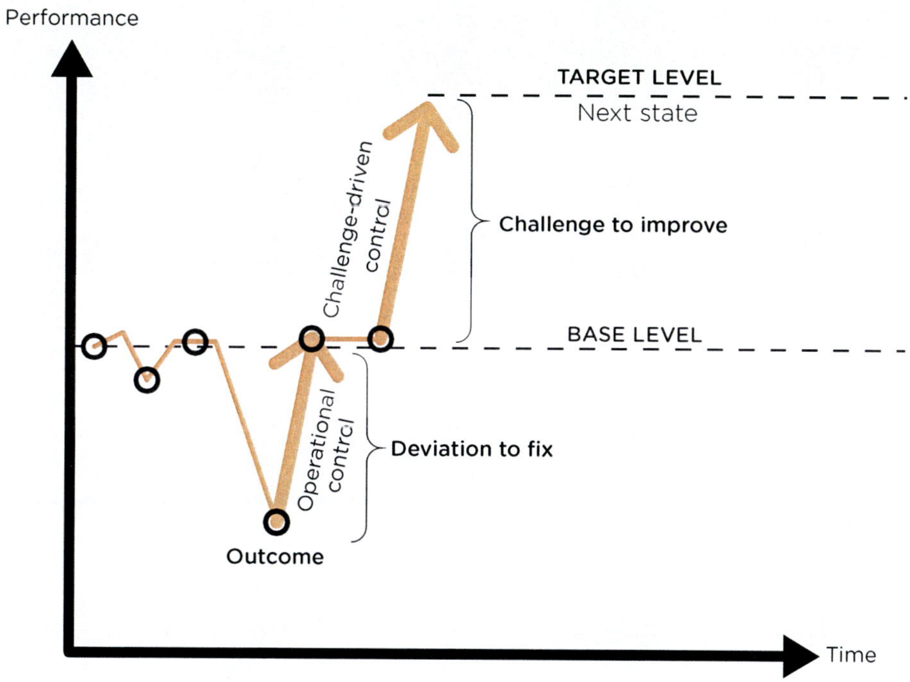

Figure 10 Fixing and improving
Combining operational control with challenge-driven control.

The lower part of figure 10 illustrates how, based on an operational deviation (the real difference between the last outcome and the agreed base level), you can do operational control by doing a quick fix in order to get back to the base level. The top part of the figure illustrates how, based on a challenging target, you can find new solutions to reach the targeted performance and make it the new base level, that is, the work of Leading by Objectives (LBO) as described in section 3.3.

The principal process is the same for both operational and challenge-driven control (as it is for any controlling device). Both rely on four recurring activities: (1) *Expect*, by setting the reference level, that is, the base or target level. (2) *Compare* the real position to the reference level regularly to find any deviations. (3) *Decide* on suitable action(s) to return to the base level or get closer to the target level. (4) *Implement* the action(s).

While the principal process is the same, there are some important differences between the two types of control. One is the pulse – the frequency of comparing and acting on deviations. As operational control is about delivering on time and to spec, it is suitable to do this often, while challenge-driven control can be performed less frequently. Another difference is that the performance measures (see the vertical axis in figure 10) usually need to be adapted to the type of control. Even if the measures are concerning the same +QTE areas (e.g. work safety, product quality, customer satisfaction, delivery and financial performance), the need to aggregate is different. In operational control, you should strive not to aggregate at all and rather *address each deviation separately.* In challenge-driven control, you normally need to aggregate the measures, for example, to monthly KPIs for:

- + **Number of near-accidents.**
- + **Ratio of absenteeism.**
- Q **Number of quality deviations.**
- Q **Number of customer complaints.**
- T **Percentage of on-time deliveries.**
- T **Average lead time.**
- E **Average output per person.**
- E **Financial result.**

A base level for operational control

The goal of operational control is to catch each deviation as it happens and immediately fix it. However, a good start for many organizations is to report and fix deviations on a daily basis, often called daily control.

If you decide to introduce daily control, you then have to decide on a base level with a set of references that should be followed up daily. In a morning meeting, each deviation from the previous day is highlighted and the fixing of it assigned to the most suitable person – hopefully so it can be reported as solved by the next morning meeting.

A base level for daily control may consist of both expectations of *what* needs to be achieved the coming day (referring to operational targets and product standards) and on *how* it has to be achieved (referring to work standards). Thus, a daily control meeting may focus on deviations in:

1. ***Operational targets*, e.g. in the form of schedules and output measures.**
2. ***Product standards*, e.g. in the form of product and quality specifications.**
3. ***Work standards*, i.e. both ways of working (e.g. as process graphs, method and operations descriptions) and standards for the workplace (e.g. as meeting rules, data storage and positions for necessary tools and consumables).**

Irrespective of whether an operational deviation stems from a gap related to an operational target or from a gap related to an agreed standard, the aim is to detect and correct it early.

Decide on the control intervals your operation requires. If you decide that the pulse has to be daily, the following questions are examples of what a daily control meeting could involve:

- \+ Have we, since yesterday, experienced any near-accidents or illness?
- Q Have we, since yesterday, had any customer complaints or out-of-spec products?
- T Have we, since yesterday, missed any delivery deadlines?
- E Have we, since yesterday, spent more time or money than estimated?
- * Have we, since yesterday, gone outside any agreed working standard?

If the answer to any of these questions is yes, the team has found an operational deviation needing their attention.

The last question is different from the first four. It is not related to the +QTE performance as described in section 3.2. Rather, it is related to how the work was done. Not following an agreed work standard is a deviation in itself, and worthwhile examining as it might also explain why a deviation connected to the +QTE occurred.

Thus, if you got a yes answer to any of the first four questions, you should automatically ask the fifth question as well. If the answer to that question is yes too, you need to find the root cause behind why the standard was not followed. Was it due to a lack of training? Or maybe lack of attitude? Does the work standard need to be improved or clarified?

And remember to always add the question: "What or who do we want to acknowledge or praise?"

A base level can be set at a challenging level, but it must be realistic in order for you to be able to make meaningful and frequent comparisons. If you and your team can, step by step, reduce uncertainties and disturbances in recurring tasks, you can make your internal performance levels more predictable. That, in turn, makes it possible to set future base levels to become both more realistic and more challenging.

Better operational control will make it possible to catch deviations early, when they are still just "buds of problems". Then they are easier to correct, and they are not allowed to grow into bigger problems that can hamper your ability to deliver.

Leader contributions through visualizing deviations

By providing structures for both operational and target-driven control, you will strengthen your subordinates' means to succeed; in other words, you will be making the first type of leader contribution as described in figure 4 in section 3.2.[32]

With a structure for operational control you, together with your team, can create more and better opportunities to make timely and quick adjustments in order to fulfill delivery commitments. With a similar structure for target-driven control, you can do the same in order to find root causes of problems and opportunities to improve.

In both cases you will be able to create more opportunities to learn. There is, therefore, a very strong connection between visualizing deviations and all three of the goals described in chapter 1: to *deliver* value, to *improve* the collaboration and to *learn* for future challenges.

Many organizations are much more used to setting long-term goals than setting good base levels for the everyday catching of deviations, continuously adjusting the daily work. Too many managers are stuck in looking at aggregated KPIs and, in so doing, they limit themselves by not acting on individual problems and their root causes. While you can, of course, delegate the running of operational control (including keeping a base level and chairing meetings), it ultimately remains your responsibility to ensure that the structure is in place and is continuously functioning better and better.

32. Such a structure can typically include partly standardized (e.g. based on +QTE reporting) daily control meetings in many teams on different hierarchical levels. See chapter 7 and Appendix A for more information.

A good base level is an absolute necessity for two reasons. Firstly, it provides reference points to compare against, repeatedly, in short intervals. Secondly, it lays down a baseline that target levels and improvement ideas could be measured against. Thus, if you don't have a good base level, you lack an absolute necessity for both controlling the daily delivery work and for supporting continuous improvements.

In summary, the second step of the Leader's Ladder, to visualize, is about making yourself, the system, the expectations and the deviations visible. By visualizing you build a foundation for your team members' work contributions. It also gives you the base for seeing new things that trigger good discussions on, for example, team spirit, root causes and alternative actions – issues that are covered in the third step of the ladder.

5. **See** the person, the game and the root causes

> “*Energize others by sharing your vision and your time.*”
> *– Scriptor*

Your time is the most precious commodity you have. To give someone else your time unconditionally is not only generous, it also shows respect. The third step of the Leader's Ladder, to *see*, is about spending some of your precious time to see every subordinate as an individual, and to see their work contributions. But it is also about trying to see the reasons behind good or bad outcomes – finding the real root causes and the related actions that are necessary to take.

The chapter includes the following parts:

- **See the person**
- **See the game**
- **See the root causes**

5.1 See the person

The third step of the Leader's Ladder, to see, is foremost an appeal to look down at the value creation and your subordinates' needs, instead of looking up, hierarchically, at your bosses' needs.

It is about not only using your eyes, but also your other senses. Many managers will become better leaders by seeing and listening more, and maybe talking a little less.

Eyes and ears

Listen carefully to what people are really saying. It will help you to understand the person and not just the situation.

Listening will bring another advantage; by letting subordinates express themselves, you also give them the opportunity to reflect and learn.

Listen for what is not said. Maybe someone is treated badly, or has too much or too little work to do without telling you outright.

Be on the lookout for signs and find out what needs to be done. It might be crucial to one of your subordinates.

Try not to have preconceived ideas about another person's experiences and thoughts, and in doing so, set an example for others to do likewise. Like the child in the Hans Christian Andersen tale *The Emperor's New Clothes*, you must also be prepared to challenge every commonly-held belief that might be false. And, if you find out that someone deliberately set up smoke screens to keep important facts hidden, you have to confront it. Remember, however, that you need to set the example of openness, as described using the Johari window in the previous chapter.

Meet everyone where they are at

There is no single right way to care for another person. We are all individuals. And we all deserve respect, to be listened to and to get the chance to contribute to the team – even the strangely quiet person or the arrogant troublemaker (however, with limited tolerance for the latter, as I will return to in the next chapter.)

We are all remarkable, as another one of Andersen's tales reminds us. Like the swan in *The Ugly Duckling*, we should look for every person's talent. Meet them where they are at and help them to develop their potential.

It is important to find a balance between too much to do and too little to do for each person in the team. Both are, in the long run, harmful to the individual as well as the organization. As the leader, you must try to find a middle way for each subordinate (sometimes called sustainable engagement), between too much challenge and too much routine or idle time.

5.2 See the game

To *see the game* means being present where the work takes place, seeing everyone's work contribution.[33] In the world of sports it is obvious how important this is; the coach sitting in the office while the team is playing will have severe difficulties leading the team to success.

To see the game is about more than walking around, saying hello and making small talk. There is nothing wrong with that, but when seeing the game, you must be really interested in the work situation and the work contributions.

Even if it is an important part of good leadership, there are plenty of managers who find excuses for not seeing the game, for example: "They would feel watched if I look over their shoulders.", "It is impractical; some work shifts and others work far away from here.", or "I would not understand what they do; it is embarrassing."

Some objections may be more relevant than others. For a manager whose subordinates work in different locations, it is, of course, harder to physically meet everyone regularly (and some of the conversations will have to be done from a distance). But if managers' objections to seeing the game are based on a reluctance to engage in dialogue and see contributions, it is time for them to question whether they should remain managers.

To grasp the importance of leaving your desk, and less important meetings, it is essential to understand that the advantages of seeing the game far outweigh the disadvantages. These are just some of the benefits: You do not have to rely on second-hand information of work situations. You get the chance to discuss deviations where they occur and with the people involved. You also get the chance to see the effects of actions and new ways of working. You learn new things about what is important to the people reporting to you. And, also importantly, your presence sends a very strong signal to every subordinate that they, and their work contributions, are valued.

33. If you are the manager of managers, seeing the game means seeing, with your own eyes, the leader contributions of your subordinates. More on this in chapter 9.

Bill Gates said: "What I do best is share my enthusiasm." One way for you to do that is to be present – giving significance by seeing the other and their contribution.

To be regarded as significant is important to all of us. Thus, create time in your agenda for real meetings, meetings when you are present both physically and mentally. That motivates.

With diary and glasses

If you have come to the conclusion that seeing the game is important, all that remains is to do it. The toolbox at the end of the book contains some tools that will help you to prioritize activities. The aim is to create time in your diary for making *leader contributions*, and then safeguard those time slots against less important activities.

Put on your "waste glasses" when you go out to see the game. *Waste* is everything that does not add value to any of the stakeholders, or more narrowly defined, everything customers are not willing to pay for.

Paying too much, or buying things that you don't need, are examples of waste. Other examples are having too many resources on hand, for example too much space or stock. Lack of quality, resulting in redoing work or loss of sales, is another type of waste. Wasting money is bad enough, but wasting people's time is often even worse.

All of us become frustrated and demotivated when faced with unnecessary work, remaining hindrances and reoccurring troubles. As the leader, you must take the lead in fighting waste. And to fight it, you have to see it. That's why you need "waste glasses".

Learn how to see the different types of waste, especially waste of time – your customers', your colleagues', your own, and of course, the time of your subordinates. Setting targets on waste reduction is a good way to challenge the team to reach a new level of collaboration.

When you really see the game, it gives you the opportunity to watch out for waste. As soon as you notice an indication of waste, it is time to bring it up – not as an accusation, but as a question, to see if others also see what you see.

Try to build a collective drive to fight waste and to see it as an opportunity rather than a problem. By fighting waste and triggering good discussions, you can help each other to acquire better "waste glasses".

Leading with questions

Asking relevant questions is an important aspect of seeing the game. Ask your subordinates what they think is functioning smoothly and what isn't, what they found out about customer satisfaction, and how they view possible improvements. Ask both for the sake of your own learning, and to help others reflect and act.

Be interested also in the details of the work, without interfering or taking over responsibilities. Act like a coach, without supplying the answers.

Especially use questions that start with *how* or *why*, for example:

- **How do you do that?**
- **Why did you do like that?**
- **Why did it turn out better/worse than expected?**
- **How should it look in the future?**
- **How do we get there?**

By asking how-questions, you trigger discussions on both the present and future ways of working. Ask, even if you think you know the answer.

By asking why-questions, you trigger thoughts on cause-and-effect relationships, as well as on purpose and meaning. If you ask *why* several times related to an extra good or bad outcome, you can reach a deeper understanding of underlying causes.

The questions are aimed at stimulating thoughts and discussions for all of you to understand more about the present situation and what needs to be done.

Avoid giving solutions, orders or criticism if it is not motivated by safety risks or obvious lack of attitude.

Continue to ask relevant questions even if it is met with resistance from people who are reluctant to answer. You have the right to learn more and to question parts of the work that can potentially be improved, and you have the right to expect good attitudes from everyone involved.

By asking questions you are coaching your subordinates to reflect, learn and make better work contributions. It is an invitation to come up with both conclusions and solutions.

Avoid becoming the problem solver yourself. The more empowered the individuals are to see problems or opportunities, as well as to design and realize solutions, the better. Try to become their improvement coach. Show your interest and use questions as triggers. Expect everyone to show interest and to participate – and give support when it is needed.

Starting conversations based on *how* or *why* can lead to good discussions resulting in a common view of what needs to be done, and who does what.

As a bonus, seeing the game gives you a golden opportunity to give feedback. From the answers to your questions, you get to see the potential of each individual more clearly, and you get facts that you can use to encourage good work contributions and individual growth.

All in all, seeing the game gives you a powerful way of strengthening motivation.

5.3 See the root causes

Your biggest opportunities to find both the clues and the root causes come if you *go and look* for them where the work takes place. At first glance there might not seem to be much of a difference between going and looking compared to seeing the game. However, there are important differences both in what triggers the action, and the aim.

Seeing the game should be done regularly, whenever you have created the time in your diary. The aim is to meet people, understand their normal work situations, seeing the individual work contributions – and giving feedback on what you see.

Go and look is something which should be done whenever there is an important deviation – positive or negative. The aim is to support finding the root causes and suitable actions – and giving feedback on what you see.

Go and look, coupled with discussions with the people doing the work, is the most natural and fastest way to start a root-cause analysis. Try to do it immediately after an important deviation has been noticed. Start with asking *why*, but remember to do it without blaming. Give credit if someone has made an extra good work contribution, but avoid criticizing if it is not obvious that somebody has shown a lack of attitude.

The 5-whys

It is rarely enough to ask "why" only once. The first answer is normally more of a reflection of the symptoms than the cause. Instead, continue asking "why" until an important root cause is revealed. This way of finding root causes is called the *5-whys*. However, sometimes it might be enough to ask twice, while at other times, you may need to ask more than five times.

You can use the 5-whys as a simple, but very effective tool for quick, everyday root-cause analyses. Figure 11 illustrates the principles behind using why-questions to drill your way down from the visible deviation to a major root cause.

Let me take a classical example from a manufacturing company. In a morning meeting you receive the information that an important machining center has been stopped. After the meeting, you go straight to the operator and ask:

You (1st why):	*Why is the machine standing still?*
Operator:	It is leaking oil.
You (2nd why):	*Why is it leaking oil?*
Operator:	The oil filter is clogged.
You (3rd why):	*Why is the filter clogged?*
Operator:	It is not large enough for this type of operation.
You (4th why):	*Why is the filter too small?*
Operator:	We did not specify the right purchasing requirements.
You (5th why):	*Why did we not put adequate requirements on the filter?*
Operator:	It is not on the checklist.

Had you asked *why* only once, your conclusion would likely have been: "Let's clean up the oil spill and get started again."

After asking five times your conclusion would, instead, probably be: "We must (a) clean the floor, (b) clean the filter and restart production, (c) order a bigger filter, (d) update the checklist used for new machine parts purchases."

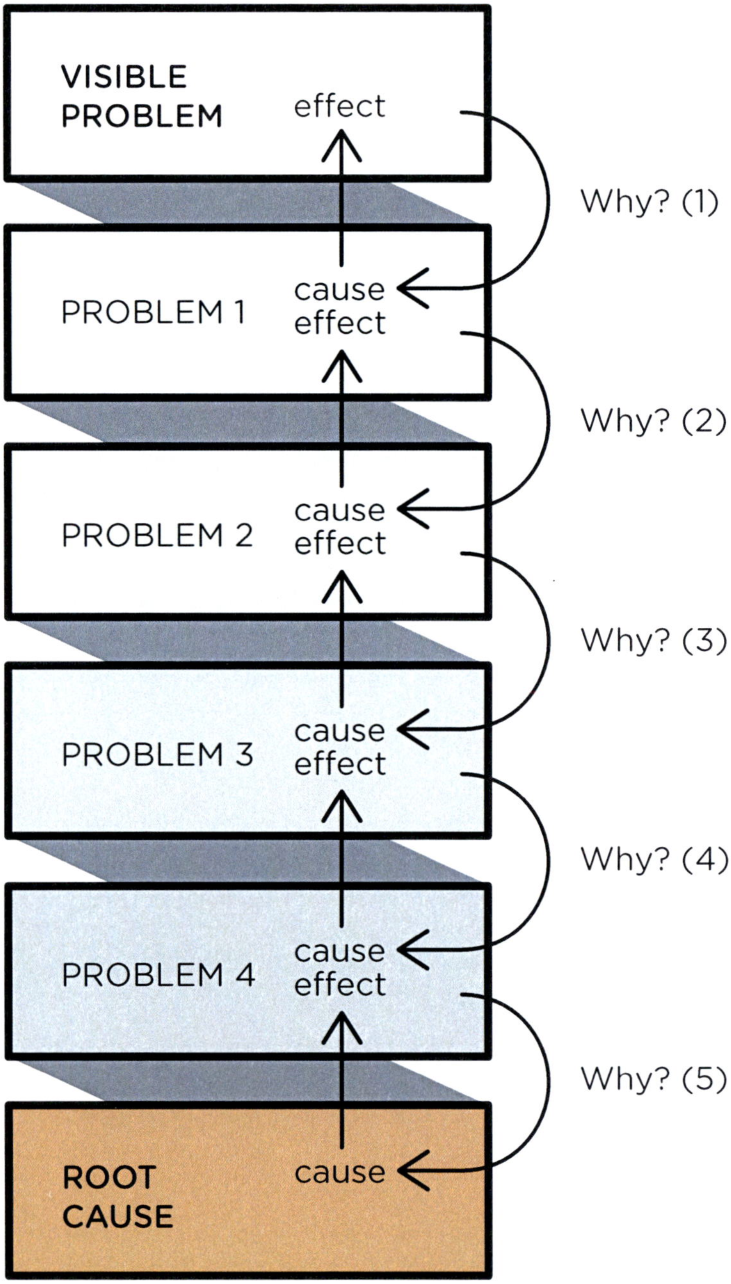

Figure 11 The 5-whys
Finding root causes by asking the 5-whys.[34]

34. There might be several causes for each symptom revealed. Hence the root-cause analysis will create a network of causes, rather than a vertical chain as in the figure. Such networks can be illustrated in so-called fishbone diagrams, as described in appendix B.

Once you have found a root cause to a reoccurring problem, it is time to find and implement a suitable countermeasure.

Remember, however, also to use root-cause analyses for positive deviations – when outcomes turn out better than expected. Then it is about understanding what was done extra well and try to find actions to turn the learning into a new base level.

A possible action for both negative and positive deviations is related to work standards. Is there no work standard in place – but ought to be? Is there a work standard in place – but it is not followed? Is there a work standard in place – but it can be improved?

Use the 5-whys often, but be careful about preconceived answers – both your own and those of others. In addition, make good use of the plentiful opportunities for feedback the method will provide you with – hopefully dominated by reasons to recognize, encourage and praise.

In summary, the third step of the Leader's Ladder, to see, is about seeing every person, their potential and their contributions. It is also about seeing the root causes behind what has gone unexpectedly well or bad. If you, preferably with the support of tools (see the appendices), create regular opportunities to do this, you will increase your ability to make good leader contributions. Moreover, you will have created the base to challenge the individual, as will be described in the next chapter about the fourth step of the ladder.

6. **Challenge** the individual to growth and accountability

> “*If I want to succeed in helping another person towards a certain goal, I must first take care to find them where they are at and begin there.*”
> *– Sören Kierkegaard*

There is a lot of wisdom in Kierkegaard’s words. It is worth noticing that he speaks about leading an individual, not a group. We are often stuck in the notion that leadership is about leading a group of people. The working team, with all its relationships, are of course extremely important to the collaboration (which we will return to in chapter 7), but your leadership must first and foremost be based on your relationship with each individual in the team, and everyone’s willingness to contribute. After all, it is the sum of all the individual work contributions that creates great collaboration.

The fourth step of the Leader’s Ladder, *challenge the individual*, is about developing good relationships with each individual in your team.

To challenge the individual means to expect learning and accountability from everyone, and to give them the related support they need. When you challenge people, you help them to grow. Challenging, however, also goes hand in hand with encouraging and giving feedback. This chapter includes the following parts:

- **Challenge with Tough Care**
- **Challenge with security**
- **Challenge and give feedback – often**
- **Challenge to accountability**
- **Challenge the attitude**

6.1 Challenge with Tough Care

> *"Expecting better contributions without giving support is as bad as giving support without expecting better contributions."*
> *– Scriptor*

We all need security as well as challenges. All of us need to find the greater meaning of our work and to experience joy and a sense of belonging in the workplace. It is, however, also essential for us to be held accountable for our contributions.

Many executive managers find it very natural to demand results from subordinates, but less natural to offer support. Others might look at their leadership only as a support function, and have difficulty formulating challenging expectations for their subordinates. A great leader shows Tough Care by both expressing clear expectations and offering necessary support.

Try to find your own balance. You are probably aware of your own bias. Do you have to practice soft care with empathy and support, or demanding care with clear expectations and direct feedback?

Neither the cold, demanding bosses, nor the sweet comfort creators exemplify good leadership. If you want to become a great leader, you must care for each person, including their growth. Tough Care means giving both soft and demanding care to others.

To show your expectations of subordinates in the right way is to show them respect.

As a leader, you are supposed to lead individuals. That is not to say that the team and its dynamics are not important. On the contrary, the team is extremely important. But only in a very well-functioning team is it possible to only challenge the team as a group, instead of challenging the team members individually.

Adjust your expectations both to the individual's potential and their present work load. Create a sustainable engagement by finding the balance for each person between too much work and challenges on the one hand, and too much idle time or routine work on the other. As the leader, your challenge is to strike these balances.

6.2 Challenge with security

Two of the three necessary conditions for good collaboration (MAA) are connected to us as individuals, namely ability and attitude. Real leaders will challenge their subordinates to grow in both.

Let us start with the first, how you as a leader can challenge someone to become more able.

Increase the comfort and learning zones

By challenging someone, you help them to develop their potential. The aim of learning at work can be translated into handling a wider range of tasks as well as enhanced contributions to both delivery and improvement.

Most people like to learn. Even if we like feeling comfortable, we also like to grow and be appreciated for our contributions. It is your task as the leader to guide each individual from clinging to complacent passiveness to active learning.

Our *comfort zones* are built up by the situations we find easy, things we are happy to do and know we can handle. When we take a step outside this zone, we go into the *learning zone*, where we try new and uncertain things, often with a bit of initial discomfort. If we go too far, we will end up in the *danger zone*, where situations are perceived as overwhelming and threatening.

A worried person has a small comfort zone and a small learning zone, as in the left hand illustration in figure 12. A more self-confident person, who really wants to learn and contribute, is reflected in the illustration on the right in figure 12.

The same reasoning as in going from worried to self-confident can be made for a transformation from lazy to active.

Figure 12 Leading growth
Providing support for personal development by reducing the danger zone.

We can all become bigger, more active and more courageous. As the leader, you have a very important task in supporting the growth of each individual, from the illustration on the left to the one on the right in figure 12. You can do that by providing more security, so that the danger zone becomes smaller, as well as by challenging and supporting the person to increase their comfort and learning zones. Continuously making the comfort and learning zones bigger, at the expense of the danger zone, will help to realize more of each person's potential.[35]

Shrink the danger zone by rewarding contributions and reducing threats

Human beings are creatures of habit – we like the familiar and often view the unknown as threatening or even dangerous. If you are confronted with something new or unexpected, your reptilian brain makes a lightning-quick assessment and decides if it is a threat or not. The amygdala in the brain's limbic cortex decides how to react to the perceived threat – whether we are to fight, flight or freeze. Although these three reactions were crucial for the survival of our distant ancestors 100 000 years ago when they were threatened by a wild animal in the natural environment, they are still as valid in today's work environment. We can flee from a threatening situation, fight it, or try to hide from it. These are still our fundamental, instinctive reactions, and it is important to keep it in mind when leading others.

35. In chapter 8 (particularly section 8.1), I describe how you can use this model for developing yourself towards braver leadership.

What we find threatening, however, varies a lot from person to person. One subordinate can find it alarming to be addressed by the manager, and might think: "What is he complaining of now?" Her response, therefore, might be to fight, that is, be aggressive or defensive without any obvious reason. Another subordinate can find it extremely unpleasant to speak in meetings, and might choose to freeze, that is, try to be invisible at a meeting or try to flee from situations that might require him to speak in public.

Irrespective of which one of the three threat reactions a subordinate chooses for a specific situation, it reduces the possibility of creating good discussion and mutual understanding.

Rewards have the opposite effect to threats. A reward causes the brain to secrete dopamine, which in return, makes learning easier. Thus, to facilitatc learning, your leadership must aim at both minimizing what can be perceived as threatening and providing as much relevant positive feedback and reward as possible. Do not be afraid of giving negative feedback when necessary, but also remember to give abundant recognition, encouragement and praise – even for small contributions. Several of the tools described in the appendices are helpful for increasing a sense of security and creating frequent feedback opportunities.

Reducing threats does not necessarily mean eliminating tasks or situations that can be interpreted as threatening by someone. It is often better to give support in order for the person to overcome an uncomfortable situation. A good discussion, with sincere listening, is one way to reduce the perception of an exaggerated threat. A general way to increase security is to provide values and expectations that are clear and consistent, as well as decisions that are clear and comprehensible.

A boss who takes the credit from subordinates and blames them unfairly, will not only miss the opportunity to encourage with positive feedback, but will add the threat of having to shoulder the blame for failures. On the other hand, leaders who highlight their subordinates' contributions to good results, and avoid blaming bad results on them when they have tried their best, make excellent *leader contributions* by both rewarding contributions and reducing threats. The research team behind *Good to Great* claims that this is exactly what the great leaders of excellent organizations do naturally.

More rewards and fewer threats will have a positive effect on anyone's behavior. This insight should also make an impact on your leadership.

6.3 Challenge and give feedback – often

Giving feedback is an invaluable part of great leadership – it means showing a response to another person's actions.

Note that it is about *giving* – you are giving something valuable to another person. Given in the right way, feedback evokes a feeling of being important, and encourages learning.

Good feedback is extremely important, but unfortunately also extremely rare. It requires knowledge of work contributions, care for the individual and the courage to be direct.

Giving feedback includes everything from expressing appreciation and praise, to correcting and disciplining. However, in-between very positive and very negative feedback, there is another type of feedback that often is neglected: acknowledgment.

Acknowledging by recognizing expected contributions

In this context, *acknowledging* people means to see them, to see their work contributions and to express recognition if it is up to standard. Many managers do not recognize normal, expected, work performance. However, they should, because not doing so makes them miss opportunities to motivate.

Recognition of expected contributions should be based on *seeing the game*, rather than on result measures. You may acknowledge with just a short "good" or an encouraging nod.

Hopefully you have reason to acknowledge expected contributions often. Do it! Of course that also applies to expressing appreciation and praise for that little extra that an individual puts in. Remember that relevant, frequent verbal recognition and appreciation are much more important than some bonus or gift that cannot be connected to an actual work contribution.

Few things are as demotivating as never getting any feedback when you try to contribute. You might even end up feeling that you would rather be seen and criticized for your job input than neglected and never hear anything – at least then someone cares.

Jan Carlzon writes about this in *Moments of Truth*: "Unfortunately, in many companies the only thing that gets attention is a mistake. ... It can be disheartening if no-one notices when there are no slumps or problem-ridden periods. 'Does it make any difference if I bungle my job? Doesn't anyone notice it? Why should I exert myself?' Everyone needs to feel that their contributions are noticed."

Create moments of feedback

If you believe that setting clear expectations and regularly taking notice of people's contributions are crucial for motivation, you have to act accordingly. You can consciously create frequent *moments of feedback* with all your subordinates. Setting up short meetings in the workplace will, for example, enable you to see everyone and acknowledge their individual contributions on a regular basis.

By using simple tools, such as the ones described in the appendices, you can create opportunities to make better leader contributions, for example through:

- Utilizing *daily pulse meetings* to see the current status, observe contributions and give feedback.
- Making room in your diary to *see the game* and to *go and look*. Utilize these moments for asking *how* and *why* in order to find new reasons for feedback.

In other words, it is essential to deliberately create regular feedback opportunities. Use them for frequent recognition of expected contributions, as well as for praising or correcting unexpected ones. Even small expressions of unselfish attitude are well worth encouraging. The opposite is also true, that is, any expression of attitude that harms the collaboration needs to be confronted.

Do not wait until you see the result. Try to give feedback on the *work contribution* rather than on the level of output. In other words, manage by contributions rather than by results (see section 3.2).

Show your appreciation to many – in front of your team, but also to colleagues and others who contribute to the collaboration. Recognition and praise are uplifting and contagious.

Using details as catalysts

With *contribution management*, supported by a structure for creating moments for feedback, you can, little by little, increase your knowledge about the details of your subordinates' working day. And details may be critical, or as the phrase goes: "The devil is in the details." It means that your biggest problem may very well be caused by the tiniest detail – a little thing that is so easy to miss or neglect.

As the leader, you must also attend to the important details, both in your own actions and in those of others. Konosuke Matsushita, the founder of Panasonic, expressed this insight like this: "Big things and little things are my job. Middle-level arrangements can be delegated."

Great leaders remind their people that even small details might lead in the wrong direction. Thus, details are important in feedback. With your interest in – and expanding understanding of – important details, you will be able to ask better questions and give more constructive feedback.

Do not underestimate your own importance. A simple question, comment or some other way of showing your interest may be a catalyst for a major change.

Show active interest in all details that can strengthen the collaboration and its value creation for your customers. In addition, if you are prepared to reprioritize your diary in order to work together with the team in securing an important customer delivery, it will send a strong signal about your priorities. What you say and do might be more significant than you think.

Problem-based, positive leadership

Many sport coaches emphasize the importance of focusing on the strengths instead of the weaknesses. And they are right in the sense that leadership must be positive.

Leading positively is, however, not the same as shying away from problems. If you succeed in creating a positive view of problems, including solving them without blaming, you will have managed to combine positive leadership with a culture of problem-triggered improvements.

To be able to look at a negative deviation as an opportunity, you must be able to make a distinction between individuals and how they act. Or, in other words, you have to distinguish between their *attitude* on the one hand and *means* and *abilities* on the other.

6.4 Challenge to accountability

> *"Nurture attitude. In the long run, there is no other leader contribution that is more important."*
> *– Scriptor*

Accountability is a corner stone of good attitude. Your accountability as the leader requires that you are informed about situations and expectations, and it grows stronger if you are involved in understanding them.

To involve someone is certainly a good start to supporting them in becoming accountable for more contributions, irrespective of whether the contributions are for delivering, improving or learning. To understand what else is required, we need to take a closer look at what it means to be accountable.

Accountability for our actions

It is important to understand the difference between being accountable and being responsible. As the manager and leader, you have been given responsibility for the organization you lead, but you are accountable only for your actions – your leader contributions – not for circumstances that are outside of your control.

In other words, individuals are only accountable for their actions, including lack of actions – not for the result. This is not only valid for you as the leader, it is also true for any one of your subordinates. Everyone is only accountable for their own actions, their work contributions. Together you share the responsibility for the collaboration and its results.

Note that the term "action" includes conscious practices as well as unconscious habits and customs. It includes everything a person does, says or writes, as well as what they express in other ways, for example by subtle hinting, snorting, ignoring or by an encouraging smile. However, the word action here also includes what a person does not do or say.

Each of us is personally accountable for our actions, but only for our actions. That goes for everyone in the organization, from the top-down.

From this, a critical question arises about leadership: "When do I have the right to make demands on other people and hold them accountable?" This question is important, but difficult to answer. Hence it is often avoided in management training courses. It is sad, but perhaps understandable – after all, requiring actions from someone else is often a sensitive thing, even when you have the formal authority to give orders. However, the answer is important. To become a great leader, you must have a good answer to this question.

An example of unacceptable behavior

Let me take a real example from a place of work:

The setting is a commercial harbor, where cranes move on a common rail. The cranes are put in a row along the docks and they cannot pass each other. If they move too close to each other, they will collide. To prevent that, each crane has an alarm system that will trigger if a foreign object is detected within its safety zone. Devices for unloading special goods, so called "pockets", use the same rail as the cranes. The pockets don't have collision alarm systems.

This particular event involves six persons: a crane driver, a pocket operator, a mechanic, an electrician, a maintenance manager, and his boss, the harbor manager. Besides the two managers, all of them have held their positions for a long time. On this particular day, Pocket #1 collided with Crane #1, which resulted in a breakdown of the crane. Besides a very costly two-day stop for the harbor, with delays affecting its customers, the collision also had health and safety risk implications for the workforce.

The investigation into the incident established that the accident was caused by a new, larger wheel fitted onto Crane #1. Neither the driver of the crane, nor the operator of the pocket was aware that a larger wheel had been put in place. Both acted the way they had always done.

When the maintenance manager is asked by the harbor manager, he explains that the new, bigger wheel was chosen in order save money. By standardizing wheel sizes, the maintenance department would save on both spare parts and handling. He adds that no-one had pointed out any risks to him.

The mechanic who changed the wheel tells the harbor manager that the collision was expected. He says he was waiting for it since the maintenance manager took the decision to change the wheel dimensions. When asked whether he tried to tell his superior about it, he answers that it is not his job to tell, just to change the wheel as he was asked to do. He adds that the maintenance manager "should have known better". When asked if he had run the usual test run after changing the wheel, he says no, and that it was neither required by a general instruction, nor by a specific order.

Shortly after the inquiry, an electrician contacts the harbor manager about what happened. He says that the collision was expected and proved that the maintenance manager was not qualified to do his job. He reveals that he had been aware of the risks since the wheel was changed. On the question if he had tried to warn the maintenance manager about what would happen, he answers that it is not part of his responsibilities to do that.

What would you do as the harbor manager in a situation like this? Would you have installed collision alarm systems in the pockets too? A cowardly manager or a manager that has not anchored sufficiently in the MAA control principles might do that – or in other words, they might act on a symptom rather a root cause.

Instead of having a justified confrontation about bad attitude, such an immature manager sacrifices their direct subordinate (the maintenance manager in this example) instead of giving him the required feedback and support to develop his leadership.

What is the most important root cause of the collision in this example? Who did the right thing and who did not? Who had a lack of ability and who needs to be held accountable for a lack of attitude?

By utilizing the *leadership diagnostics tool* in appendix B, you can map the relationships between actions and accountability. It may be used for situations that have turned out very well, or as in this case, developed into a major problem. For every root cause you find, and for every person who may have contributed to that cause, you perform an analysis of the contributions made, and the appropriate feedback.

In this case, the leadership diagnostic shows that the mechanic should have been held accountable for his lack of attitude and that the maintenance manager must be given training and support to prevent and handle similar situations in the future.

The leadership diagnostic done for this example is presented in section 9.2 and is further explained in appendix B.

Contribution management with MAA

The harbor incident was most likely preceded by years of deteriorating leadership, coupled with an acceptance of bad attitude, and will, in all likelihood, take a big dose of good leadership to correct.

If you want to avoid getting stuck in a negative spiral such as the one in the harbor example, and instead create a positive one, you need to challenge everyone to growth and accountability. To be able to hold someone accountable, the person must understand the expectations, as well as have the means and abilities required for doing the job. Checking these necessities is the foundation of contribution management.

Contribution management means challenging people to making better work contributions, including securing mutual understanding, as well as providing support, follow-up and frequent feedback. It aims at improving the three necessary conditions for good collaboration, that is, the MAA. The logic behind contribution management is that collaboration becomes better if the MAA conditions are improved. This logic is based on the Care and Growth Model statement that you have the right to hold people accountable only if they have the required means and abilities to do the job.

Thus the core of contribution management may be stated as: If a person has both the *means* and *abilities* required to perform the committed work contribution, it is their *attitude* that determines the outcome – and whether they can be held accountable for doing the job to the agreed standard or not.

When a new task is formulated, a leader has to ask if all the necessary MAA conditions *are in place*. And, along the same lines, if something goes wrong, the leader must instead ask which necessary MAA condition *was not in place*. This can be summarized in three parts, each comprising one question.

If the contribution meets or exceeds expectations, you should acknowledge, or praise. If the contribution falls short of the expectation, you should ask the first question:

1. Were the available *means* sufficient for the person to do a good job?
If the answer is "no" you (often together) need to secure that the means are improved. This might involve clarifying targets, tasks and priorities, or it might require better tools and work descriptions. If the answer to the first question is "yes", you have to ask the second question:

2. Did the person have the required *ability* to do a good job?
If the answer to the second question is "no", you need to ensure the improved ability of the individual, supporting them to learn. If the answer is "yes", it is a clear indication that there is an attitude problem involved. Thus, you have to ask the third question:

3. Did the person have the right *attitude* to do a good job?

If your investigation of the third question shows that the person really did exhibit a lack of attitude and had, for example, been careless or demonstrated selfish priorities, you must hold them accountable for insufficient work contribution.

Contribution management according to MAA is illustrated in figure 13.

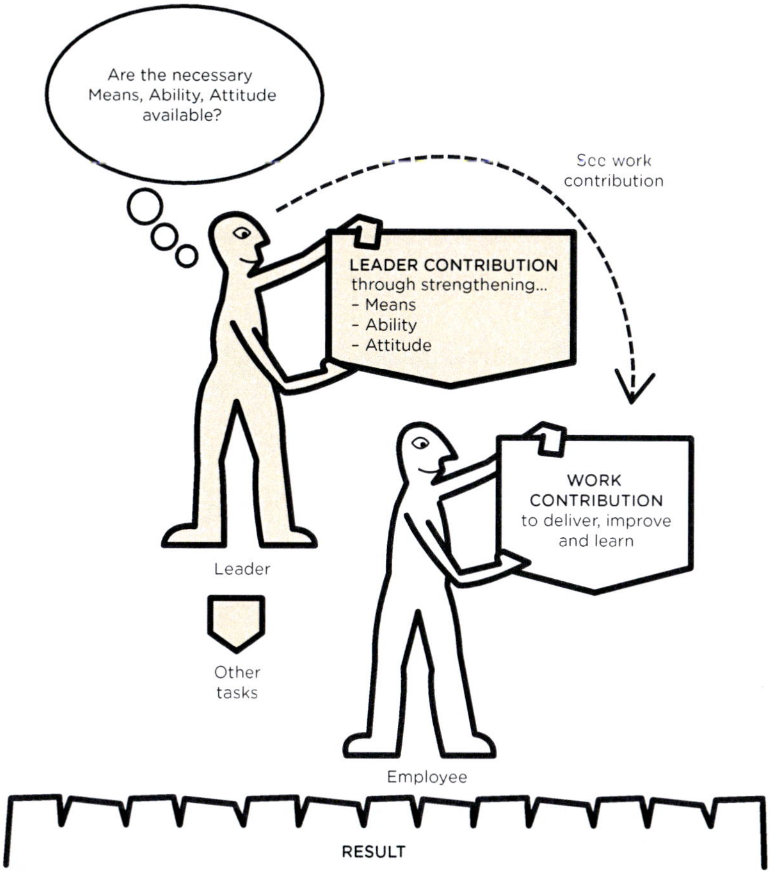

Figure 13 The Contribution Management Model
The leader sees the work contribution (dotted line) to be able to create a good discussion and feedback about means, ability and attitude (MAA).

When preparing for future tasks, or in analyzing actual situations that the leader has not been able to see firsthand, the assessment of MAA must be based on a verbal description of the contribution rather than on seeing it.

From expectations to a positive spiral

If you use contribution management you challenge each individual and hold each of them accountable for their work contribution – provided that you have first verified the understanding of the task, as well as that both the required means and abilities are in place. By doing this, you create the base for both positive and negative feedback.

Understanding the task requires that you and your subordinate share a realistic expectation of the work contribution. In a repetitive and predictable work environment, this is fairly easy because the expectation can be closely linked to best practice, for example a standardized work description.

This is more difficult to achieve when it comes to work that is more unique and unpredictable. The expectations must then be based less on standards and more on rigorous dialogue around the unique task, its targets and the appropriate approach. In such work environments, the learning becomes even more important. If the result does not turn out as well as expected, there may still be reason to praise a whole-hearted contribution if it turns out that both of you knew too little about which means and abilities were required to achieve a good result.

Thus, clear expectations of the work contributions are important both in repetitive and unique work environments in order for your subordinates to accept accountability for their actions and for the leader to be able to give appropriate feedback. Formulating such expectations (and making it mutually understood), is the start of a positive spiral – the *Contribution Spiral* – which consists of four stages:

1. ***Challenge the individual* to clear contribution expectations that are mutually understood.**
2. ***Ensure* that the necessary means and abilities are available. Let the subordinate confirm their commitment when the means and abilities are in place.**
3. ***See the game* and the contributions in the workplace. Use the opportunities created to give regular feedback on specific contributions, including the attitude shown.**
4. ***Summarize the feedback* in regular growth dialogues.[36] Connect the feedback to an appropriate next step in order to challenge the individual to continued growth (returning to stage 1).**

36. Sometimes called Individual Performance Management (IPM) meetings.

In appendix C, I describe how you can use the Contribution Spiral to make better leader contributions.

Holding people accountable

A manager has both the right and the obligation to hold a subordinate accountable when that person has the means and the abilities to contribute well, but don't. However, many managers neglect to do so. There are four main reasons for this:

1. **Lack of drive and courage.**
2. **Lack of ability.**
3. **Lack of support.**
4. **Lack of mutual understanding of the expected contribution.**

Do you have difficulty holding your subordinates accountable for their contributions? If yes, which of the above factors do you need to improve?

Do you have sufficient drive and courage to engage? Do you know how to act? Do you need to secure support from your superior (and HR)? Or, do you need to be clearer with each individual about the expectations of work contributions? Use the Contribution Spiral in appendix C1 to support you in this.

6.5 Challenge the attitude

Based on Tough Care, leaders have both the right and the obligation to confront lacking attitude. They also have the right to expect the full support of their superiors to do this, as well as expecting unions and coworkers not to back any such lack in attitude.

A while ago, there were numerous newspaper articles about a man who worked for a railroad company who had, on several occasions, been caught surfing the Internet for pornography, as well as sleeping on the job. His behavior led to him neglecting to control the train signals in the correct way, risking hundreds of lives. Despite the repeated offenses, and the huge consequences involved, the reaction from his employer was to give him yet another warning. What is your view on the appropriate sanction of this kind of behavior?

Attitude problems

A disappointing work result may depend upon external factors or insufficient contributions – leader and/or work contributions. Insufficient contributions, in turn, depend on lack of means, abilities and/or attitude.

The attitude shown by individuals mirrors their intent to be accountable for their contribution to the greater good of all. In a work context, this means making their best work contributions towards better collaboration – to deliver, improve and learn.

Note that there is an obvious risk of misinterpreting the attitudes of subordinates, that is, the reflection of their intent. Actions that, at first glance, may look like expressions of bad attitude, might be due to other causes or circumstances that you are not aware of. The risk of misinterpreting attitude is, however, not a reason for you not to act on what seems to be a lack of intent to contribute.

In a well-functioning workplace, attitude problems are rare and relatively minor.[37] However, there are two reasons not to neglect to act on them:

- **Even small attitude problems can affect the team spirit and collaboration.**
- **Small attitude problems may grow bigger, and spread, if not confronted.**

A potential attitude problem signals a lack of respect and egoistic priorities. Carelessness, laziness, whining, blaming, hiding facts and backstabbing others are all signs of bad attitude. Think about what will happen if you do not confront these types of behavior. Also think about what attitude you, as the leader, display outwardly.

The team player and the egoist

Great leaders base their actions on the assumption that everyone really wants to contribute their best. But there are limits to their tolerance of behavior that hurts the collaboration. A subordinate who shows an egoistic attitude must be handled in a different way than the team player. However, both should be invited to belong to the team. And they must both be given the chance to understand the vision and goals, as well as the tasks and expectations.

To be able to take the next step, the team player needs your attention and feedback, as well as your challenge and support.

37. When Wendy Lambourne was studying deviations in a factory, she found that 70% of the deviations depended on lack of means, 20% on lack in ability and 10% on lack of accountability. She writes in *Dealing with Exceptions*: "In all the diagnostic exercises that I have participated in since then, means issues have always been the most common, followed by ability, and lastly accountability issues. This makes sense to me. The majority of people come to work wanting to do the job right. The leader's task is to make it possible for them to do so."

The egoist, who continues to show a lack of attitude despite your feedback, needs clearer expectations and tighter follow-ups from your side. Give immediate corrective feedback on continued bad behavior, as well as prompt positive feedback if there is an improvement.

We all alternate between being team players and egoists. We deserve to be confronted when we hamper other people's attempt to cooperate. Corrective feedback gives us the chance to understand (compare figure 9) and improve. A great leader acts early on bad attitude – first to understand, but later tougher and stricter if necessary.

A base level for attitude

It is obvious that a leader must confront clear defiance of formal rules. It becomes more difficult, however, when a subordinate shows bad attitude without clearly breaking explicit rules. Bad attitude actions are, in fact, often very subtle. It might be a small cutting remark (taunt) or a slight grimace.

A friend of mine told me about an incident at his first job. One day, he almost fell over a broom that was halfway under a desk and halfway out in the aisle. He asked the colleague at the desk why the broom was there. The colleague gestured with this head towards the manager's office and explained: "Naturally, there should not be a broom lying here. But do you think he has the courage to tell me to put it away? The broom shows who is in charge here."

How do you handle a situation like that? Sometimes the lack of respect is directed at you as the manager. In other cases, it might be directed at someone else. What is an appropriate reaction to a subordinate who openly discredits a colleague – or sighs or raises their eyebrows to show disrespect?

The talks that happen behind someone's back might easily have serious consequences, for instance, people might start to treat someone unfairly based on gossip. If this behavior spreads in a team, it can be devastating for the collaboration. Therefore, you have to act when a person shows a lack of respect for a colleague or another stakeholder.

For example, when the elderly research leader at a university hospital refuses to follow the new, agreed-upon way of working, that was concluded would benefit both his colleagues and the patients, he has to be confronted. This might obviously be difficult. Teaching old dogs new tricks is not easy, especially if the person feels that it comes at a risk to his own prestige and/or freedom to act. However, it is important to take up the fight – both for the best of the collaboration and for the best of the person. But only take it on if you are likely to win. If you anticipate that the issue will end up with your superior or the HR manager, first ensure that they are on your side.

If subordinates break formal and binding rules regulating their obligations as employees, they are guilty of misconduct. For you to refer to such misconduct in a dispute, you need to be able to show both how you have made the rules clear and what has happened all the way since the first breaking of the rule, including your feedback. You therefore need to document all your feedback interactions – all the way from gentle discussions about what really happened, and why, to formal warnings.

Base levels are used to visualize deviations from expectations. You can define a base level for expected attitude in exactly the same way as you would define a base level for expected results or ways of working.

Let the team define its rules and values on top of what is formally required by centralized regulations. Involve your colleagues and superiors if possible. And most importantly, put them in writing together with your team, so they become a clear base level for when you need it. Keep the base level alive as a natural part of the workplace standard by referring to it every time you have reason to recognize good attitude.

Look for the real intent

It is the intent behind an action that determines how you as the leader should respond. Therefore you have to be able to interpret intent. Anyone can conceal egoistic attitude. And sometimes a person might signal a bad attitude despite actually having good intentions. Let me take a real example from health care. A woman was asked to perform a new task by her boss, a task she was judged to have both the means and ability to handle. She answered "I refuse, I just won't do it." The manager first interpreted the answer as pure disobedience, but decided to find out the reasons behind the refusal. It turned out that the woman didn't believe she was capable of doing the new task. A manager who could not be bothered to examine the intent behind the defiant answer would likely have responded too harshly. But in this case, the manager met with the woman and succeeded in building her confidence to learn and take on the new task.

The example pinpoints the reason why, as the leader, you have to look for the real intent behind the actions you see. For example, if a subordinate's refusal to contribute their best is egoistical or selfish, you have to act in a tough manner. If it is due to a lack of confidence, your approach should be softer, as the supporting coach. Let your best interpretation of the attitude, the intent to contribute, determine your response.

It is often difficult to be completely sure about the intent behind an action, for example a short comment, a snort or a sigh. Asking "Why did you do that?" can be a good start to finding the real intent. Just as with attempts to find the root cause of problems, it might take several "whys" to really understand the intent behind an action. Therefore, the 5-whys method is also relevant when investigating a potential attitude problem.

Individualize your corrective feedback

According to the MAA logic, it is only justified to criticize someone if they had the appropriate means and abilities to perform a good job, and still did not do it.[38] If the problem springs from a lack of means or abilities, you have a joint responsibility to try to compensate or provide the missing conditions.

Try to learn from the reason why a condition is missing. It might be because someone in the leadership failed to do something. The leadership diagnostic in appendix B is a very powerful tool for analyzing a leader's role in a situation that has turned out worse, or better, than expected. By using it, you can avoid similar problems in the future and strengthen good leadership behavior.

Expected work contributions should be acknowledged, while unexpected work contributions require stronger feedback. If the contribution is better than expected based on the means and abilities at hand, praise is due. If it is less than expected, and is related to a lack of attitude, corrective feedback is required.

Remember that giving corrective feedback is much more difficult than praising. Adapt your wording to the situation and the individual's personality. The basic rule is to give your observations in a straightforward manner, eye to eye, and to be prepared to listen to the other's point of view. Refrain from criticizing an individual in public if you do not have very good reasons to let more people hear it.

Strive for eye contact to ensure a real connection. Be clear in your message, but be willing to understand the person's motivations better. Try to start a good discussion, always with the aim of improving the attitude to contribute.

Be gentler to the sensitive person and harder with the thick-skinned. Observe the other person and try to understand how they perceive your comments.[39] Keep looking for any signs of attitude improvement so that you can recognize small changes for the better. However, continue to be clear about your expectations and keep referring to the agreed attitude baseline.

38. Note that if you expect subordinates to improve the means and their abilities to perform certain tasks, this effort to improve also becomes a task that, in itself, requires means and abilities.

39. You can adapt, by either softening or hardening your reactions, as the situation requires. Someone once said: "No-one can make you angry if you do not allow it." The Greek philosopher Aristotle expressed a similar sentiment when, in the 3rd century BC, he wrote: "Anyone can become angry. That is easy. But to become angry with the right person, to the right degree, at the right time, for the right purpose and in the right way – that is not easy."

If necessary, you have to escalate your corrective feedback. Remind yourself that you are doing it for the sake of the collaboration, the team and other stakeholders, and for the sake of the individual involved. Care for the individual's growth as a person and as a team member. And remember that caring does not always mean to be soft.[40]

Play down hard mistakes

You commit a *hard mistake* if you criticize someone on false grounds, that is, when their lack of contribution is due to insufficient means or abilities. You commit a *soft mistake* if you do not criticize insufficient contributions caused by poor attitude. Hard mistakes are uncommon in most organizations, while soft mistakes occur more regularly.

There are two main reasons why you as a leader would commit soft mistakes. One is that you lack information, and the other is that you lack courage. You can, therefore, avoid making soft mistakes by gathering information about the root cause(s) of the event at hand, and by plucking up the courage to confront any signs of bad attitude.

The risk involved in avoiding soft mistakes is that you will make a few hard mistakes instead. It is, however, possible to limit the consequences from hard mistakes. If you have created an open climate where you are prepared to admit mistakes, you will most probably learn when you have made a hard mistake. If you realize that you've been too harsh in a situation, you can make an apology, which will most likely be accepted.

Few, and well-handled hard mistakes are better than too many soft ones. I would like to suggest that the dysfunctional culture illustrated by the harbor example from section 6.4 was the result of many, many soft mistakes over a long period of time.

Remember that you should confront bad attitude both for the sake of the collaboration and for the sake of the individual's growth. If your subordinates see that intent in your behavior, they will most likely overlook a few rare hard mistakes.

40. Nelson Mandela underlines that care sometimes needs to be hard. He writes in *Long Walk to Freedom* how Jongintaba Dalindyebo, king of the Thembu people, took care of him after his father's death: "The king and his wife, No-England, raised me as if I was their own child. They worried about me, guided me and punished me, everything in a spirit of love and fairness as if I had been their own child. Jongintaba was strict, but I never doubted that he loved me."

Untrained or incapable?

Let us take a closer look at the term "ability". If someone lacks the ability to perform a certain task, they are *unable* to do it. The reasons for them being unable can be twofold. They are either capable of doing the task, but *untrained* to do it. Or they may be *incapable*, which means that it is impossible for them to learn how to do the task properly (in an acceptable amount of time).

There is nothing dramatic about being incapable; it has nothing to do with our individual value as human beings. All of us are capable of doing lots of things, and simultaneously incapable of do many others. Most of us are incapable of becoming the first violinist in a symphony orchestra. Some of us, however, might well be able to play the tambourine in a garage band, or handle the itinerary and bookings for a band.

There is a role for everyone, but maybe where you are right now is not the best place for you. You might need to reconsider and change roles and/or organizations in order to grow and deliver your best. It is, therefore, important to distinguish between being untrained or incapable.

Imagine that some of your subordinates are untrained for a new task that they are capable of learning. They have the means to develop their abilities, but have not done the training as agreed. The reason might be an attitude problem that, if confirmed, you must confront and try to change (see arrow-box 1 in figure 14). Fortunately, most people want to contribute and only need training opportunities to learn a new task that they are capable of performing (arrow-box 2). The subordinate who is incapable of the job must, however, get your support to find new tasks, either within or outside the organization (arrow-box 3).

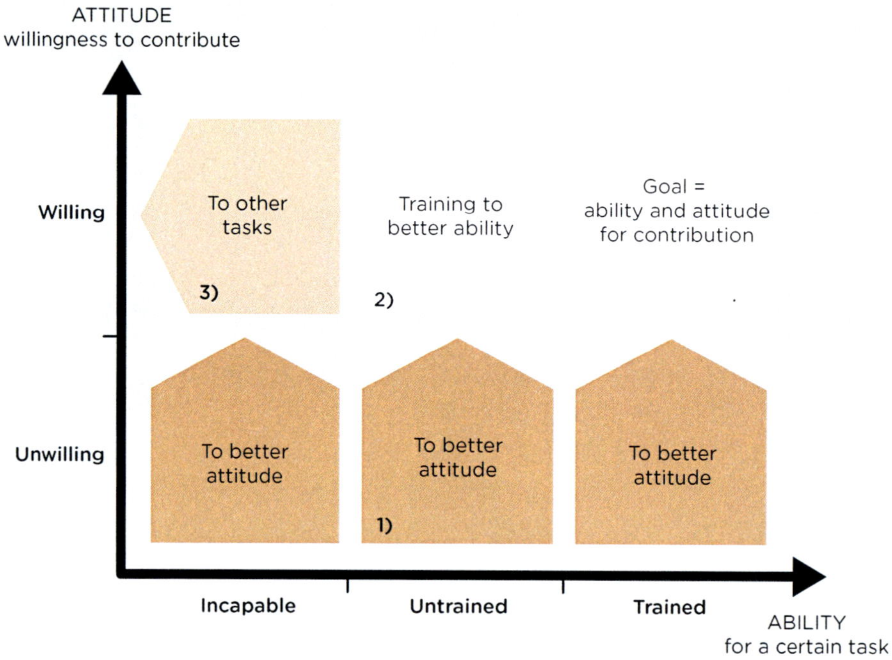

Figure 14 The Attitude-Ability Matrix
Find everyone where they are – and help them to get where they need to go.

The three bottom arrow-boxes in figure 14 illustrate how important it is to address the willingness to contribute. Any unwillingness needs to be turned around. This is a key task for any leader.

The wanted position is illustrated by the white "+box" in the top right of the figure. If you have the whole team in that position, you are in the enviable position of being able to concentrate on challenging everyone with new goals and the corresponding training opportunities.

Incapable persons can, and should, be held accountable for their performance failures only if they have deliberately misled you to believe that they were capable. An incapable person with good attitude cannot, and should not, be held accountable for not being able to perform a task. Such persons must be met with understanding and respect while, at the same time, you collectively try to find new tasks for them.

From the *Attitude-Ability Matrix* in figure 14 we can derive important conclusions for a leader. One is that you must treat fellow human beings who are willing to contribute with the greatest respect, and support them to find their niche where they can make their best contribution. If it means finding them new places to work, the decision might be hard, but the execution must be soft.

Another is that you should try to simplify the working tasks so that a normal person with a good attitude can be trained to do them. Do not create processes and tasks that demand superheroes.[41]

Even if you can minimize cases of incapability by focusing on simple and effective work processes, there will still be work tasks that not everyone can do, even with proper training. If you realize that some people are incapable of contributing sufficiently, it is better to start finding them new tasks, in the organization or outside; and to do it as quickly as possible – not least for the sake of the individuals in question. Everyone needs to feel useful and needed.[42]

In summary, the fourth step, to challenge the individual, is about giving everyone the opportunity to learn and grow closer to their full potential. This is a prerequisite for building a great team, which is what the fifth step is about.

To be able to challenge individuals in the best way, you need to humbly find them where they are at in order to support them in the direction where they can best use their capabilities. The continuation of this chapter's introductory quote from Kierkegaard highlights this:

> ***"If I want to succeed in helping someone towards a specific goal, I must first take care to find them where they are at and begin there. If I cannot do this, I am under a delusion if I think I can help someone else. In order truly to help people, I need to understand more than they do, but first I need to understand what they understand. If I do not do that, my greater understanding does not help them at all. If I nevertheless want to assert my greater understanding, then it is because I am vain or proud, and that I want to be admired by them instead of helping them. All genuine helpfulness starts with humility. The helpers must first humble themselves to the ones they want to help, and therefore, understand that to help is not to dominate, but to serve. If I am unable to do this, then I cannot really help anyone."***

41. Managers at Toyota have pinpointed this as one explanation for their success. They say that the company has focused on developing work processes that allow ordinary people to create extraordinary results, instead of the common notion of looking to hire extraordinary people.

42. Jim Collins' *Good to Great* research showed that the extraordinary level 5 leaders acted quickly when they realized that a person was incapable.

7. **Build** team, flow and structure with pulse

> ***"Our advantage lies in our ability to cooperate and to create team spirit."***
> ***–Bert-Olof Svanholm***

The fifth step of the Leader's Ladder, *building team, flow and structure*, is about creating team spirit, creating effective workflows and providing supporting tools that improve collaboration. That is also what Bert-Olof Svanholm, the former executive of the international engineering giant ABB, highlights in the quote above. Good interplay and team spirit are fundamental to our ability to deliver, improve and learn – as well as for us to enjoy our working days. On the fifth step we focus on challenging the team instead of the individual, as on the fourth step. It also stresses the importance of using a support structure to improve the interplay and the spirit. The chapter includes the following parts:

- **Build team and flow**
- **Build good discussions with a pulse**
- **Build systematic improvement**
- **Build structure for PDCA**
- **Build learning opportunities**

7.1 Build team and flow

"We are going to win, and the industrial West is going to lose: there's nothing much you can do about it, because the reasons for your failure are within you. Your firms are built on the Taylor model; even worse, so are your heads. For you, management is the art of smoothly transferring the executives' ideas to the workers' hands. We are beyond that: business, we know, is now so complex and difficult, the survival of firms so hazardous in an environment increasingly unpredictable, competitive and fraught with danger, that their continued existence depends on the day-to-day mobilization of every ounce of intelligence."
–Konosuke Matsushita

Despite the quote being almost 30 years old, it is still very relevant. Real leaders work hard to mobilize the best in every person – in order to improve the collaboration through increasingly better MAA. And to do that, they build team spirit.

The team and the team spirit

More than just a group of people, a team is characterized by the members sharing the same goals, and a desire to cooperate with and support each other. The motto of the three musketeers, "all for one and one for all", from Alexandre Dumas' book with the same name, perfectly sums up team spirit.

Great leadership turns groups into teams. The result is that all the team members feel they belong to and are needed by the team. For a team to be strong, it is also important to create a feeling of security, so that there is less need for people to protect their own interests. Less need to act selfishly enables more of a focus on collaboration. As the team leader, you have more impact on those feelings than anyone else.

Diversity is often a real advantage for creativity. Invite different people into your team, regardless of gender, age, ethnicity or expertise. The differences will most likely increase your common ability to see different perspectives, for example on problem-solving and finding new ways of fulfilling customers' needs.

Build your team on a foundation of caring – the care for colleagues and customers, as well as owners and society. Inspired by your good example of Tough Care with Courage, the team will eventually develop the kind of dynamic where they all fully respect each other, contribute their best, dare to speak up and have the courage to test limiting boundaries.

Enabling structure and discipline

It is not uncommon to find managers who see a contradiction between structure and system thinking on the one hand, and creativity and flexibility on the other. They look at structure as negative limitations that prevent them from acting spontaneously.

However, I have seen that a good structure provides positive means to increase both the quality and the speed of decision making. On top of that, proper structure can be an aid for building better team spirit.

The term "structure" here refers to common rules and guidelines (e.g. work standards), as well as the tools and habits that you deliberately develop in order to support the work of adding value. Both the method that guides how you set goals, and the resulting document with the goal statements, are examples of essential elements of a structure.

A good structure simplifies the job. It clearly sets the limitations, but supports flexibility within the given framework.

Work towards strengthening a structure that simultaneously gives transparency and routines, as this encourages initiatives, testing and learning. In the following parts of this chapter, as well as in appendices A and B, two such sets of structures are described, namely *pulse meetings* and *PDCA supporting tools*.

Good housekeeping at the workplace (e.g. on your own hard drive or on the company server), is a way to build and retain structure. Methodologies that support you in maintaining order (e.g. 5S[43]), can be incorporated as part of the structure. As the leader, you can choose to view such methods from a broader perspective as tools for practicing sound discipline for everyone in the team, including yourself.[44]

43. 5S is the name of a method for organizing a workspace for efficiency and effectiveness. It uses a list of five words that all start with the letter "S". These are: "sort", "set in order", "shine", "standardize", and "sustain".

44. Sound discipline here means that everyone adheres to agreed principles, rules and ways of working, and is prepared to improve upon these guiding rules. Ikea Swedwood's success under the leadership of CEO Roger Svensk is partly explained by such a sound discipline, including a zero tolerance of late arrivals at the daily pulse meetings.

A structure is not worth much if it is not used. And worse even, the team spirit is undermined if some people in the group think that they are above common rules and agreements. You should, therefore, intervene when signs of lack in attitude risk undermining the purpose of your structure. Ensure that you create an open atmosphere for discussions, but ensure also that decisions are implemented. Such a sound discipline will strengthen the team spirit.

Us and them

Team spirit emanates from a feeling of togetherness – this cohesion is often expressed with words like "us" or "we". While this is good for the team, you should guard against it becoming divisive and fostering a sense of "us and them", especially towards other teams within the same organization or within the same cross-organizational workflow.

Do not allow yourselves to neglect the legitimate interests of the people outside your team. If you allow the team to look at others with suspicion, or regard them as troublemakers with the wrong attitude, you limit the potential of creating a more holistic collaboration.

Thus, you have to intervene as soon as your team members start speaking badly of those outside your team. Demanding that they meet the others to clarify the situation or possible disagreement is a good start.

Us-and-them talk becomes even more serious if your team works together with the others as part of a larger value-creating workflow. A great leader safeguards the long-term holistic best outcome of the whole workflow, independent of organizational borders. This revolves around creating maximum customer value with a minimum of waste. It also involves strengthening a more inclusive sense of "us", and fighting any exclusionary expression of a sense of "them".

The tricky part, therefore, is to strengthen the team spirit without overdoing it. In other words, you both draw and blur demarcations, that is, both strengthening and weakening borderlines between people. The term demarcation here includes the feeling of belonging as well as the formal division of work responsibilities. The formal part clarifies the boundaries between which tasks belong to us, which belong to other teams and which responsibilities are shared. The emotional part of demarcation is the feeling of belonging.

It is possible to have a strong sense of belonging to the small team, while at the same time feeling part of the greater group of people. This leads to an important conclusion for your leadership: Try to cultivate an expanded sense of belonging in your team.

To act in the borderline areas

The demarcation of your team from its surroundings also highlights a question about your own position relative to the team: Should you belong to the team or act from outside of it? To answer that question, let us look at three managerial stereotypes:

The demanding boss is an authoritarian manager, often an expert. These bosses choose to stand outside the group, focus on results and manage by demands and orders.

The buddy boss focuses mainly on relationships and very little on results. They try to belong to the group, to create comfort and see their role as supporting and coordinating the work.

The leader boss can focus simultaneously on results and relationships – cultivating both effective and harmonious collaboration. These leaders position themselves at the demarcation boundary of the group so that they can act with Tough Care for what is in the long term the best for everyone, as well as for the collaboration.

These three types are illustrated in figure 15.

Figure 15 Three managerial stereotypes
Learn to lead at the border.

The alternative to the extremes of the demanding boss and the buddy boss is therefore a leader who can be caring and demanding, oriented to both value creation and relationships. This is a form of leadership that neither stands outside the group to give orders (unless an extreme situation demands it), nor melts into the group. Such a leader defends the team's interests when challenged by outside forces, but also defends the holistic perspective of value creation when it is challenged by people from within the team.

The simple rule is: *Defend the interests of the people who are not present.* This requires braver leadership.

The maturity of the team determines distance you need to keep. If you lead a mature team, you can become more at one with the group than when you lead a dysfunctional group. The demarcation of the responsibilities of the individuals in the team also needs to be adapted to the team's maturity. In a less mature group you need to specify clearer demarcation, for example through formal documents on the responsibilities attached to specific positions. In a well-functioning team you need to give more freedom, supported by clear directions – so-called aligned autonomy. In such a team the members themselves are mature enough to coordinate who does what, and to adapt to new situations.

However, even a mature team may need someone to direct and take decisions when there are disagreements, as well as to support the strengthening of MAA when needed.

This is not only valid for clarifying duties within a team. The same reasoning goes for the demarcation of responsibilities between teams and departments. An immature organization calls for very clear demarcations. In a mature organization, on the other hand, more general agreements of which team does what should suffice. In such an organization, the teams will help each other with borderline tasks whenever it is needed.

Thus, you need to be able to handle not only demarcations between individuals, but also between groups. If you've undertaken the task of leading immature individuals who try to avoid accountability, or immature groups that blame common problems on each other, you must start by clearly demarcating responsibilities. Gradually, with increasing maturity, you can allow these lines to blur more and focus on collaboration along more holistic workflows.

See the customer and the flow

A process is a set of activities that creates value for one or more stakeholders.

Often the activities in the process are sequential, forming a workflow. When improving a process, it is essential to focus on the real value created for the customer who receives the output, irrespective of it being an internal or external customer. It is also important to have a holistic view of the process – from start to finish, from the experienced need to the fulfilled need.

You can both secure and improve the complete value flow if you look at the big picture, starting with the customer's real need. Focusing on flow efficiency rather than on resource efficiency will not only remove bottlenecks and therefore speed up the flow, but it will, in the long run, also increase the resource efficiency, and thus reduce costs.[45]

You can choose to start small – with the part of the flow that your team is responsible for – and focus on the value the team creates for its customers, for example for colleagues in a neighboring department.

There are several good *value flow analysis tools* available to support you in describing, analyzing and improving your processes. These methods include different ways of illustrating the flow. But irrespective of how the process graph is drawn, it always visualizes the activities and its relationships – from inputs and a trigger to start, until the delivery of an output that satisfies the customer.

One such way is called role-activity diagrams, where the activities are mapped into "swim lanes", one lane for every role involved in the work. In this way, every handover from one person to another becomes very visible as an arrow passing a lane border going from one activity to the next. A role-activity diagram also makes it very easy to see the different activities that a role owner is responsible for – you just have to look at the activities in the swim lane belonging to that particular role.

In some cases, such as in processes for the production of goods, it is very easy to see the objects flowing from activity to activity, as well as understanding who the end customers are – the people paying for the products. In other cases it is more difficult, like in service delivery. In schools or hospitals, for example, people might be viewed as "the objects" flowing through the system, receiving value through activities.

45. See for instance Eli Goldratt's *Theory of Constraints* (TOC) that describes how to control and improve systems starting with bottlenecks, or Niklas Modig and Pär Åhlström's *This is Lean*, that describes how a strategy based on flow efficiency will create many advantages.

In some cases it can even become difficult to identify a single customer group. Take, for example, a school where the pupils receive the main value created, but someone else pays for it. Both the persons paying for the value and the persons receiving the value can be seen as customers.

Adding value is the purpose of any work process. The non-value-adding things you do should be seen as waste. Between obvious value-adding activities and waste lie the activities that are (so far) necessary, but hardly value-adding. These activities also need to be questioned and challenged. Most quality checks would fall in that category. They have often been added to the process to compensate for deficiencies in *means*, *abilities* or *attitudes*. If you tackle the root causes in MAA instead, you will be able to remove the quality checks.

Management's unwillingness to address deficiencies in ability and attitude is a common source of the vicious cycle of adding more and more quality controls. With contribution management, you avoid this pitfall and clear such non-value-adding activities from the process.

The operations of all types of organizations are built up by processes.[46] Many of these are less significant and hence do not need your full attention of being mapped and improved. But the important ones do. As the leader, you must ensure that the essential workflows are identified and mapped to the level of detail necessary to ensure the securing, learning and improving of safety, quality, speed and effectiveness.

In his book *The Process Edge*, Peter Keen warns us about the process swamp, or more specifically, to get stuck in describing the many less important processes, which keeps us from concentrating on the important ones. So, focus your attention. Directed (re)designing of your system is, after all, a far better way to gain effectiveness than evenly distributed cost reduction initiatives.

Keen also warns us not to forget the soft processes, the ones that do not lead to concrete products, but instead create value such as improved operations or a stronger brand.

Both of Keen's warnings are worth taking seriously. Thus, avoid getting stuck in a too formalized and too extensive staff-led version of process management. And avoid missing the important soft processes – especially the ones that create better collaboration, learning and leadership.

The risk of forgetting the soft processes stems from the difficulty of seeing them as processes because they are so different from the sequential workflows

46. In some organizations, the term process has been misused and misunderstood. Some people have come to think that processes are a pile of documents, formally needed to keep auditors happy. In reality, processes are very real sets of activities used to produce value – sets that can be made more or less effective. These processes exist, whether you have documented them or not. So you may as well document and improve them – at least the more important ones.

we normally associate with processes. In contrast to a production process, many important soft processes are, however, not sequential, and do not have either a clear starting point or a clear end point. Take a learning process, for example. If you see it as limited to a specific course, it might look sequential. Seen in a broader context, however, learning is less like an arrow with a beginning and an end, and more like a spiral where the ability is increased layer upon layer.

Soft processes may be harder to visualize, but that should not keep us from trying. The important soft processes need to be described, improved and sometimes linked to the more sequential delivery processes, for example through a new bullet on the agenda, or an adjusted template or checklist.

Leading process improvements

Process management aims at producing maximum value with minimum waste – fulfilling the real customer needs in a way that secures quality, efficiency and flexibility.

It is not just about *assuring* the correctness of what we deliver today, but also *improving* it for tomorrow. The former calls for the right means, abilities and attitudes in order to deliver what has been agreed, and is fulfilled when everybody delivers "right from me". The latter also calls for the right MAA, but connected to systematic improvements rather than delivery. It is, to a great extent, about improving both flow efficiency and effectiveness, striving towards "the right product, the right way".

As there is an obvious risk of underestimating the power of good process management, there is also a risk of overdoing the formal aspects, including controlling it from too far from the people doing the job. There are three basic rules to avoid this: (1) Focus only on the most important processes, including the soft ones. (2) Break down activities only as far as it is necessary for quality assurance and improvement reasons. (3) Decentralize the process management and share best practices between teams.

The latter means involving people in improving their own work. Give them trust and freedom, as well as expectations and support, and you will most likely see more improvement than you expected. Let them try value-flow analysis in their own part of the flow (as described in appendix B).[47] In the next

47. The proper balance between centralized and decentralized process management might be hard to strike. Some processes need to be standardized across an organization, while others are better improved by each team working in them. Financial control is an example of a process that normally needs to be centralized. For other processes, it might be enough to specify the frames centrally, such as some coordination points and a common terminology – and leave the details, and the improvements, to each team. When you decentralize process management to different teams that all work with very similar tasks, it is important to ensure that the teams meet regularly to share best practice with each other.

phase, you can let them zoom out and analyze a bigger chunk of the value flow together with colleagues from other teams. This will create understanding of the whole system and also provide improvements from a more holistic perspective. And, most importantly, it strengthens the team spirit – from the small team to a larger "process team".

7.2 Build good discussions with a pulse

Communication is the lubricant of collaboration – and of leadership. We learn from discussions, both from listening to others and from formulating our own views. Open and honest dialogue brings about new perspectives and new knowledge.

Good discussion

The term "good discussion" here means a conversation in which each person who can contribute, or needs to understand, actively listens and talks about an important subject. Many vital issues, such as those related to delivery or improvements, need repetitive *good discussions* – with the frequency, or pulse, that the particular topic requires.

Good discussions, with sufficient pulse, prevent problems from growing bigger. You can deliberately create such pulsed discussions by combining structure and good leadership. Deliberately creating a structure of short and frequent pulse meetings involves gathering the *right people* with the *right attitude*, to talk about the *right subject* with the *right facts*, at the *right time*.[48] And, if the situation requires it, be flexible and adjust the agenda, participants, visualized facts and frequency to create better meetings.

To lead, and to let others lead, such meetings in a good way might be one of the biggest challenges for you as a leader. It is simultaneously difficult and easy. The most difficult part stems from the differences between us as individuals. We come to meetings with different backgrounds, different professions and different personalities, and we all need to be understood and be able to understand each other. The easy part is that you, as the leader of a good-discussion meeting, can get far by adhering to some basic rules, see table 1.

48. The "right subject" can for instance be to coordinate and secure the everyday deliveries (delivery-pulse meetings) or to find and follow up improvements (improvement-pulse meetings). The "right facts" here mean presenting the necessary data in a way that supports good discussion, understanding and well-informed decision making. Little by little both the facts and the way they are presented can be improved. The "right time" means making the meetings as short as possible and as often as needed.

Remember to ...	Remember not to ...
... invite all who can contribute or need to understand – but no one else.	... discuss in a too limited group – it will harm the result and maybe also the motivation of those who are not present.
... listen and encourage the others to listen.	... do too much talking and convincing.
... allow time for everybody to reflect and comment.	... allow some to dominate.
... see everyone by seeking eye contact with each and every one.	... ignore someone.
... act immediately on disrespect.	... let expressions of bad attitude pass.
... differentiate between topic and person.	... blame people who act with good intent.
... involve everyone in the actions decided in the meeting.	... let someone (including yourself) take on too many of the chosen actions.
... steer the meeting back to the agenda with respect for persons you have to interrupt, and without losing an interesting thread that needs to be continued in another forum.	... let the discussion go in circles or drift too far off from the agenda.
... be curious and open to new facts and opinions.	... get stuck in preconceived ideas about what the others think, what has happened, or about what needs to be done.

Table 1 Basic rules for leading a good discussion

What are your own strong and weak points as the leader in a meeting? If you are the talkative type, you can decide to practice silence, to hold back early comments or advice that constrain your coworkers' reasoning, creativity and learning. If, on the other hand, you are the quiet type and usually let some other individuals in the group dominate, you can choose to practice giving other meeting participants a chance to speak.

Do not forget that all of us are sensitive about feeling excluded or ignored. Include everyone in the meeting, through eye contact if it is a physical meeting, or through verbal invitations if it takes place over distance. If possible, make time for individual silent reflection before important issues are discussed – and ask the quiet ones for their opinion. If the required time is not available, call a special meeting for that particular issue.

Remind yourself that there are causes behind every deviation, and individuals behind almost every cause. Regardless whether the cause to a problem lies in means, ability or attitude, there is often a person who could have acted proactively to prevent it, for example the leader. However, never blame anyone who has acted with good attitude. In other words, make a distinction between the topic and the person. Or put differently; play the ball and not the person.

Different types of pulse meetings

Pulse meetings provide the opportunity to create the right frequency of effective sessions for good discussions. Together they form the beat, or takt, of good discussions with topics complementing each other. The term "pulse meeting" is used with different meanings in different organizations. Here it means *rapid and frequent* meetings that use visualizing techniques to make important *facts, statuses and progress clear to all* the participants.

A pulse meeting should be kept so short that it can be repeated as often as required without creating waste. It requires that only the important facts are made visible to steer the discussion so that the aim of the meeting can be achieved effectively.

Based on this definition we can conclude that pulse meetings can be divided into two basic categories:

1. ***Delivery-pulse meetings*** **– the purpose of which is to find deviations early and to act on them in order to deliver in accordance with short-term commitments.**
2. ***Improvement-pulse meetings*** **– the purpose of which is to improve the long-term performance through enhancing MAA, e.g. through developing better ways of working, better supporting tools and enhanced skills levels.**

Delivery-pulse meetings can be divided into three sub groups: line-pulse, project-pulse and matrix-pulse meetings (see appendix A for details).

Improvement-pulse meetings can be divided into meetings focusing on (a) securing the base-level performance on the one hand, and (b) raising the base level on the other (see figure 10 in section 4.3 for an illustration of the difference). Meetings to secure base levels should be held frequently and be based on deviations and their root causes. Meetings to raise base levels can be held less frequently as they are based on challenges and the activities necessary to meet them. But this challenge-driven improvement may also be carried out frequently with several minor experiments, with the aim to iteratively breach knowledge gaps.[49]

The goal of both (a) deviation-driven and (b) challenge-driven improvements is to improve the long-term collaboration performance, as opposed to delivery-pulse meetings, that focus on how to deliver in accordance with commitments already made. However, all pulse meetings can deliberately be set up to learn as much as possible from every meeting.

Delivery-pulse meetings

Delivery-pulse meetings are the meetings that require the highest pulse. The pulse of these is normally set to once a day, which often means that they are called daily control meetings. In some operations, a longer time between meetings might be sufficient, while in others it might be necessary to hold them many times a day. The aim, however, is the same – to see deviations before they become big problems and to coordinate work in order to deliver on time, with the expected quality.

The meetings are often very short – with participants standing in front of a board that supports energetic, good discussions. The main reason for having frequent but short meetings can be explained with the metaphor of driving a car. When you steer a car, you have to be very observant about where you are and where you are heading. The driver constantly corrects the direction of the car by many – and small – movements of the steering wheel.

How often you observe the position and direction of the car does of course affect the quality of your driving. A less focused driver means a jerky ride. This principle also applies to the delivery processes at work. With more frequent delivery-pulse meetings, you can correct deviations earlier, when they are still small, resulting in smoother control.

Delivery-pulse meetings work well for both repetitive work in a line organization, and for one-time work run as a project. Control boards and ways of working will, however, differ depending on the type of job you perform. Thus, there are different tools for supporting different types of delivery-pulse meetings (see examples in appendix A).

49. Compare with the Improvement Kata method of Lean management, which uses experimenting, supported by coaching, to learn and reach the set target states.

A coordinated meeting structure

While delivery-pulse meetings have great effects on the individual team, the effects can be multiplied by connecting the pulse meetings of teams that depend on each other. Such a structure of synchronized meetings has the potential to increase effectiveness between hierarchical levels, as well as between functions along a process flow. The aim of such a structure is to synchronize levels and functions, as well as transferring problems and actions to the right owner with the right ability and authority.

By setting up a holistic daily control structure, you gain the advantage of quick communication between pulse meetings on different levels. It works both for line organizations and for multi-level projects. In both cases the working day starts with short stand-up meetings at the working level, where "previous-day deviations" and "coming-day tasks" are visualized and briefly discussed, for example, based on the +QTE grouping. One aim of these meetings is to assign quick actions to fix problems, or rather potential problems, which have been found since the last meeting. By regularly fixing small things early, getting the team back to the agreed base level, you will be able to deliver according to plan.

When necessary, deviations can be escalated level by level until the proper ability and authority are available. Rapid response from upper levels to delivery problems found at lower levels builds trust in the hierarchy. Pulse meeting escalation also helps to pinpoint ability issues: Do we need to delegate authority? Where and how do we add expertise wisely without creating unnecessary expenses?

After interlinking delivery-pulse meetings, you are ready to continue the work of creating a holistic and coordinated meeting structure. A natural path is to connect improvement-pulse meetings to the hierarchy of delivery-pulse meetings. The carrying out of both deviation-driven and challenge-driven improvements need to be connected to the delivery-pulse meetings, irrespective of function and level in the organization.

Setting up a special visual control room is a powerful way of connecting different pulse meetings and making the information from the different pulse meetings visible to all the participants. In this way you can create synchronization between delivery pulse and improvement pulse.

7.3 Build systematic improvement

> *“People don't resist change. They resist being changed.”*
> *– Unknown*

Improvement work is driven by people and affects people. If you really want to turn changes into lasting improvements, you have to involve the people who will be affected.

Systematic big and small improvements

Improvement work can basically be run in two different ways. You can either run it through *improvement projects*, which have a specified end, or as *continuous improvements* that don't have a final deadline. The former is about affecting large boosts in performance, often requiring the aid of external experts. The latter is about the many small improvements that can be done locally by the team. The two ways are illustrated in figure 16.

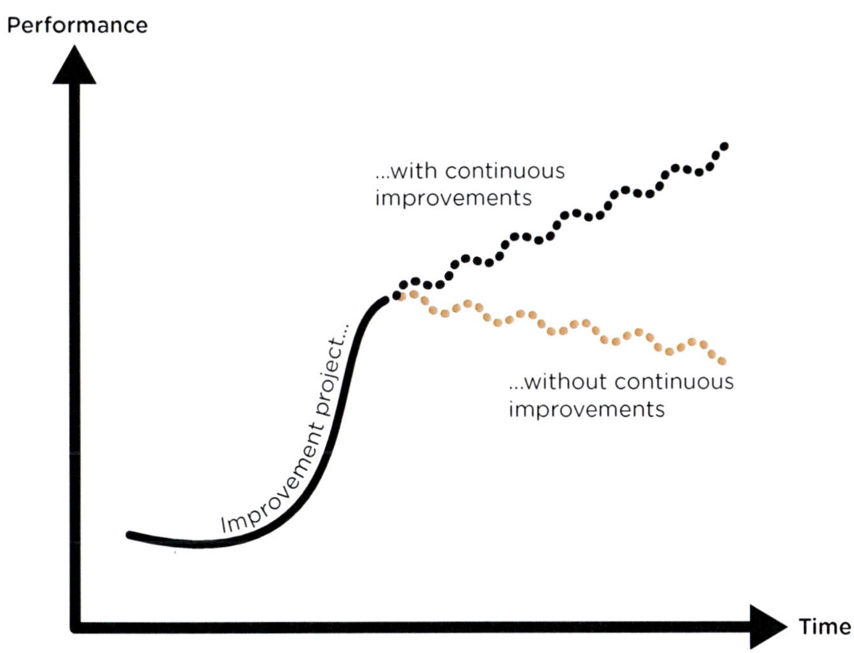

Figure 16 Systematic improvement
... by combining projects and continuous improvements.

Many management teams seem to believe that improvement projects are the only way to improve performance, and start such a project when a problem has grown too big. I call it *the project trap.* The risk is that projects are used reactively to solve problems that have been allowed to grow way too large.

It is like driving a car with a blind drawn over the windscreen and only lifting it once in a while. When you find that your car has drifted halfway out onto a field, you are forced to make very late and large corrections in your steering – or even force some of the passengers out to push the car back onto the road again. Using the same simile, continuous improvement would correspond with very active driving, with constant observation through a clear windscreen, using small steering adjustments, in order to remain well positioned on the road all the time. This way of improving is about converting small deviations into small actions, using every opportunity to both secure and raise base levels.

Unfortunately, there seem to be several reasons why organizations fall into the project trap, and stay in it. One reason is that it feels good to be able to tick off things as ready, especially if it means following a trendy buzz approach, even if the actions came late and with only limited lasting results. Another reason is that starting a large project gives the impression of powerful management. But the major reason is probably that the project path to improvements is easier than the continuous path. If you have the authority and the funding, it is simpler to initiate a project than to lead your organization onto the path of continuous improvement.

While improvement projects are definitely needed from time to time, small continuous improvements are more important in the long run – especially for your leadership.

A combination of improvement projects and continuous improvements is, of course, the best. I have seen this in an operation that I have been able to study closely for more than a decade. By combining the two ways of improving, the number of deliverables per employee and per week was improved by a factor 2.5 over a period of eight years. Of the 150 percent increase in productivity, the initial improvement project accounted for only slightly more than one third.[50] The rest came from continuous improvements, see figure 17.

50. The initiating project was a mixture of redesigning the product and redesigning the production system. No investments in automation were made that can explain the productivity increase per person. However, some investments were made in new tooling in a takted moving line. Very minor investments were made after the start of the continuous improvement phase.

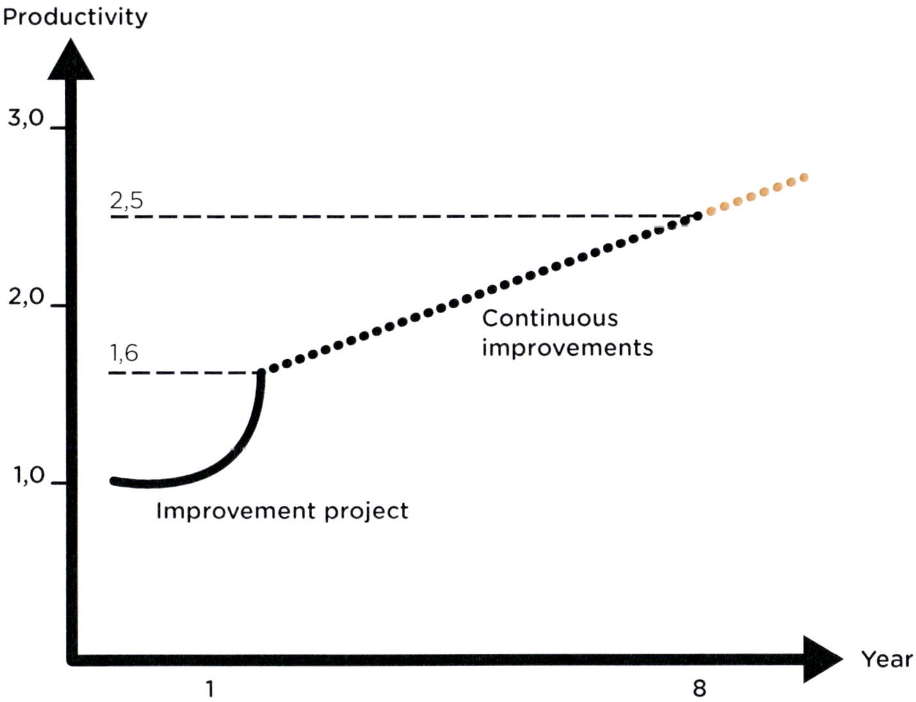

Figure 17 The power of continuous improvements
A real case study, showing the effects of combining an improvement project with continuous improvement.

You might object that figure 17 shows that the speed of the productivity increase is higher in the project phase compared to the continuous improvement phase. However, the effects of a project will typically decrease if the receivers of the output are unable to continuously take care of it. Therefore, it is essential to add continuous improvement ability to improvement projects. If not, the project result will eventually fade away as illustrated by the red dotted line in figure 16.

The principal shape of the curve in figure 17 is not only related to productivity. You will be able to achieve the same effect for other performance measures, such as for quality improvements, whether you work in an industry company, school, municipality, care home or hospital.

Thus, a great leader works on improving the team's ability to make systematic improvements, especially continuous improvement. I will return to how you can accomplish the latter, but first a section on how to manage change through improvement projects.

Change management

Strangely enough the term "change management" is rarely associated with continuous improvements. Rather, it has to come to stand for managing large, revolutionary projects. Such a transformation endeavor often takes a long time and requires a unique project organization, including external experts. (Building continuous improvement ability, on the other hand, is also a revolutionary challenge, but it requires able leaders rather than able experts.)

Large change projects are often triggered by big problems. That in itself is a problem. It is obviously better to solve a problem while it still is small.

But whatever the reason why you start a large change project, it needs to be managed differently in different phases – from dissolving old ways of thinking, via finding solutions, to establishing the habits of the new. Probably the most well-known models describing this are Kurt Lewin's three-stage process: Unfreeze – Change – Freeze, and John Kotter's 8-step process for change management that starts with establishing a sense of urgency and ends with anchoring new approaches in the organization's culture.

The models that attempt to describe the necessary phases in change management typically begin with creating understanding and motivation. The logic is simply that no-one drives change without being motivated, and few resist change that they interpret as being meaningful. This is captured in the phrase: "First sense making, then change making."

Thus, a large transformational change-management project starts with creating the drive for the change, based on understanding and attitude, and it ends when the changes are entrenched as habits. (In that respect, it is similar to the short loops of continuous improvement.)

Time is central to change management. One reason is that there is often very little time to act on a problem that has been allowed to grow too big. Despite the urgency, all the people involved need to be given time to understand the need for change, and the options available. Executives often take lots of time to understand the situation and the preferred solution, but then allow those on the lower levels only a fraction of this time.

Endurance is another aspect of the importance of time. Lack of endurance might become a problem in large change projects, but the risk is even bigger in change processes that involve shifts in behavior, for example those related to Lean and leadership transformations. In such cases the time needed could have been underestimated, as well as the importance of the example set by management. This leads to motivation deteriorating before the large results become visible. It is not uncommon to see impatient management, lacking an anchored vision of the future, giving up on a major transformation and, instead, start communicating the next big campaign. Apart from wasting time and money, this demotivates subordinates, who will regard the next loud announcement with well-founded skepticism.

Thus, if you want to lead a successful transformation project, direct your energy to persistence towards a communicated vision and target conditions by using frequent dialogue in a low-key manner rather than a noisy initial campaign.

In change management, as in leadership in general, it is important to see and utilize the different individual's strengths and growth potential. One simple model divides people into four stereotype groups based on how much influence they have on the others, and whether they have a positive or negative view of the change in question.

It is very natural for all of us to show an immediate negative reaction to a proposed change – the unknown can be threatening at first glance. Therefore, you should see the questioning of ideas for change as something natural, and positive. It opens the floor for good discussions where different perspectives and arguments can meet. By listening and arguing, you can increase understanding and thus the quality of the solutions. Open resistance is only a problem if a person refuses to listen to others and continues to oppose a well-communicated decision.

Hidden resistance, however, always constitutes a major problem. It is an indication that the culture of dialogue is lacking. Highly influential individuals who counteract in the shadows (denoted in the model as sharks), must be forced to the surface. Highly influential individuals who help drive the change (denoted in the model as tigers), are, on the other hand, crucial for major transformations. However, as a change leader, you must not forget the less influential team players, who are often modest, loyal and knowledgeable. Their motivation and support are extremely important for the long-term result.[51]

51. See e.g. Thomas DeLong and Vineeta Vijayaraghavan's article *Let's Hear It for B players.*

Systematic improvement

Sometimes you need external support to ensure the success of improvements. But remember never to let go of your responsibility as the leader. Delegating improvement to external experts is often inappropriate for leading improvement projects, and is always inappropriate for leading continuous improvement. Thus, build and strengthen your own ability, both personally and in your team, to lead systematic improvements of both kinds. By using this dual capability you will be able to follow the upper curve in figure 16. The ability to lead continuous improvement is, however, the more important of the two. It is based on a positive view of problems, and it can be supported by simple methods and tools.

7.4 Build structure for PDCA

> ***"Embrace your problems and opportunities,***
> ***... to become a little better every day."***
> ***– Scriptor***

Establishing and improving upon a culture of sustainable innovation is a great leadership challenge, nursed by your passion for excellence and supported by structure. The basic tool in the toolkit for continuous improvement is called PDCA.

PDCA – the flywheel of systematic improvement

PDCA (*plan, do, check, act*) is a method for systematic improvement and learning. It is often used for guidance in problem-solving. PDCA can be illustrated as a wheel that should always be kept in motion, see figure 18.

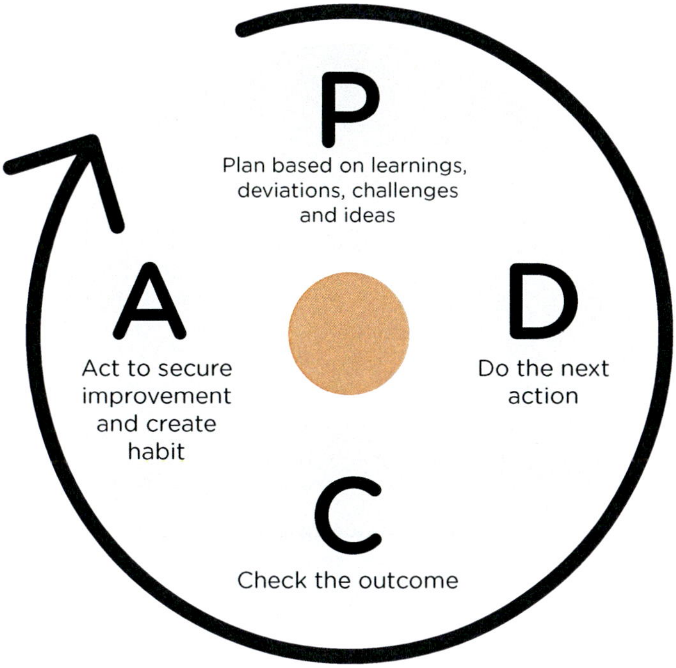

Figure 18 The PDCA wheel
... describing the recurring work for continuous improvement and learning.

Heavy wheels, like water wheels and flywheels, store kinetic energy. They are difficult to get in motion, but once they have come up to speed, they are fairly easy to keep going. That is also the case for the PDCA wheel.

The four parts of the method – plan, do, check and act – might be easy to remember, but they are insufficient for understanding all the important aspects of systematic improvement.[52] I have found the following seven steps necessary to explain the essence of PDCA:

Plan (P)

Step 1 **Capture and visualize problems, challenges and ideas. Prioritize and choose.**

Step 2 ***Go and look* to clarify the real problem or challenge and find the major root cause or obstacle.**

Step 3 **Decide on the next appropriate action (or experiment). Specify the expected target state and the sub-activities necessary to reach it.**

52. Different variations and extensions of PDCA have been developed, e.g. Toyota's 8-step problem-solving process described by Liker and Osono, Rother's Kata, Boyd's OODA (observe, orient, decide, act) and Kennedy's LAMDA (look, ask, model, discuss, act).

Do (D)

Step 4 Do the action (or experiment) decided upon – preferably by first trying it on a small scale.

Check (C)

Step 5 Check the outcome of the action by studying measurements, seeing the work and listening to the people involved. Analyze, learn and adjust the improvement effort if needed.

Act (A)

Step 6 Secure the improvements, e.g. by training in new ways of working. Document and spread it when appropriate.

Step 7 Create a habit and verify the improvements by scheduling occasions for go-and-look audits.

When applied to an operational deviation, step 1 should be augmented with: "Correct the immediate problem through a quick fix!"

A reminder can be added to step 2: "Form a suitable team!" While PDCA can certainly be used by an individual, team work is usually preferred in order to get more perspectives on problems and solutions, but also to increase learning and motivation.

Remember that facts are more than mere data. Hence, *go and look*! It is better to return to the workplace often rather than staying behind the desk, relying on data from rumors and computers. Watch out for knowledge gaps or other obstacles that might be hard to spot at first glance. Maybe it is such an obstacle that it needs to be addressed with a countermeasure in the next action step.

Many organizations get stuck in step 3 and 4, in the sense that they decide and do, decide and do, ... and so on. This behavior might look strong and decisive, but it has severe disadvantages because it risks addressing symptoms rather than causes, creating jerky motions and failing to bring about learning. So, even if it is better than passivity, being caught in step 3 and 4 is definitely not the same as systematic improvement.

The other five steps are more natural in theory than in practice. The systematic capturing of deviations, challenges and ideas (step 1), is alarmingly uncommon. The same is true for the ability to define the real problem and dig down to its root causes (step 2).[53]

It is also very common to neglect to analyze the real effects of an action taken as prescribed by step 5.

On top of that, the important steps 6 and 7 are often forgotten. They are about taking the time needed to secure the improvements made and turn them into habits, for instance through training, documentation and persistently following up. It is a good idea to schedule go-and-look occasions both in the near and distant future, in order to see firsthand what is working well and what is not.

Dare to try

While some people risk getting stuck in doing, others risk getting stuck in analyzing. These people often know very well what needs to be done, but still don't do it. PDCA reminds us of the importance of doing both the action and the reflection. Neither too much hesitation nor too much shooting from the hip are good in the long run. It is important rather to combine the trying and experimenting with systematically searching for facts and building new knowledge.

As the leader, you need to support others to master the different steps of the PDCA wheel. It requires the will and courage to get going, or in other words: "Don't be afraid of failing. Be afraid of not trying." And remember to stop and reflect on the successes and as well as on the failures – regard them all as learning opportunities.

Three "taps" for controlling your improvement flow

Operational deviations, preferably visualized and handled in frequent delivery-pulse meetings, are the main sources of possible improvement triggers. These deviations can be handled in two ways – with quick fixes or with root-cause countermeasures.

A *quick fix* is an action done immediately to get you back to the base level in the easiest and quickest way possible. A *root-cause countermeasure*, or root-measure for short, is an action directed at removing the source of a negative deviation. Improvement-pulse meetings should be designed to take care of these actions according to the PDCA wheel.

53. Thus, remember to ask yourself: What is really the problem that needs to be solved in order to reach your targets more optimally? Which processes and shortages in MAA are causing it? What would the objective measurable evidence be that the problem has been solved? Complement by adding two important questions: Are we stuck in preconceived ideas about root causes and solutions? Do we need more facts and/or outside expertise to challenge our bias?

The wheel moves with every such task you undertake. The tasks you choose to handle are a subset of possible triggers that come from operational deviations, target challenges or improvement ideas. You can control all three these forms of influx with three valves or taps, one for each flow, as shown in figure 19.

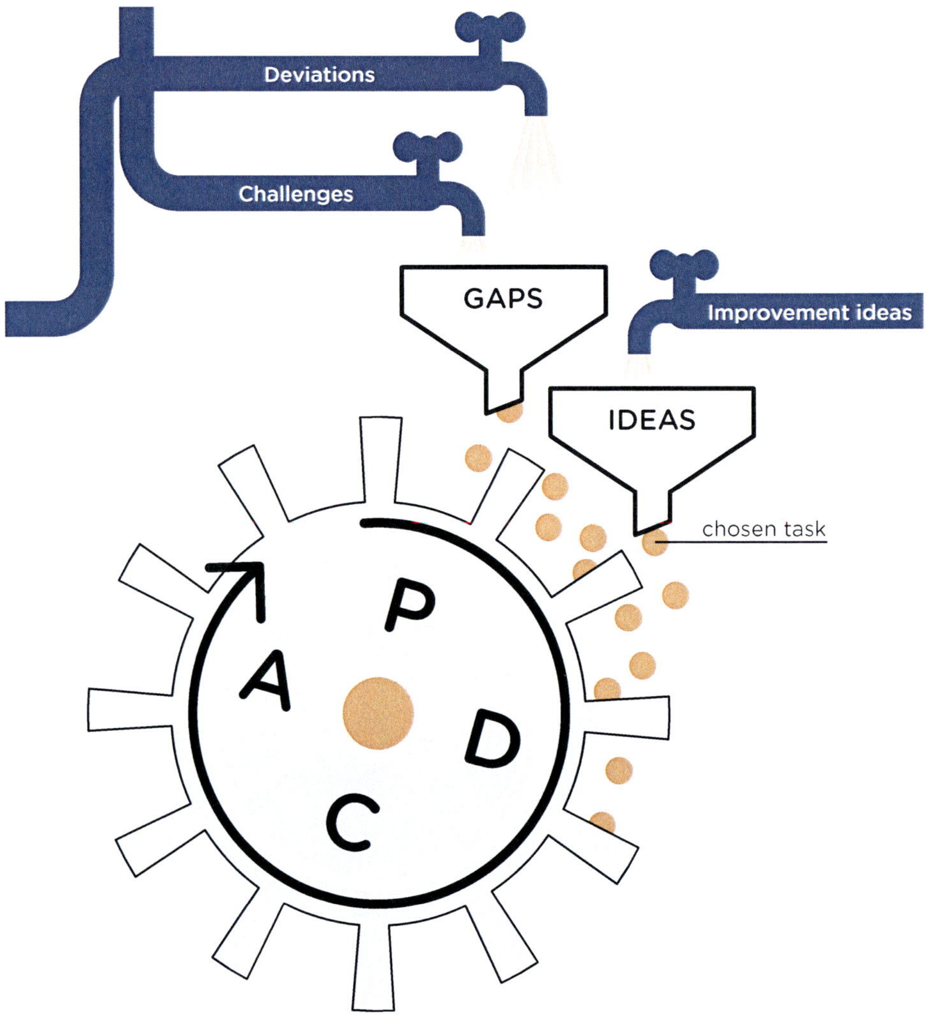

Figure 19 The PDCA taps
Your three means for controlling the influx of tasks for continuous improvement.

The pipe leading to the tap on the right of figure 19 symbolizes the influx of ideas from all participants of the improvement-pulse meeting. The *Pick Chart* in appendix B is an effective tool for regulating the corresponding tap.

The two pipes at the top left illustrate the two other sources of triggers for improvement. The corresponding two taps illustrate your ability to regulate the inflows related to operational deviations or challenging target gaps.

It is very important that, as the leader, you understand how to create the right quantity of improvement tasks by adjusting both the base level and the target level (see figure 10 in section 4.3).

If you set them too ambitiously, you overestimate your ability to deliver and improve. Your pulse board will light up completely red and demotivate rather than inspire. It is better, rather, to lower the less important parts of the base and target levels in order to direct the fixes and root-measures to the most important tasks that can be handled next.

If, on the other hand, you set the base and target levels too low, the pulse board will stay completely green. Working life might seem comfortable (at least for the time being), but without challenges and learning. Ask yourselves if the base level is set too low, and if you have run out of challenging targets. A completely green board is actually a warning sign; it could possibly be time to raise the bar.

Use this insight when, little by little, you improve your delivery-pulse meetings and improvement-pulse meetings in parallel with the team's ability to perform systematic improvements. Boards with color signals help you see the balance between being satisfied (green) and needing to improve (red). By enhancing your team's improvement capability in symbiosis with the right ambition levels – the appropriate number of red signals – you will, together, be able to create the best possible progress.

Loving problems and hating waste

Prosperous organizations tend to create a culture of seeing problems as opportunities. They talk about *loving the problems*. As such a culture matures, the number of problems, or rather visible opportunities, usually increases rather than decreases. Immature organizations, on the other hand, have fewer visible opportunities, but nevertheless, a lot of hidden problems. The rewarding of the presence of fewer deviations – and even worse, the acceptance of a culture of blaming – can lead to a habit of hiding problems. Such organizations become predestined to fall into a negative spiral.

An organization that is geared to continuously performing better, welcomes problems. Thus, it is essential to scan your leadership, your teamwork, your processes and the environment for opportunities. It does not mean that you should try to solve more problems than you presently can handle. Still, it is

good to visualize opportunities. When they are visible, you can prioritize and handle them in the right order.
Loving your problems goes hand in hand with hating waste, in other words, everything at work that keeps you from adding value.

By reducing waste you will free time for improvements, for example, to enhance all aspects of +QTE performance, as well as finding new ways to increase customer value and develop new growth opportunities for the business. This use of the freed time for new challenges is important. People with the ability and attitude to drive change need security in order to improve wholeheartedly. They deserve having new challenges awaiting them when they managed to free their working time from waste. An organization that lays off people who have committed to rationalizing their own jobs is in trouble. Its PDCA wheel will be very hard to restart.

The ability of your team to visualize problems and opportunities, as well as to look for and reduce waste, can be enhanced by your *curiosity* – to experiment and learn more. Albert Einstein complements this view with his wise words: "Imagination is more important than knowledge."

The ability to solve problems and reduce waste is also enhanced by *humility*. You need to be humble and honest enough to admit things you did wrong, did not see or do not understand sufficiently. And you need to show your dependence on other people's contributions, and give them full credit for it.

The vision for continuous improvement can be summarized as "all the people, all the time". It means that everyone in the organization should be thinking about what can be done better – and do it regularly, every day. Unfortunately, most organizations are far from realizing that vision. Instead of involving everyone in PDCA work, the norm is to turn the making of improvements into a profession of its own. Executives have a tendency to look at PDCA as something other people can do instead of actively, with their personal support, introducing it on all levels and functions. This missed opportunity might be caused by their limited understanding of PDCA, or an inability to recognize their own importance as leaders and role models.

Frame management – leading with expectations and freedom

As their manager, you have been given the power to order what your subordinates should do. But you can also choose to give them total freedom of action. Most managers position themselves somewhere in-between being the autocratic dictator who orders everything that should be done and the laissez-faire person who is not at all involved in the work. The perfect balance between tight control and wide-ranging freedom is hard to strike, and it must be adapted both to situations and persons.

Creative continuous improvement calls for you to give both freedom and trust. To give freedom means, for example, to give decision-making power to people who are more capable than yourself for the situation in question, or to people you want to coach through trial and learning.

However, freedom is not enough. It must be combined with an expectation of improvement, a common understanding of which direction to go and the boundaries that has to be followed. Together this puts up the frame that your subordinates could work freely within. This type of leadership can be called *frame management*. By giving freedom within a frame,[54] you lead with structure rather than solutions. At Toyota, this has been called "push the form, pull the content" because you give the form and expect subordinates to fill it with content.[55]

Take as an example that you have decided on the frame that every work team in your area must have a morning meeting and that all customer complaints must be handled in accordance with the PDCA wheel. By communicating this, you have been very clear about your expectations on a high level, but left it to every team to solve it in their own way. You have given them both the frame and the freedom. Then it is up to each team to design their own morning meetings and their own problem-solving techniques (e.g. by choosing tools from appendix B). You can now concentrate on *seeing the game*, combined with providing your own coaching when necessary or, even better, relay tips on best practice in order for them to learn from each other (or from teams in other organizations).

Thus, do not look at yourself as a problem solver, but rather as someone who teaches problem-solving. For this, you need to know the PDCA essentials yourself. Furthermore, it also calls for you not to interfere too much – even when you believe you have the solution.

Involve everyone – expect improvement and a trusting attitude. Offer support with training and tools. *See the game* with genuine interest, and ask supporting questions about the PDCA work. Ask about root causes, obstacles and waste. Encourage experimenting and ask about what was learned from them. And, importantly, acknowledge all new knowledge and recognize even small steps in the right direction.

54. Such a frame can be that a work standard that must be in place and followed. The freedom is then to give the team the responsibility for the content, updates and training. A frame for a product development project team may be expressed as to create maximum customer value to an attractive price level. Such a wide frame gives the team the freedom to be creative. If the steering committee instead controls the product specification in every detail, it will limit the creativity.

55. As it has been reported by Niklas Modig after studying Lean services in Japan.

7.5 Build learning opportunities

> *"In a time of drastic change it is the learners who inherit the future. The learned usually find themselves equipped to live in a world that no longer exists."*
> *– Eric Hoffer*

Eric Hoffer's words are truer today than ever before. In a leadership context you can expand it to: Do not worry about having to cope with losing subordinates whom you have helped to grow. Worry instead about having to cope with subordinates whom you have not enabled to grow.

It is also important to remember the dependence between learning and the two other branches of the Collaboration Tree. Mr. Akinori Hyodo has wisely stressed the connection between to learn and to improve: "Development of people comes first. Continuous improvement is just a result of developing people."

The ability to learn is generally more vital than knowledge – for individuals and for organizations. An inherent problem is, however, that we tend not to miss the knowledge that we do not have.

Reflect and learn

To be able to learn, one needs to stop and reflect. It takes time, time that is often hard to free up. Still, try to do it. Set aside some quiet time for self-reflection in your agenda. Ask yourself about your *leader contributions* since last time, and ponder on what you need to practice until the next. (Do not be too hard to yourself – your attitude of wanting to improve is, in itself, already worthy of praise.)

Make sure to also build in time for team reflection. You can do it quickly as a last question of the daily meeting: "What did we learn yesterday?" and "What is worth praising?" Alternatively, you can do it more thoroughly as a scheduled "lessons learned" point at the weekly meeting. Ask the questions: "What did we do well?" and "How can we do better?" and relate the answers to MAA.

From learning to habits

While learning is essential, it is not enough. The learning has to be turned into actions. And the actions need to be turned into habits. Aristotle once stressed the importance of this: "We are what we repeatedly do. Excellence, therefore, is not an act, but a habit."

This often calls for documentation, such as a task in an action list and/or as an improved working standard. But it often also calls for follow-up. Use your diary to schedule go-and-look occasions for the weeks to come. See with your own eyes that the learning has turned into actions, and do it as many times as needed until you are confident that it has become a habit.

Let us return to the fourth quadrant of PDCA – act. Look at steps 6 and 7 as if you are putting a wedge behind the wheel so that it won't roll back, see figure 20.

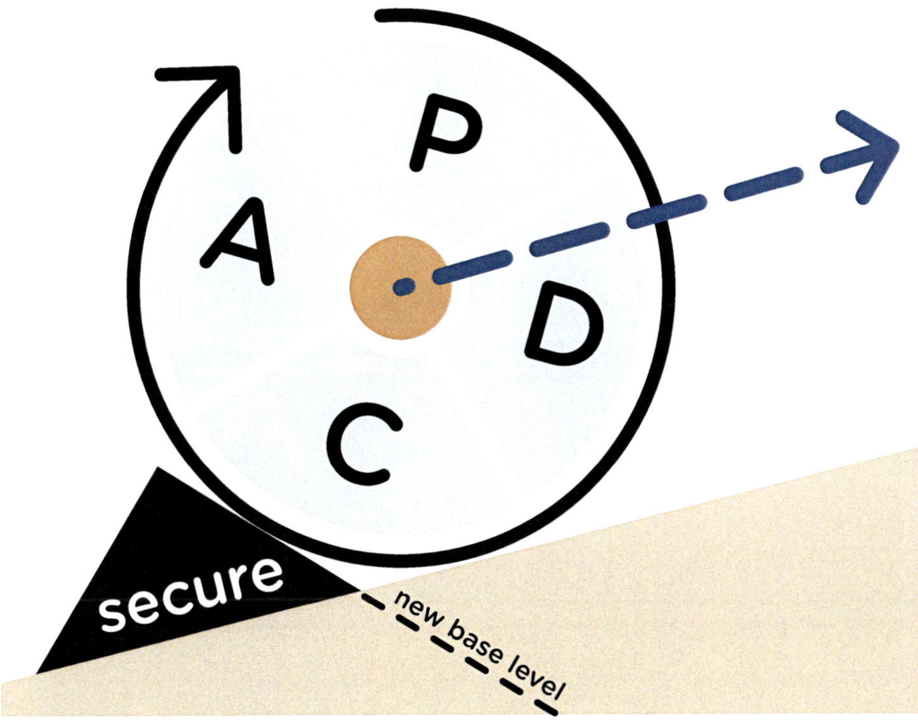

Figure 20 Securing progress
With the A in PDCA, the wheel is secured so that it does not roll back.

Let the team secure what they have achieved, and show your expectation that it should become practice and not fall back to the old ways. Ensure also that the new knowledge you have created is taken forward, for example by spreading it orally and by updating standards. Moreover, use the new knowledge for innovation, in other words, combining it with other inputs to create completely new solutions (for new products, new tools or new ways of working).

In summary, the fifth step, build team, flow and structure, is about using the fundamentals from the first four steps to get better and better. Team spirit is fundamental to this, but so are the holistic view on value flows, coupled with the structures you create to support delivery, improvement and learning.

Moreover, spirit, flow and structure can be developed in harmony. It is possible to design your structure, such as tools for visual control in pulse and improvement meetings, so that it supports both team spirit development and value flow development. Use that opportunity.

8. Braver Leadership

"To dare is to lose one's footing momentarily.
Not to dare is to lose oneself."
– Sören Kierkegaard

All five steps of the Leader's Ladder can put you in situations which require courage. This chapter summarizes and gives examples of what *braver leadership* is about. The chapter includes the following parts:

- **Be braver**
- **Courage to anchor**
- **Courage to challenge the individual**
- **Courage to build team spirit**

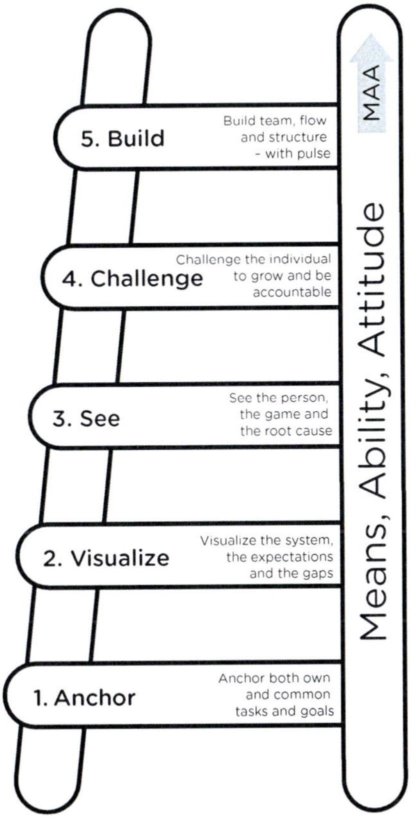

8.1 Be braver

> *"For if you're not afraid, how can you really be brave?"*
> *–Moomin according to Tove Jansson*

To know what ought to be done is one thing, but to do it is another. There can be several reasons for not doing what we know is right. The reasons can range from laziness, or a lack of ability, to a lack of courage. This chapter is about the latter, because fear often makes bosses and their subordinates avoid doing what they know is right.

Braver leadership

Courage is not about being fearless. Courage is about conquering fear – to act in spite of fear. Our bravery is as subjective as our fears. Thus, what is bravery for one person might not be so for another. It depends on whether one is anxious about the outcome or not. In the context of leadership, the courage needed by a leader can be summarized as *braver leadership*: to more regularly act and do what is long-term the best for the collaboration and its stakeholders – despite uneasiness or fear of personal consequences.

I use "braver" instead of "brave" to highlight that it is not a black or white issue. Sometimes we are brave and sometimes we are not. And we are all able to become braver, to show glimpses of courage a little more often. In fact, we all have a cowardly mouse and a brave lion within us. Which of the two will grow and dominate? It is simple; it is the one you feed the most. You starve your mouse and feed your lion every time you do something right even though you may be putting yourself at risk of negative consequences.

Thus, braver leadership is about more often acting contrary to your own short-term self-interest. The fear you might experience can emanate from the risk of making mistakes, losing status, or even being excluded from the group. Conquering such a fear requires both the will and the underpinning values to do so.

You only show braver leadership when you are acting in line with your value base. That often requires courage. And it can be hard. But if you deliberately try to become braver, you can find some strength in the opening quote of Kierkegaard: "... Not to dare is to lose oneself."

It is both difficult and admirable to be braver in this sense, but remember that such an evolution does not take place overnight. Practice becoming braver in small steps. Use the small opportunities that your everyday life presents to overcome the unease in each particular situation. See it as a learning opportunity, regardless of it being related to losing control, trying something new, engaging in a conflict or something else.

From the comfort zone to the danger zone

Let us return to the development zones presented in figure 12 in section 6.2. There it was about challenging your subordinates to growth. Here it is about challenging yourself to grow as their leader, see figure 21.

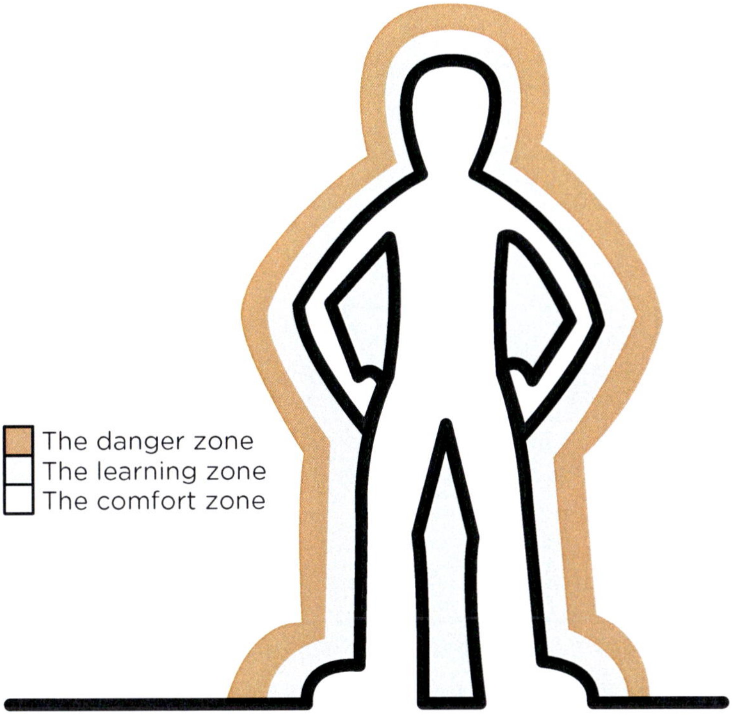

Figure 21 Braver leadership
... daring to grow as a leader by challenging yourself.

The feelings you experience when facing a challenging situation or task can be divided into three zones. When you are in the *comfort zone*, you will say and do things that you feel safe to do, that are in line with what you have done before, and what is expected. In the *learning zone*, you act outside of what you have already mastered – learning new things, but still without any major discomfort. It might involve trying harmless new things or attending a training course. In the *danger zone*, however, you experience unease, or even fear, of risking negative outcomes. The situations triggering the threat are different for each person. For one, it can be triggered by making a speech in front of a large audience. For another, it may be opposing a discriminatory joke, giving feedback to the boss or putting an end to gossip about a colleague.

You are brave when you act unselfishly within your danger zone. Each time you do it, you will grow as a leader. To be able to do that, you might need coaching from your superior or someone else.

Be proud each time you succeed, exactly as proud as you would be of subordinates who overcome their fear in order to do the right thing. A person trying to act braver is worthy of praise. The Swedish nurse, Sarah Wägnert, who took personal risks to expose conditions at her workplace, is a good example of such bravery. Her actions triggered improvement of the conditions and new legislation.[56]

The consequences you risk as a leader are hardly a matter of life or death. But you may risk your career, your reputation and/or your belonging to a group. And that is scary enough. It is, therefore, brave to follow your internal compass, despite the personal risks involved. There is indeed good reason for praising even small brave actions – your own as well as those of others.

8.2 Courage to anchor

Courage to anchor is about finding your own value base regarding what is right or wrong – and then following it despite unease or fear. It may take quite some bravery to anchor in what is most important in leadership and then do it. Let me quote three wise men in order to explore what this type of courage means. I start with the 19th century Danish philosopher, Sören Kierkegaard, who wrote:

56. The law, called Lex Sarah, regulates the duty of employees in social services to safeguard the well-being of those in their care (such as the elderly or handicapped), as well as the duty to report bad conditions. It furthermore also grants such whistleblowers protection from being fired or in any other way sanctioned for reporting any wrongdoing.

> ***"Truth is not introduced into the individual from without, but was within him all the time."***

Kierkegaard claims that we all know the truth from within. That is kind of hopeful, isn't it? Kierkegaard's contemporary, Abraham Lincoln, takes it a step further, by arguing for what you have to do with the truth inside you:

> ***"I am not bound to win, but I am bound to be true. I am not bound to succeed,but I am bound to live up to what light I have."***

According to Lincoln, we have an obligation to act from our innate wisdom. Quite a serious responsibility, don't you agree? The Chinese philosopher, Confucius, put his finger on the sore point 2 500 years ago:

> ***"To see the right and not to do it is cowardice."***

What is your view on these three statements? Do we have the truth within us? Are we obliged to act on it? And are we cowards if we don't?

Dare to take a position

As social creatures, we need to belong to groups, and to do that we feel the need to conform. To behave like the other managers, especially your superior, feels safe (and seems like a good strategy for your career). It is also more comfortable to conform and do what is considered normal, even if it sometimes contradicts your own convictions of what is right. Take, for instance, the courage needed to question poor attitude, old truths or habits that have become as natural as they are bad.

Of course, you have the choice not to take a stand. It might look like the easiest alternative if you are employed in an organization where, in your eyes, the superiors show a severe lack of attitude or integrity. Besides remaining silent, you also have the choice to try to turn the value base around, or to quit and do something else.

Dare to go against the flow

It takes great courage to contradict a domineering boss. You might even risk your job. Is it worth it? You are the only one who can answer that. If the particular issue is serious, and you have failed to establish a dialogue, you may decide to risk your position.[57] That is brave. But again, you have to choose your own battles.

One special situation that can force you to choose between going against the flow or not, is if you find their reasoning too narrow-minded or short-sighted. This is not uncommon; what is in the long term the best for the stakeholders (including owners) may not always be compatible with maximizing results in the next quarter. Sometimes it is hard to strike a good balance between the short and long term, but you have to try.

Daring to live your values means that you strive for more than being liked. What is good about that, however, is that it will most probably result in you being liked by most. Not compromising your intent to create the best for all stakeholders in the long term, will build the foundation for your pride in yourself, and pride in you from others. Others will follow your example. Braver leaders who consistently try to stick to their value base will create trust, motivation and stability.

8.3 Courage to challenge the individual

There are several types of situations in which it requires courage to challenge another individual. One is when it is appropriate to let go of power. Another is when the situation calls for straight and honest feedback. A third is when you need to be uncompromising with details and limits. These three scenarios that call for braver leadership are described in following three passages:

57. How persistent do you need to be in protesting? A simplified answer is called "the rule of three". It means that we are morally obliged to raise an important question, such as an objection to a bad decision, three times before giving up.

Dare to let go of power

You can share your power in many ways. You can delegate a task to a person, with a corresponding well-defined way of working. Or you may empower them to find their own way of solving the task, and give them trust and sufficient authority to make their own decisions. The latter, empowerment, can be naturally interlinked with *contribution management* (see appendix C).

Empowerment demands two types of courage. One reason for being brave is when you (falsely) start to believe the other's increased power decreases your own. The other reason is when you assume that entrusting another with an important task might lead to poorer results. The former demands the courage to fight your own purely egoistic motives, while the latter requires the courage to risk some short-term goals to reach better long-term effects.

Dare to give honest and frequent feedback

Braver leadership is also about the boldness of looking another person in the eye, and being honest. In chapter 6, I described the difference between making soft and hard mistakes. The former is about excusing someone's lack of attitude, while the latter is about reprimanding someone's action despite their good intent.

Managers who find it unpleasant to give feedback easily find many excuses not to do so. They may justify it by saying they don't want to run the risk of hurting someone, or that they don't have enough facts about the situation in question. The fear of an unpleasant conflict makes them wait too long before confronting the signs of lack of attitude, such as carelessness, lack of respect or selfish actions. It takes courage to override that fear and act early. And it might also take courage to apologize in the event that it turns out to be a hard mistake.

It takes even more courage to give feedback when you manage by contributions rather than by results (see section 3.2). The reason is that work contributions are open to more subjective interpretations than hard figures.

It is cowardice to criticize a group instead of the individual(s) accountable for the bad attitude actions in question. A braver leader also takes on the strong individuals with straight feedback.

But more importantly – the braver leaders also remember to use positive feedback with acknowledgements and praise as the everyday source of encouragement. And they do it to everyone, not only the stars of the team. That may also demand a bit of courage.

Dare to refuse compromising on details and limits

The braver leader follows up work contributions, and if necessary, without compromise. Details are often important and you have the right to demand that commitments are followed even when it comes to details. The same goes for agreed limits or rules. Be clear about your expectations and do not excuse below-standard contributions caused by lack of attitude. If there is something wrong with the limits or rules, change them.

But what do you do if you yourself are challenged? A skilled leader once said to me: "My experience is that if you do not set limits, the other takes over." Lack of respect is never okay. You must take on the fight against it – not least if it is directed towards you. Just ensure that you are well prepared in order to win the battle.

Limits for bad or lacking attitude must be made clear, not only in defense of the respect between people, but also in defense of the respect for the work. Workers on all levels can, at times, refuse to accept responsibility to learn new things and contribute to the common improvement work. Irrespective of whether the reason is a prior lack of leadership or something else, you should not back off from the legitimate demand that everyone contributes to the three goals of collaboration – to deliver, improve and learn.[58]

8.4 Courage to build team spirit

Even team building may require braver leadership, because providing the freedom, structure, clarity and openness that the team spirit depends on, might cause you some measure of discomfort.

Dare to both give freedom and to interfere

As the leader, you may be forced to micromanage things down to the last detail if, for example, you are in a crisis situation, or if the group you lead is very immature. However, micromanaging is not something you should strive towards. Seek instead to give the team greater and greater frames of responsibility (see section 7.4), which may demand courage from you to really let them act within the frame.

58. The reason for someone not being part of improvement work can of course be legitimate, for instance lack of means (e.g. time) or ability. However, the attitude of being willing to contribute to the best of their abilities must be there.

A well-functioning team should be given the trust to try new things and to make mistakes. Ensure that the direction and the frames (as well as the PDCA way to systematic improvement and learning) are clear to everyone before starting. Give freedom, but show interest according to the motto: "Eyes on, but hands off." Let the team sort out their own problems and conflicts as long as it is done with mutual respect. But do not hesitate to interfere at the first sign of disrespect.

Dare to create structure and discipline

Work standards and rules are important parts of a structure for collaboration, but are only meaningful if they are followed. A balanced standardization, combined with the discipline to follow the standards, support your value creation. In the 1990s, Ingvar Kamprad, founder of the multinational furniture giant IKEA, initiated the standardization of the showrooms in all the IKEA stores around the world. In *The Truth About IKEA*, Johan Stenebo, a former IKEA executive, describes both the resistance to, and the effect of this standardization. He was himself very skeptical about the conceptualization down to the very minor details and was, as many other colleagues, repelled by the lack of freedom. He concludes, however, "... but Ingvar was right, again".

Standards need sound discipline. Jim Collins' study of great enterprises and their level 5 leaders highlights this. He writes: "When you look across the good-to-great transformations, they consistently display three forms of discipline: disciplined people, disciplined thoughts, and disciplined actions. When you have disciplined people, you don't need hierarchy. When you have disciplined thoughts, you don't need bureaucracy. When you have disciplined actions, you don't need excessive controls. When you combine a culture of discipline with an ethic of entrepreneurship, you get the magical alchemy of great performance."[59]

However, an attitude of sound discipline does not come about by itself. It is the result of good leadership. Thus, you must lead not only by creating structure, but also by creating habits and improvements. It requires your endurance and courage to stand up for agreed standards and discipline.

But do not overdo it. Standardize the right things to the right levels. Freedom within larger and larger frames is the basic rule for the mature team – complemented by your encouragement to have fun while experimenting with new products, new ways of working and new knowledge.

59. From the article *Level 5 Leadership: The triumph of humility and fierce resolve.*

Dare to take decisions, and dare to wait

Decision making may require bravery in different ways. The most obvious is when you have to take a decision that you know will be disliked by influential people. And your unease would probably increase if you are uncertain of what is best. Nevertheless, you sometimes have to take unpleasant decisions based on unreliable facts. In those situations, the alternative is often worse – not making a decision might lead to paralysis of the organization.

To rely on clear and well-anchored principles (as described in section 3.3) is one way to reduce paralysis and secure a stable direction.[60]

Sometimes you must take a decision, while in other instances it is better to wait. A memorable rule of thumb says: "Take your time with the decision making, but execute fast."

It may require some bravery for you to stop in order to gather more facts or to reflect, especially when the people around you are expecting action from your side. Do not be ashamed of showing uncertainty when it is needed – it is a sign of maturity.[61]

You may also need courage to stick to a well-founded decision if it is heavily criticized, or to swallow your pride and change an untenable decision that you realize is wrong.

The conclusion is that you need to be both consistent and flexible, both fast and slow, in your decision making – and all of these might demand braver leadership.

Dare to be open

One important aspect of openness is the sharing of information and knowledge. Cowardly managers act selfishly and do not share facts, so that they can look better and avoid the risk of subordinates growing past them.

Braver leaders dare to share. They also dare to confront everyone who, for egoistic reasons, keep information or abilities to themselves.

However, the aspect of openness that requires the most courage from the braver leader is probably to be transparent about their own weaknesses and mistakes. They ought to do it for the greater good, with the logic, "let's learn from this", and "if I'm open, others will dare to be too".

60. Jim Collins emphasizes the importance of principles in *Good to Great*. He compares the level 5 leaders in great organizations with hedgehogs. These leaders looked at the complex world and turned the important parts into simple principles that they consistently kept as their steady, strategic compass. The managers of the companies that Collins used for comparison acted like foxes, shattered and inconsistent.

61. Etsko Schuitema brings this to a head when he writes: "Immaturity is about a tolerance of mediocrity and intolerance of ambivalence, whereas maturity is about an intolerance of mediocrity and tolerance of ambivalence."

Think about an organization where the top manager never admits any wrongdoing, but instead looks around for a scapegoat or something else to blame. Are people further down the hierarchy in such an organization likely to visualize problems in their own area? No, they will most likely try to hide small indications of problems until they have grown too big to hide, and then they will try to find outside factors to blame – just like their boss. This inevitably leads to a negative spiral[62] that can only be broken by role-model leadership.

Such leadership requires courage from you to openly and honestly search for root causes to problems, and being prepared to admit that your leadership might be part of the root cause. You can create miracles if you, together with your colleagues, help each other to find and remove leadership waste.

This, however, requires insight and maturity from upper management to get going. That is what the next chapter is about.

62. The opposite, a culture of looking at problems as possibilities, combined with the openness of admitting one's own mistakes will, on the other hand, lead to a positive spiral. That insight was probably the reason for the company that instituted "The-biggest-confession-of-the-year award" to do so.

9. Leading Leaders

"Sweep the stairs from top to bottom."
– Unknown

The five steps of the Leader's Ladder can be used by all managers, irrespective of their level within the hierarchy. If, however, you are a manager over other managers, there are some special aspects that need to be highlighted compared to if you are a first-line manager. I have gathered the most important of these aspects in this chapter. It's about leadership development – both your own and that of your subordinated managers. The chapter includes the following parts:

- **Leader contribution management**
- **Tools for the management team**
- **Trust and responsibility**

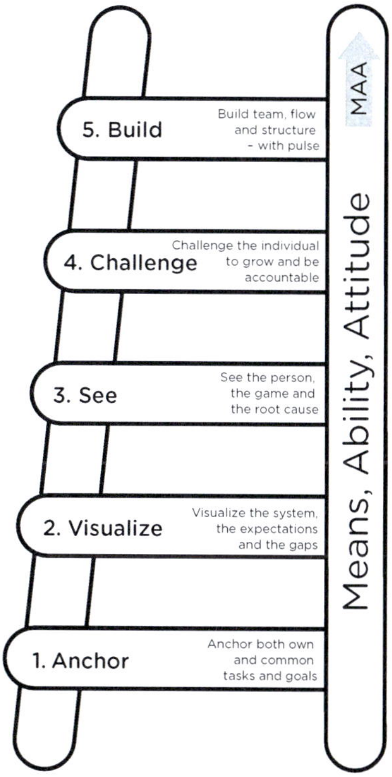

9.1 Leader contribution management

Your behavior has brought you where you are. If you have been assigned a management position, you must have done things right in the eyes of those who promoted you. If you have been promoted several times, you probably have a pretty good notion of what management behavior is valued by your superiors.

In fact, the reactions you got from the people around you have shaped your view of behavior for success. That is good *and* bad. It might help you to become an even better manager, or it can prevent you from ever becoming one. For example, many managers have learnt that results focus is central to management, which in turn might prevent them from developing their leadership based on *contribution management*. That's a pity as it limits the growth of both people and organizations.

Therefore, I sincerely hope that you read the following text with an open mind and give yourself the time to take in the message behind it.

From your own leader contributions to others

Figure 22 illustrates *the Contribution Management Model* from section 6.4, extended with one more management level. The darker person at the top left of the figure symbolizes you as the manager over managers (in the figure all the managers reporting to you have been reduced to the single semi-dark person in the middle of the figure). The figure highlights your most important leadership tasks, namely to make the three types of *leader contributions* to each and every one of the managers reporting to you.

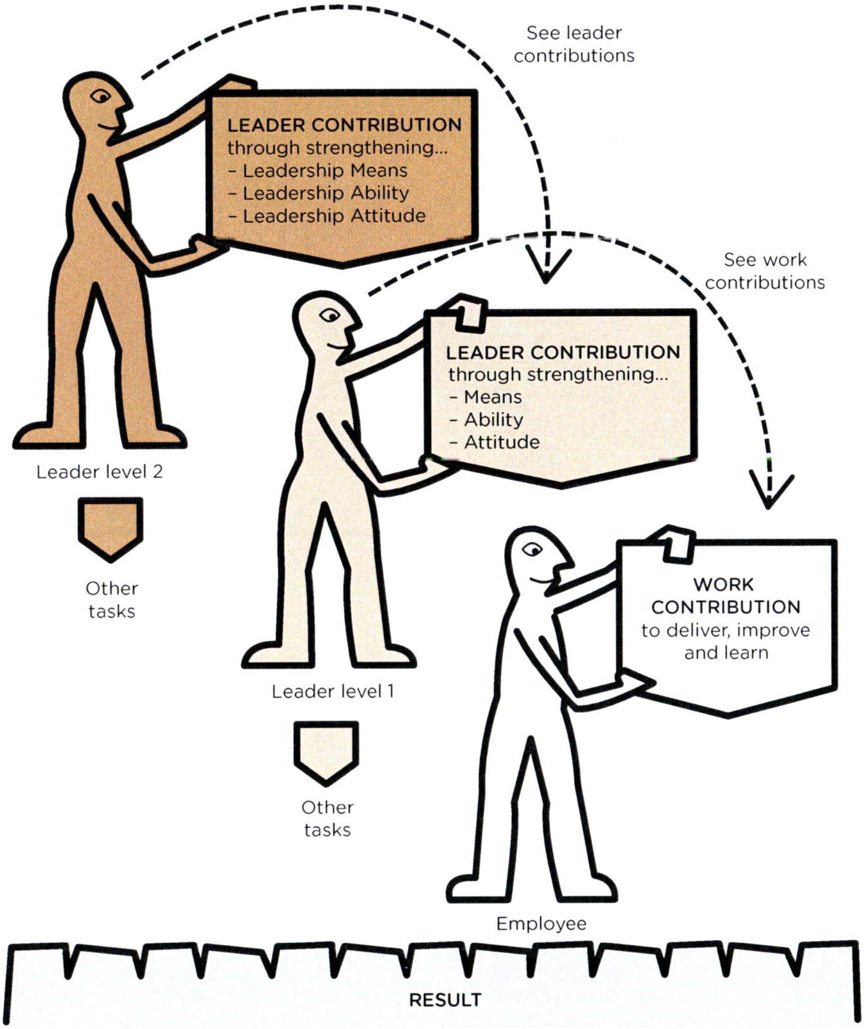

Figure 22 The Contribution Management Model – the 3-tier version
The first-line manager sees the work contribution (dotted line) of the worker, while the upper-level manager sees the leader contribution of the subordinated manager.

The Contribution Management Model conveys an extremely important message to you if you want to facilitate other leader's growth: Do not become obsessed with the results. Instead, watch how they make their leader contributions – and make your own leader contributions based on what you have seen.

The core issue is to *see the game* and then use the leader contributions you have seen,that is, *the means, abilities and attitudes (MAA) they have strengthened* for their subordinates, to guide your efforts to further develop their leadership.

In other words; you need to be present in order to see *how* your subordinated managers strengthen (1) *means*, (2) *abilities* and (3) *attitudes* for their subordinates. Based on that, you can determine which leader contributions you need to give them to support their next growth step. One of the basic contributions you can make is to hold regular good discussions on leadership within the management team.

Keep your eyes on the contributions

In most organizations, managers are rewarded based upon the results their subordinates produce. That behavior makes the work that creates the result secondary to the result itself.

The alternative is to reward managers based upon their leader contributions, in other words, their actions that strengthen MAA. The logic behind focusing attention on contributions before results is that you can't have excellent results without good input from the people involved.

Remember that any person, such as any manager reporting directly to you, is only accountable for their own actions, their own contributions.

Let's use farming as a metaphor to explain it. Farmers are accountable for cultivating the land in the best way possible. Thus they are accountable for fertilizing, sowing, reaping, etcetera in accordance with best practice. But they cannot be accountable for a hail storm that destroys the crop.

In the same way, everyone who directly reports to you is not accountable for everything that happens in their area – they are only accountable for their own actions, including lack of action. Their most important actions are their leader contributions; the strengthening of MAA, including holding their subordinates accountable for their respective work contributions. In other words, just like the example of the hail storm in the metaphor of the farmer, you cannot hold anyone accountable for things outside their control. You can only hold someone accountable for not using their means and abilities to make their best possible contributions to the collaboration.

As a manager of managers, you need to practice *leader contribution management* to avoid neglecting the things that produce the results. If you decide to stick to management by results and spend most of your time setting and following up targets, you will miss great opportunities for leadership development. Exaggerated result management can even lead to loss of motivation for the lower-level managers. And worse, if you are a top executive, this will probably spread downwards, layer by layer, severely restricting leadership development in the whole organization you are in charge of.

I have heard many excellent lower-level managers say, when their boss's behavior is brought up: "I get my motivation from others." That's sad, isn't it?

Leaders who are not seen for what they really contribute, experience a lack of support of their development, and will gradually lose their will to continue.

With leader contribution management, your genuine interest in leadership behavior makes the leader contributions of your subordinates take centre stage, and deservedly so.

This can be done following the same contribution management principles as described in section 6.4 (further detailed in appendix C), but with the difference being that it is now about leader contributions instead of work contributions. That means that you follow a spiral with four stages that gradually builds better leadership abilities: (1) *Challenge* to the next step in leadership development. (2) *Secure* together the necessary means and abilities needed. (3) *See the game* regularly to observe the leader contributions and engage in feedback discussions. (4) *Summarize* the feedback in regular growth dialogues. Then start over again at (1).

To succeed with leader contribution management, you and your team need to have become anchored in what the most important elements of leadership behavior are that you need to improve upon. Keep the focus on the contributions rather than on the results. This will require your time, so safeguard it in your agenda. It is very easy to fall back to an overstated focus on the result, without the proper reflection on how it is created. Do the reflection together in the management team, so that, step by step, you can develop a joint *leadership standard*.

Leadership standard

To grow the leadership abilities in your management team you need a shared understanding of what good leadership is about in concrete terms – a leadership standard. Such a standard establishes model behavior and the tools required for the leadership you have agreed to practice.

Neither you nor the rest of the team need to have the perfect standard formulated beforehand. But you have to start somewhere. The Leader's Ladder is meant to be such a starting point. You can use the ladder, or parts of it, to anchor together the most important aspects of your leadership – and based on that, set up your next leadership standard.

A leadership standard, as all other standards (see section 4.3), constitutes the tangible base level that you can compare the real situation to every day.

It needs to be complemented by a vision and your leadership principles (see section 3.3), as well as the next challenging target level.

When formulating and improving your standard, you have to start out from what is needed the most, and turn it into very concrete descriptions of what behavior is expected from all of you as leaders. Then it's time to see the game – observe the leader contributions made by each individual and engage in feedback dialogue on what you have seen.[63]

Leadership development takes time. Do not overreact to uncertain or conflicting signals.[64] Instead, stay with your principles and maintain good discussions about attaining the next level of important leader contributions within your management team.

That dialogue, together with each new level of your agreed-upon leadership standard, will provide you with a more precise discourse on leadership. This, in turn, forms the base of your common support and growth as leaders.

Using the Leader's Ladder to lead leaders

The five steps of the Leader's Ladder are designed to support all managers, regardless of the type of organization or hierarchical level. So far, I have covered aspects that are common to all leaders, irrespective of rank and position (chapter 3-8). There are, however, some aspects of the Leader's Ladder that need special attention from an upper-management perspective. Let's look at them step by step:

Step 1 ***Anchor* yourself, and your team of subordinated managers, together in what the long-term goal of your leadership is. Continue by clarifying your common leadership standard. Finally, ensure that everyone understands the expectations and how progress in the leadership development will be followed up.**

Step 2 ***Visualize* your common leadership ambitions, e.g. by picturing a leadership vision and principles, as well as posting long-term targets. Also, make the current base level of your leadership standard visible, for instance, in the form of a see-the-game checklist as illustrated in figure 26.**

63. A see-the-game checklist, that highlights important parts of the standard, reminds you what to look for. It can support you in setting up regular see-the-game sessions. One important aspect that normally needs highlighting, is how the leader creates and uses opportunities for feedback, including acknowledging even small contributions. (See the next section and figure 26 for an example.)
64. Remember that it sometimes requires a significant amount of time even for a superb leader to create a well-functioning team out of a dysfunctional one (for instance the Harbor example from section 6.4). Do not panic about outcomes from an employee survey. Employees with lacking attitudes may distort the survey results, even in a team with excellent leadership. If the survey results from one of the teams managed by a subordinate of yours look alarming, you need to focus even more on contribution management – encouraging and coaching the manager to make even better leader contributions.

Step 3 *See* the game by blocking time in your agenda for you to be present and observe your subordinates in leadership situations. Use your observations to create the opportunity for concrete feedback discussions around your common leadership standard. When appropriate, and if the situation demands it, perform leadership diagnostics (as described in section 9.2) to find root causes for leadership improvements. Arising from that, you can bring general leadership issues and conclusions to your management team for discussion. But do it with zero tolerance for any blaming of people with good attitude.

Step 4 *Challenge* every subordinated manager to take the next step in their development as leaders. Use the methods of leadership contribution management and be generous with feedback and support. Challenge everyone's abilities and attitude while, together, you improve the means that support better leadership. If you have to give up and conclude that someone is incapable of good enough leadership, you must help them to find other positions – both for their own sake, and for the sake of their subordinates.[65] Challenges are based on how the managers make their leader contributions according to MAA. Give them feedback on what you have seen, especially on how they involve everybody, create good discussions, give feedback, hold individuals accountable, and how they build structures that support deliveries, improvements and learning.

Step 5 *Build* team, flow and structure for leadership. The team spirit in a management team is as important as the spirit of a working-level team. A working-level team is responsible for delivering products (services and/or goods) to internal or external customers, and to keep doing it better. A management team is responsible for delivering leadership to the people in the organization, and to keep doing that better. This joint endeavor calls for collegial support and leadership structure with supporting tools.

65. Jan Carlzon, the former CEO of SAS, touches on this in his book *Moments of Truth*. He means that it is unfortunate that removing someone from a management position often is seen as a punishment, irrespective of the person being both happier and more suitable for the new position. He concludes that is easier for upper management to let bad managers stay even though they are causing problems for their subordinates: "To save one person, the boss, they let all the others suffer – because of cowardice, rather than out of goodness."

9.2 Tools for the management team

Most of the tools described in appendices A-C are suitable also for you in upper management. Use them for improving both the performance in general, and for leading the growth of your leaders. The following tools are extra important for upper management:

- *The LBO process* (chapter 3 and appendix B) with the purpose to share and coordinate long-term goals and shorter-term targets over time and between different functions.
- *A coordinated pulse-meeting structure* (chapter 7 and appendix A) with the purpose to tie short visual control meetings together for driving deliveries and improvements on all levels.
- *Systematic improvement with PDCA* (chapter 7 and appendix B) with the purpose to support and expect from all teams on all levels to systematically use problems, challenges and ideas to improve in their own area of responsibility.
- *Root-cause analysis and leadership diagnostics* (chapter 9 and appendix B) with the purpose to find the right issue(s) to improve – also when it concerns immature leadership.

In addition to the tool descriptions you will find in the appendices, here I want to go a little deeper into how you, in upper management, can use the last three of the tools listed above, complemented by a description of the powerful tool of *leader-pulse meetings*.

Together these tools give you excellent support for leadership development in your management team. Let's start with looking at leadership diagnostics, the crown jewel of tools for generally improving leadership within an organization.

Leadership diagnostics

Leadership diagnostics based on an MAA root-cause analysis is probably the most powerful tool to support all managers in an organization to grow in accordance with the Leader's Ladder. You can use it by yourself, but it becomes much more effective if you use it together in your management team(s).

However, with the wrong attitude, it will create more harm than value. A diagnosis must never be used to find scapegoats. Upper management must involve lower-level management with the open and honest purpose of helping everyone to grow their leadership, including their own.

Assume that everyone has a positive attitude and really want to improve their leadership ability. Wait until you are mature enough in that sense before you start using the leadership diagnostic tool. Of course, if you later run into attitude problems, you have to deal with them decisively.

The aim of leadership diagnostics is to honestly, with focus on leader contributions, find and address the major root cause to a deviation – without putting the blame on people because they lack some means or abilities.

The deviation used as the trigger may be positive (an unexpected achievement) or negative (a disappointment). The analysis is done by checking if the means, abilities or attitudes (MAA) have been unexpectedly good or bad. Start with the people involved in the event that caused the deviation and continue this MAA-analysis, level by level, upwards in the hierarchy.

Let us look at the harbor example from section 6.4 to understand what leadership diagnostics is about. In figure 23 you can see how a diagnostic template is filled out by the harbor manager.

	Prepare	
1	EFFECT Main problem or other effect	*Collision between Pocket #1 and Crane #1 on Monday xx-xx-xx.*
2	CAUSING EVENT that led to the effect (only needed when effects are too comprehensive)	*The new line wheel mounted on Crane #1 was too large, causing it to collide with the pocket.*
3	WORK CONTRIBUTION to study (a behavior contributing to the event)	*The mechanic NN did not tell the maintenance manager about the risk of collision when he was asked to change to a larger wheel size, even though he knew what would happen.*
	Diagnose	
4a	**WORKING LEVEL**	
	NAME of the person responsible (partially/wholly) for the event	*The mechanic (NN)*
	REAL ACTION What did the person do?	*NN changed the wheel without warning his manager about the risk. Instead, he told his colleagues that an accident was going to happen.*
	EXPECTED ACTION (What would ideal/expected behavior have been?)	*NN ought to have to have warned his manager of the risk when he was asked to change the wheel.*
	EXPLANATIONS OF THE DIFFERENCES between real and expected (note different explanations if stated)	*NN blames the system for not requiring him to warn anyone in a situation like this. It seems that NN's intent was to discredit his manager for not knowing that the collision would happen.*
	MAA-GAP CONCLUSIONS (What M, A or A gaps are involved?)	*NN had the means and the abilities required to do the right thing, but did not do it. NN showed a severe lack in attitude by not wanting to do the best for the collaboration. Thus, NN needs to be censured.*
4b	**MGMT tier 1**	
	NAME of the leader	*The maintenance manager (MM)*
	REAL ACTION What did the person do?	*MM decided that the wheel size should be altered in order to save costs. He took part in the investigation of the collision, but did not do anything besides supporting the repair of the crane and the pocket.*
	EXPECTED ACTION (What would ideal/expected behavior have been?)	*MM ought to have censured NN for behaving in an unacceptable manner.*
	EXPLANATIONS OF THE DIFFERENCES between real and expected (note different explanations if stated)	*MM was wrong when he decided to change wheel size, but he took and communicated the decision with good attitude. However, he did not reprimand NN, which amounts to an insufficient leader contribution.*
	LEADERSHIP MAA CONCLUSIONS (What could have been or needs to be done regarding leadership MAA?)	*MM obviously did not possess the ability to handle challenging behavior from subordinates. He needs feedback and leadership training to be able to handle similar situations in the future.*
4c	**MGMT tier 2**	
	NAME of the leader	*The harbor manager (I)*
	REAL ACTION What did the person do?	*I have given MM feedback and started coaching him in handling bad attitude.*
	EXPECTED ACTION (What would ideal/expected behavior have been?)	*See "REAL ACTION" above.*
	EXPLANATIONS OF THE DIFFERENCES between real and expected (note different explanations if stated)	*N.A. (no major difference).*
	LEADERSHIP MAA CONCLUSIONS (What could have been or needs to be done regarding leadership MAA?)	*I have so far given sufficient leader contributions related to this particular event. However, I have underestimated the lack of attitude, here shown by NN and others. Thus, I have shown weakness in my ability to see and act proactively. I should become more active in seeing the game as well as in allowing time for reflection. I also need to be clearer with all employees of my expectations regarding attitude, e.g. by updating and communicating our policy (a mean), highlighting requirements for safety, openness and honesty, as well as for everyone's accountability for contributing their best to the greater good of the collaboration.*

Figure 23 MAA Leadership Diagnostics

The template is filled in by the harbor manager after the accident in the example described in section 6.4. (The numbers in brackets refer to the method description in appendix B.)[66]

66. The method is based on leadership diagnostics as presented by Etsko Schuitema in *Leadership: The Care and Growth Model.*

The diagnostic in figure 23 shows that the harbor manager did the right thing when he gave his subordinated manager (the maintenance manager) feedback on how he should have handled the lack of attitude shown by the mechanic. The harbor manager also showed a good learning mindset by looking at what he could have done differently before.

You can find more details on the diagnostic method in appendix B.

A coordinated pulse-meeting structure

A management team has a lot to gain from connecting short and effective pulse meetings to a holistic system which quickly refers each problem (or opportunity) to the right function or level where it can be handled effectively (see 7.2). You can create an initial setup of such a meeting structure together with your management team and then, little by little, optimize it to secure both deliveries and improvements.

Such a structure is ideally based on well-designed and well-coordinated delivery-pulse meetings and improvement-pulse meetings in all working teams, as well as in each management team. That, in turn, requires upper management to set good examples. They can do it by handling escalated delivery problems quickly, or at least with prompt feedback.

And they can also do it by using root-cause analysis to solve important reoccurring problems once and for all. Such systematic improvement rest on the PDCA wheel described in section 7.4, and it should be carried out by all teams in an organization, as illustrated by figure 24.

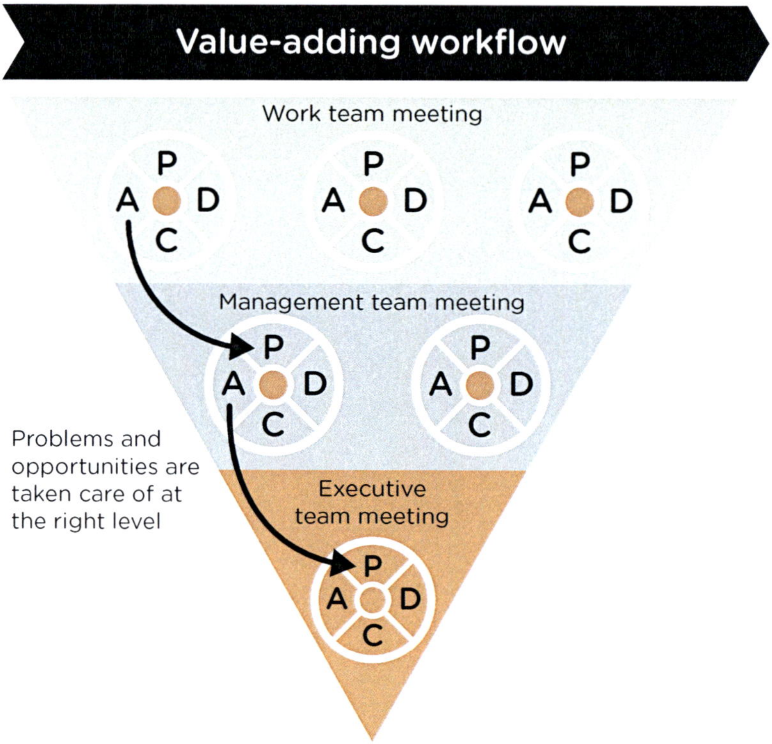

Figure 24 Using PDCA everywhere
Systematic improvement utilizing PDCA in all teams on all levels.

The figure shows how each team is trying to solve reoccurring problems and address important challenges using PDCA on a regular basis. If a team runs into a problem or a challenge that they do not have the ability or authority to handle themselves, they should be able to escalate it to an appropriate team (illustrated by the two arrows in the figure). The receiving team must be able to provide the needed capability, or they must pass the issue on to the next level.

To avoid so-called upwards delegation that risks creating a bottle-neck at the upper management level, you must secure enough authority and ability at the lower levels. The basic rule reads: "Problems should be solved, and opportunities embraced, on the lowest possible level."

There are of course increased costs involved in doubling capabilities, but there are also motivational, quality and speed aspects to consider. Thus, let every team grow their systematic improvement capability, including using own measures and setting own targets (as described in section 3.3), parallel to the growth of their team. Coach the individuals through the process and see to it that all teams, on all levels, are engaged in systematic improvement.

To get a new pulse-meeting structure to function effectively, you must safeguard it from disturbing events. Do not allow other meetings to compete. A good solution is to keep each morning free from everything besides pulse meetings and go-and-look time. With a bit of planning you can secure both the escalations from level to level and the needed attendance from support function representatives. If you safeguard enough time, you can also expect managers, including yourself, to *go and look* directly after the meetings in order to observe new deviations as well as to support the problem-solving. Figure 25 illustrates the basic principles of such a meeting schedule.

Time	Monday	Tuesday	Wednesday	Thursday	Friday
8–10am	Pulse meetings at different levels	Pulse meetings at different levels	Pulse meetings at different levels	Pulse meetings at different levels	Pulse meetings at different levels
10–12am	Meeting-free time Go and look	Meeting-free time Go and look	Meeting-free time Go and look	Meeting-free time Go and look	Meeting-free time Go and look
1–3pm					
3–5pm					

Figure 25 A meeting structure
... that safeguards pulse meetings as well as time to go and look.

With a setup in line with figure 25, a manager typically takes part in two short (typically 10-15 minutes each) interlinked delivery-pulse meetings between 8 and 10 in the morning – one with their own team and one, normally a quarter or half an hour later, with the management team above. The rest of the morning may be utilized to improvement-pulse meetings as well as to see causes of deviations and work contributions out in the workplace.

Managers who face going from conventional meetings to coordinated pulse meetings are often concerned that the increase of the number of meetings will take too much valuable time away from the delivery process. However, once they try it, it doesn't take long to convince them that the opposite is in fact true. Soon, several of the old meetings can be canceled or drastically shortened because many issues are solved earlier, faster and better in the new pulse meeting structure.

I have heard several upper managers bear witness to this, and saying things like: "It has actually freed my time. Before, I had a situation where the phone was ringing all day and I ran around putting out a lot of fires. Now we can sort most things out in the morning meetings."

Adding more new meetings than the old ones you cancel seems like a bad idea at first glance – but not if the new ones are much shorter, better designed and better coordinated. Use the time freed from longer meetings and putting out fires to grow everyone's ability to solve root causes of reoccurring problems. That will free even more of your time.

Leader-pulse meetings

Leader-pulse meetings are regular meetings with the aim of growing the leadership ability of every manager in your team. The meetings are built around leader contributions, both the actual ones and the expected ones. In that respect, a leader-pulse meeting is similar to an ordinary delivery-pulse meeting. The latter focuses on the actual delivery status compared to what is expected (the base level), and on the action needed to handle the deviations found. The former does the same, but for delivery of leader contributions.

Thus both are about delivering what you have agreed to. The basic process is therefore the same, that is: (1) determine the expectations, the base level, (2) visualize the deviations and (3) do something about them.

Your agreed leadership standard is the base level that provides leadership expectations concretely enough for you to catch deviations (1). Seeing the game and visual control techniques then support the visualization (2). At the regular pulse meetings, you decide what actions need to be taken and follow up their execution (3).

One way to make expectations and progress visible is to show every manager's commitment on a common board. That board then becomes a regular (e.g. weekly) meeting focus point for the management team. Everyone's commitments and actions since the last meeting form an excellent base for good discussions – preferably enhanced by color signaling of contribution types and deviations.

Using regular leader-pulse meetings will enable you to raise the standard and update your common leadership standard little by little.

If you run out of interesting discussion triggers, it is time to do a few more leadership diagnostics. Another way of securing good discussions is to institutionalize seeing the game of peer leaders. Start by creating a see-the-game checklist[67] based on the prioritized leader behavior pinpointed by your leadership standard, see figure 26 for an example.

67. The same type of tool can be used for other purposes, such as to observe how principles are used or how housekeeping base levels are adhered to (compare with so-called 5S-audits).

Type of leader contribution	Leadership standard for leading pulse meetings	Status	Notes
Secure Means	Are expectations of contributions made clear — with distinct actions if means are missing?		Good ...etc
	Are deviations in SHE, quality and timing captured and acted on?		Good ...etc
	Is a good discussion created — and is it based on facts experienced in the workplace?		Opportunity to ... etc.
Support Learning	Is the common need for different abilities visualized both for the short and long term? Is it adequately updated and used?		
	Are deviations naturally connected to individuals' ability development plans with a plan for following up when necessary?		Opportunity to ... etc.
	Are new opportunities for learning created and used?		Good ...etc
Strengthen Attitude	Are discussions based on respect and care for others?		Good ...etc
	Are opportunities for feedback created and used, e.g. by acknowledging base level contributions?		
	Are both short- and long-term targets visualized clearly and used — and connected to agreed value creation for all stakeholders (+QTE)?		

Figure 26 A see-the-game checklist

The list highlights important parts of the underlying leadership standard and is a reminder of what to look for when observing leader contributions at a pulse meeting.

The purpose of the checklist is to support every leader in your team to observe a colleague in a leadership situation, and then give constructive feedback afterwards. By reading the checklist before going to see the game, you will remind yourself of what to look for. Afterwards you can note what you have seen on the checklist (the two grey columns in the figure) before giving the feedback in private with the colleague you have been observing. By using it as a trigger for a good discussion you will probably both learn a bit about your leadership and its potential. You can also bring interesting general conclusions or questions flowing from this exercise to the next leader-pulse meeting.

A meeting board for this type of meeting should clearly visualize expectations, status and planned actions for different kinds of leader contributions (see section 3.2). It can be done in different ways, for example, by using the project-VP tool (a variant of visual planning) described in appendix A. With a VP-board you can show all the important activities that have been planned in the near future – one row per manager. Besides the different types of leader contributions connected to each leader and their team, you can also choose to show upcoming shared activities, as well as personal responsibilities for common improvements, such as for doing a leadership diagnostic triggered by a recent deviation.

9.3 Trust and responsibility

The leadership of an organization is the sum of all its leaders and their leader contributions. Everyone is accountable for their actions towards improving as leaders. The person at the top, however, has the biggest responsibility, as well as the greatest leverage, to develop the total leadership ability of the organization.

A really miserable organization has probably had terrible top management for a long time. There is a lot of truth in the saying: "A fish rots from the head."

The opposite – that great organizations have great leaders – is also true. The level 5 leaders found by Collins' research team is evidence of that (see *Good to Great* by Jim Collins).

From honesty to trust

Great leadership emanates from honesty. Dishonesty ruins collaborations. One type of dishonesty is to pretend that the impossible is possible. This is, unfortunately, quite common both in politics and in management. Take, for instance, when upper management forces a project leader to accept an impossible budget or schedule. If the people involved in the project know from experience that the targets are completely impossible, they will lose motivation. The only thing that might change their view is a drastic improvement of MAA – for example, of the ways of working, or new tools. If not, seeing that they have to accept the view of upper management and their protests are ignored, they may resign themselves to collective denial to hide the real situation.[68]

68. Stefan Bükk presents one example of this type of denial when he describes how an experienced project manager was overrun by his steering committee and ordered to shorten the project lead time estimate by 30%. The manager knew that refusal from his side would have resulted in the project being transferred to a younger and less experienced person, which in turn would have resulted in an even longer lead time. He therefore decided to stop protesting and to carry on. Bükk writes: "The project manager was caught in an impossible situation, and what's worse, the organization turned into a lying organization instead of a learning organization. Why? Well, the opportunity to say no to an impossible project can be seen as an Andon string, i.e. when the project leader says NO, there is a signal going upwards in the organization to trigger support and special attention... Many companies seem to have cut that string and instead lend themselves to 'Management by Lies'."

Upper management is heading the wrong way if they promote a culture where managers are expected to play hard and cut budgets. It sends the signal that they distrust their people. This will in turn create denial of reality and a dishonest culture, for example, by people building margins to prepare for the cuts.

Of course upper management and steering committees have the duty to challenge budgets and schedules, including setting higher targets, but it should never be done based on distrust.

If you believe that too many safety margins have been built in, start by asking why this is the case. Do the people doing the estimates and the scheduling have attitude problems, or do they lack the abilities needed? In both of these cases you need to address the deficiencies in MAA. And if it is an issue of bad attitude, first ask yourself if your own previous behavior might have played a part in causing it.

It is sad, but very human, how easily people fall into groupthink and distrust. That's why we have to fight it with the courage needed to challenge it – not only in others, but also in ourselves.

In other words, try to create trust both downwards and upwards. Don't just outright reject an honest "it is impossible" as the response when you challenge someone. Respond by asking and coaching: "Why is it impossible?" and "How can we remove obstacles or find new ways to make it possible?"[69]

After all, raising the target from today's base level requires at least some improvements in MAA.

It starts with you

There is no doubt that leadership, and development of leadership, is important. There is also no doubt that all managers are accountable for developing their own leadership abilities. But who is responsible for the general leadership development in a large organization? The simple answer is: All managers who have managers reporting to them.

Sure, it is natural to give the HR department important roles to play, but it is when the top manager takes the lead that good things really start to happen. It should ideally start all the way at the top, for that makes it possible to coordinate the leadership development in terms of direction and speed.

69. It can be very destructive if a manager ignores warnings with comments like, "Why are you being so negative?" or, "Just do it, how hard can it be?" If you take such a distrusting approach to people who are expressing concerns with good attitude, you risk the unique opportunity to make adjustments and learn from the situation. But even worse, you also risk losing the general motivation and commitment of the people producing the results.

The basic rule, irrespective of how high up in the organization your transformation starts, is to set the leadership development for every single management team, level per level, that is, with each superior manager bearing the responsibility for their own team.

Do not give up if leadership development is not yet driven by your own superior manager. Start at your level. Your example, and your interest, is very important to the managers placed under your command. Together you can make a difference that will be noticed and spread to other parts of the organization.

10. The Collaboration Tree: a framework for value-based leadership

> *"We make a living by what we get,*
> *we make a life by what we give."*
> *–Winston Churchill*

Churchill's statement is very relevant for leadership. Giving is vitally important. Collaboration rests on giving in the form of making work contributions and *leader contributions*. Giving in this context is about unselfishly contributing to the collaboration, but it also opens up a pathway to growth – to mature as a human being.

In this last chapter, I clarify the foundation of the Leader's Ladder. It serves both as a summary and to expand upon some important concepts. The first part of the chapter is about how the Collaboration Tree can be used as the framework for great leadership, followed by an explanation of how Tough Care with Courage is fundamental for leadership development. The rest of the chapter is devoted to the maturation process as a leader, and as a person.[70] The chapter includes the following parts:

- **The Collaboration Tree as a framework**
- **Value-based leadership**
- **Give and grow**
- **At last – your ladder against your tree**

70. The section about maturing, as well as other parts of the chapter, are very much inspired by *Leadership: The Care and Growth Model* by Etsko Schuitema.

10.1 The Collaboration Tree as a framework

> *"My leadership is meaningful only when I'm heading in the right direction."*
> *– Scriptor*

Leadership exists within a context. In working life that context is about value-creating collaboration. The Collaboration Tree from chapter 1 thus becomes a natural foundation for a framework for leadership in working life.

The Collaboration Tree

The Collaboration Tree visualizes the context of joint value creation, and thus the context also for leadership. It is against this tree that the Leader's Ladder rests steadily.

The Collaboration Tree and the Leader's Ladder, supported by the Leader Contribution Model and the tools in the appendices, form a holistic model for leadership development, covering everything from values and principles to concrete behavior in different situations.

The Collaboration Tree symbolizes how increasingly better value can be created for all four major stakeholders based on the three necessary conditions of MAA (*means*, *abilities* and *attitudes*). Figure 27 illustrates this, highlighting the special importance of leader contributions and a value base for leadership.

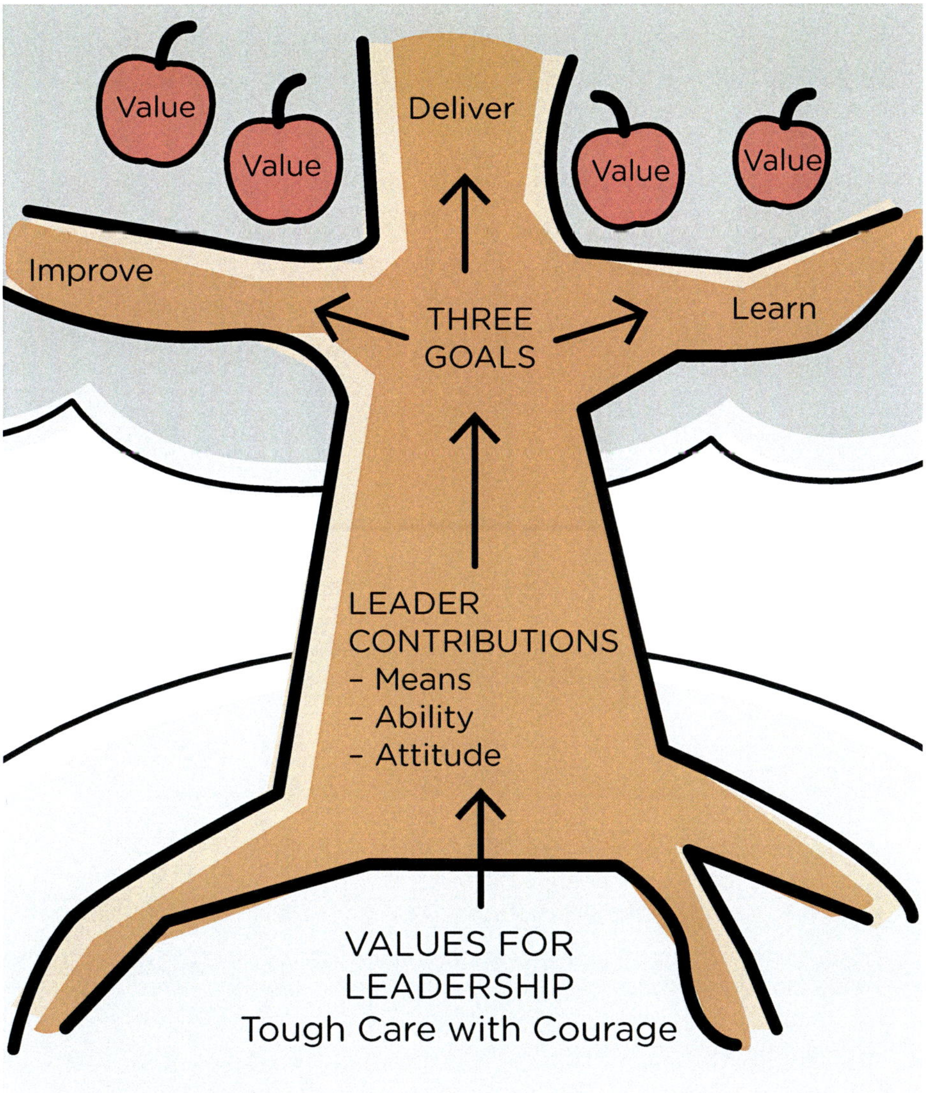

Figure 27 The Collaboration Tree
... from a leadership perspective.

The Collaboration Tree provides the framework for value-based and braver leadership. The following section describes the four parts of the tree, from top to bottom – from the value that is created, to the basic values needed.

The fruits – the four receivers of value

Leadership in working life concerns leading the collaboration to create value. There are normally four major groups of receivers of the value created, called stakeholders, namely customers, coworkers, owners and society.

The customers ought to receive products (goods and/or services) of high quality, in time and at a reasonable price. *The coworkers*, the people making contributions to the value-creation processes, receive value in the form of salaries and security, but hopefully also in terms of personal development and meaning. *The owners* receive value from the organization reaching its targets, often in the form of a legitimate return on their capital investment. *Society* receives value from taxes, but also via good products, new knowledge and other contributions to its common, sustainable welfare.

You create greater meaning and a broader legitimate base for your leadership if you try to give all four stakeholder groups the value they deserve. That balanced intent does not remove all conflicts of interest, but it does make it possible to "bake a bigger cake to share". At the same time, it reduces the risk of a disappointed stakeholder destroying value for the others, such as customers leaving, employees working at half speed, or owners closing down the operations to move their capital elsewhere.

Even though the daily delivery of products to customers and the periodical delivery of return on investment to owners are extremely important, you as a leader must make the learning and growth of your subordinates your prime priority. This is simply because leadership is about relationships with individuals. But it is also because the sum of the abilities of all the individuals aggregates to the ability of the whole organization – the ability to create value for all four stakeholder groups.

The branches – the three goals

You create value when you *deliver*, *improve* and *learn*. The most obvious value creation is done in the delivery processes, in other words, in the workflows that result in products needed by the organization's customers. The delivery processes should, as a rule, create value that is worth more than the cost of producing it. The resulting financial surplus normally benefits all stakeholders, directly or indirectly.[71] Thus, the *delivery branch* of the Collaboration Tree illustrates value creation to all four stakeholder groups; or, put differently, provides nutrition to all four apples.

71. E.g. directly through dividends paid to owners (after the employees got their remuneration and society got its taxes), or indirectly through reinvestments that build sustainability, growth and job security.

In order to secure sustainable value delivery over time, the collaboration needs improvements of products, ways of working and supporting structures. This value creation is done in improvement processes. They result in better products and less waste during production, making sustainable progress possible. Good systematic improvements will also lead to other effects such as increased speed and flexibility, or to a better workplace, increased personal growth and a smaller environmental footprint. Therefore, the *improvement branch* of the tree also illustrates value creation to all four stakeholder groups.

It is, however, not only the organization that benefits from better collaboration. Everyone who puts in the work effort should gain from it, for example by learning. The learning process enables growth in a number of different ways. One such way is that you grow your individual ability to perform today's and tomorrow's tasks. Another way is that you grow your ability to contribute to excellent teamwork, as well as your ability to learn. The *learning branch* of the tree illustrates all such value creation from individual learning. While each person directly gains from this, the other stakeholders will benefit indirectly.

Everyone's responsibility to deliver and improve is sometimes called the dual task. I assert that it should be enlarged to *the triple task*: We all have three duties to the collaboration – that is to contribute our best in terms of delivery, improvement and learning.

The trunk – the three leader contributions

The trunk of the Collaboration Tree depicts the three necessary conditions for collaboration, MAA. Strengthening the three conditions is the most important contribution you can make as a leader. You do it (1) by improving and securing the *means* – the resources and structures needed, (2) by providing challenges and learning opportunities for every person to grow their *abilities* and (3) by helping individuals to grow their *attitude* based on your Tough Care for them.

You might need to spend more of your time on making leader contributions. And you probably need to improve the way in which you provide them. Spend your time wisely and avoid leadership waste.

The roots – the value base of Tough Care with Courage

A value base for great collaboration is to a large extent about respect for all the people involved in, or affected by, the collaboration. But it is also about the will to contribute to effective and harmonious teamwork.

The value base for great leadership can be summarized as Tough Care with Courage. That base is about acting outside your comfort zone (if necessary) for the holistic greater good – including both soft and hard expressions of care, and including both respectful and efficient teamwork.

To lead others requires a good attitude from the leader, anchored in clear leadership intent. Try to visualize your own intent by asking yourself these questions:

- **Do I have a strong will to create value for all stakeholder groups?**
- **Do I really care for all the people I have set out to lead?**
- **Am I prepared to act a bit more courageous every day in order to respond appropriately to the challenging situation I am faced with?**

Your honest answers to yourself will bring some of your own values to light. They become a starting point for your next step towards better and braver leadership.

10.2 Value-based leadership

> ***“If it is not right, do not do it.***
> ***If it is not true, do not do it.”***
> ***–Marcus Aurelius***

Acting based on what is right and true is not always simple.[72] Firstly, you need to understand what the particular situation requires, and secondly you need to have the courage to act accordingly.

72. Marcus Aurelius probably succeeded quite well in that as he was regarded (especially by the philosopher Niccolò Machiavelli) as one of the five good emperors who ruled the Roman Empire from 96 AD to 180 AD.

All of us have insights within us about what is right or wrong, but we need to be true to ourselves about it. Then, to become braver in following that compass, we need to give ourselves enough time to reflect – to anchor our own mission and tasks.

Power, manipulation and honesty

To have power is to be able to influence other people. To lead is to really do it. Thus leadership is about using power.

In working life, the power to lead emanates from both the formal managerial power given by *the superiors*, and from the leadership power granted by *the subordinates*, through their willingness to contribute.

As I mentioned in the introduction, leadership is *not* about creating good results through other people. It is not about using others by forcing or manipulating them. It is not even about buying their labor.

To manipulate someone to work for your own interests is often the worst management strategy – it will undoubtedly create resistance once it is revealed. We tend to expose egoistic persons who try to fool us. To buy, or force, someone to work is better, because it is at least done openly.

Real leadership, however, is about facilitating everyone's willingness to contribute to the goals of the collaboration. In other words, real leadership is about growing everyone's attitude to deliver, improve and learn in order to create real value for all the stakeholders.

In contrast to buying, forcing or manipulating subordinates, real leadership creates the positive will to follow the leader. That intent will grow when you, as the leader, transparently and honestly, work for what is the long-term best for all the organization's stakeholders, including the individual coworkers. In turn, it requires you to be honest with yourself about your own value base, and it probably also requires many small steps of personal growth.

A value base for leadership

A value base is built up by values. In this context, a value is a basic understanding of how a person *ought to act* in a specific situation.

Values vary from person to person. Thus we all have our own value base. It is more or less shared with the people we work with.[73]

The dominating values within an organization, together with basic assumptions and repetitive behavior, eventually form the culture of the organization.

A value base for leadership is formed by the basic understanding how a leader ought to act in specific situations. You can clarify it by yourself – and it can be jointly formulated by a management team.

A leadership value base might be summarized on a high level, for example, as Tough Care with Courage. Your own summary forms the base for your leadership mission – what you want to achieve with your leadership.[74]

The more you actualize your leadership value base, the more it can become the compass that guides your everyday behavior. You can also view it as an anchor that provides the stability for acting consistently.

A distinct value base is easier to follow. If it is properly anchored inside you, it helps you to become braver – acting in line with it even when it would involve taking personal risks.

A successful Lean transformation require the combination of a proper value base and good leadership. The many failures to gain lasting effects from Lean efforts are most often caused by a poor value base and a lack of leadership. Peter Hines et. al. refer in *Staying Lean* to a research study of the major reasons for failing with Lean. The top reasons were found to be lack of vision and communication. The authors conclude: "Indeed, poor leadership has been identified as the reason for poor sustainability of Lean change."

73. When formulating a common value base it is important to remember that it can only be a vague reflection of the individuals' value bases. Formulating a shared value base for an organization is a way of signaling the guidelines for agreed appropriate behavior. If it is true (i.e. if it is widely accepted and followed at least by management), it can be used for improving attitudes. If it is false (e.g. formulated as a wish list for others and not for yourself) it is hypocritical and demotivating. You and your leader colleagues must exemplify really living the values you propagate.

74. You are free to shape your own leadership mission exactly as you wish. I have heard a manager summarize it like this: "My leadership is not about my success, nor even is it primarily about my organization's success – it is about the success of the people I have set out to lead."

The word "respect" is often used, within and without the Lean context, to describe the core of a successful collaboration value base. One of my two favorite Richard Branson quotes highlights this: "Respect is how to treat everyone, not just those you want to impress." The other quote emphasizes another important issue: "Happiness is the secret ingredient for successful businesses. If you have a happy company it will be invincible."

Compared with what has been written about Lean tools, very little has been written about Lean leadership.[75] Jeffrey Liker, who has been studying the reasons behind Toyota's success over many years, is one exception. He has been highlighting the need for new types of leadership and values (compared to typical Western companies – see *The Toyota Way* and *The Toyota Way to Lean Leadership*). He describes how Toyota's approach to leadership differs from traditional Western leadership and how they build from a long-term mission that includes the company and its owners, the customers, the employees, as well as the broader society. According to Liker, the managers at Toyota strive for sustainable value creation, especially for their customers.

Toyota has summarized its value base in two pillars: *Continuous improvement* and *Respect for people*. These are further divided it into five parts:[76] (1) Challenge to maintain a long-term vision and meet all challenges with the courage and creativity needed to realize the vision. (2) Continuous improvement, as no process can ever be declared perfect. (3) Going to the source to find the facts to make correct decisions, build consensus and achieve goals. (4) Toyota respects others, makes every effort to understand others, accepts responsibility and does its best to build mutual trust. (5) Teamwork – Toyota stimulates personal and professional growth, shares opportunities for development and maximizes individual and team performance.

This (and similar) value base descriptions are meant to be valid for all employees. But it leaves one important question unanswered: What are the most critical values needed to become a great leader? The answers can be found by describing how a leader ought to act in different types of situations.

Hence, let us look at crucial leadership behavior.

75. I have tried to compensate for this lack of literature by discussing different Lean leadership aspects with experienced people from all over the world whenever possible. In this way, I gained new perspectives from many experts, such as Jeffrey Liker, Tatsuhiko Yoshimura, Sumida Toshinobu, David Meier, Takayuki Shimizu, Gert Frick and Niklas Modig. I thank all of them.

76. According to Toyota Material Handling Europe. They write in their internal brochure, *The Toyota Way*, that it "expresses the beliefs and values shared by us all", and that it is based on "the value the company delivers to customers, shareholders, associates, business partners and the global community".

Leader behavior

> *"Leadership behavior is company culture."*
> *– Unknown*

Our value base decides our behavior and our behavior, in turn, reveals our value base.[77]

The leadership you are able to practice depends on how your subordinates perceive your actions (the values you indicate, what you say and what you do), in other words, how they view and understand your behavior. This means that the only way to develop your leadership is to adjust your behavior.

Table 2 shows leadership actions in the form of contrasting positions. Use it for considering, alone or together with colleagues, which types of behavior are preferable in different concrete situations – and where you have the greatest potential to improve.

77. Compare with figure 7 (in section 3.3) that illustrates how the value base – via principles, ways of working and tools – guides our actions.

Leader A ...		Leader B ...
... regularly shows care for all stakeholders.	↔	... is completely focused on reaching the next financial target.
... focuses on the process (how things are done and can be done better).	↔	... focuses on targets and outcomes – letting others take care of methods.
... takes personal risks to do what is required.	↔	... does not take personal risks.
... cares for every subordinate's growth.	↔	... concentrates on looking good from above.
... shares a clear vision and clear expectations.	↔	... is satisfied with the current state and avoids conflicts.
... acts on what is most important.	↔	... acts on what is most urgent.
... returns to discussing common tasks and targets – connecting them to individual contributions.	↔	... finds tasks and targets obvious.
... makes expectations, contributions and deviations visible with a daily pulse.	↔	... follows up results on a monthly basis.
... visualizes problems to find root causes (also in their own leadership).	↔	... tries to avoid problems or finds someone to blame.
... designs a structure of many short and focused meetings.	↔	... uses long meetings with broad agendas.
... listens attentively and sees every individual.	↔	... talks a lot and addresses the whole group.
... is present and watches the game in the workplace.	↔	... primarily uses numbers and reports at his/her desk or in meeting rooms.
... searches systematically to understand root causes.	↔	... trusts the first obvious solution.
... challenges and gives frequent feedback based on contributions.	↔	... challenges with targets and gives feedback on numbers in monthly reports.
... challenges and holds people accountable.	↔	... makes soft mistakes based on questionable excuses.
... involves people and asks questions.	↔	... directs and answers questions.
... manages with frames, i.e. with both expectations and freedom.	↔	... manages with orders and detailed rules.
... continuously builds improvement and learning abilities – strengthening the team spirit.	↔	... lets outside experts take care of all major improvements.
... builds team spirit along complete work flows, independent of organizational borders.	↔	... concentrates solely on his/her own function.

Table 2 Examples of leader behavior to be used for good discussions

An unselfish value base

> *“Many men go fishing all of their lives without knowing that it is not fish they are after.”*
> *–Henry David Thoreau*

Your integrity and legitimacy as a leader are based upon really acting in line with your value base. If you are not living it, it is a base without value.

By anchoring your value base, you gain the insight of your own intent. The anchoring gives you a stable reference point for the many choices you have to make in a normal working day.

We all have values that are more or less unselfish. An unselfish value is a basic understanding of how you should act in a certain type of situation despite that it might hurt your self-interest.

Unselfish values are prerequisites for great collaboration and thus for great leadership. A person who goes to work only to get maximum pay for minimum effort becomes neither a good coworker nor a good leader.

A common value base must therefore contain mostly unselfish values. Leading by setting an example of really living such values improves both meaning and team spirit.

Leadership and an unselfish value base are linked in two ways. Firstly because good leadership depends on the leader’s intent to give unselfishly to their subordinates (through their leader contributions). Secondly because everyone in the team should be led to give unselfishly to the collaboration (through their work contributions).

My summary of such a generous value base for leadership is Tough Care with Courage. It means leading unselfishly – for the long-term good of all stakeholders – by caring for each coworker with both hard and soft expressions, and doing what each situation requires more and more courageously.

10.3 Give and grow

"The goal is to be able to give with gratitude."
– Scriptor

When we give unconditionally, without expecting something in return, we are generous in the true sense.

However, the term giving can mean lots of different things. You are generous when you give unconditionally of your money or belongings, as well as when you give of your time to someone to support them, or doing other favors for them. Such giving is rarely connected to taking serious personal risks.

The most unselfish and generous acts are connected to giving both unconditionally and courageously. This means that you show the strongest expression of generosity when you give what someone else needs by acting courageously, such as saying or doing something even when you face negative personal consequences.

Generous giving (whether it demands courage or not) will benefit not only the receiver, but also the giver. You have reason to be thankful both for having something to give and for the maturity of wanting to share it, or put shortly: *Grow with the goal of giving with gratitude.*[78]

The Maturity Staircase

Personal maturity is normally built in small steps. Each such step is taken in the moment, by giving instead of taking. Each time that we are fully present in the now, trying to grasp the situation without bias and acting generously, we have grown a bit. It is true for me, for you and for your subordinates.

Maturing is not about becoming hard or soft, but rather about giving what the situation requires, irrespective of having to act hardly or softly, courageously or not. As you mature, you will more seldom put self-interest first, or act greedily or cowardly. Instead you will be able to more often act unselfishly and sustainably. This is illustrated by *t* in figure 28.

78. I have based this statement, as most of the content in this section, on my interpretation of Etsko Schuitema's teachings. Read more in his books *Leadership: The Care and Growth Model*, *Intent: Exploring the Core of Being Human* and *The Two Sandals: Intention, Attention and the Journey of Becoming Human.*

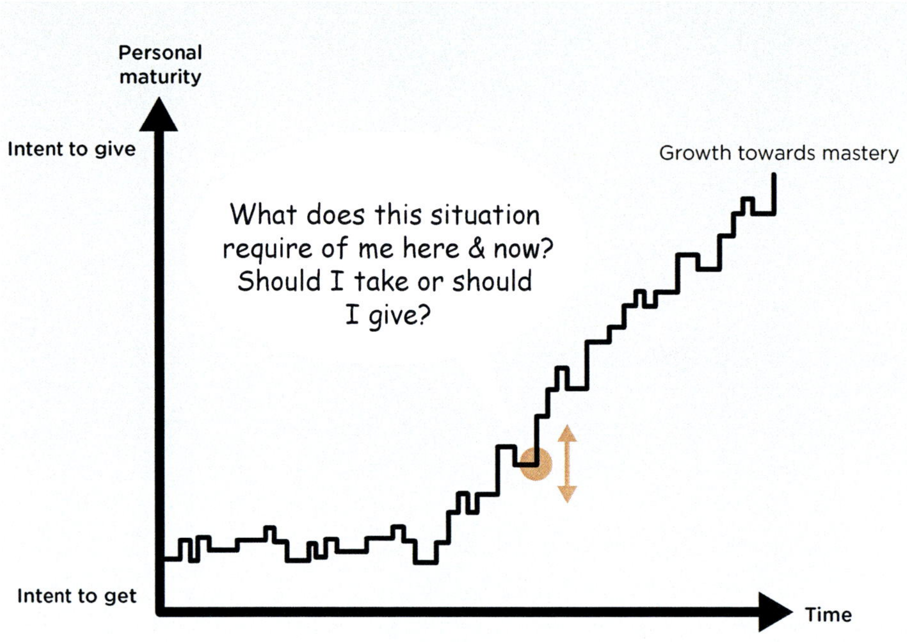

Figure 28 The Maturity Staircase
Growing as a leader by shifting intent. (Based on *Leadership: The Care and Growth Model* by Etsko Schuitema.)

You define yourself in every situation where you make the choice between giving and taking. When you make the choice to give, you grow.

Your maturation as a person is based on unselfish acts, which will enable you to climb up the stairs in figure 28. Selfish acts will, on the other hand, pull you down.

As you grow upwards (towards mastery), you will become more authentic and less focused on what you believe others should give to you. You will become more responsible, seeing your duties, and demanding your rights less frequently. You will be driven more by values and less by needs – and the less you need from others, the more independent and powerful you will become. In short, by giving more often, you move from craving to contributing. You grow from being a victim of the behavior of others, to become the master of situations.

People who mature in this way will, little by little, take more holistic responsibility for the collaboration. They will complain less and act more – becoming less dependent and more influential. This applies not only to you, but also to every one of your subordinates.

Etsko Schuitema explains in *Leadership: The Care and Growth Model* how this process from victimhood to mastery works:

> ***"In any situation there are two possibilities. One relates to what you want to get and the other to what is correct, what you should give or put in. If you ruthlessly pursue the second possibility you will transmute and continue transmuting. Hour after hour, day after day, week after week, you will change and continue changing. You will not recognize yourself after a week, and every week subsequent to that you will continue to surprise yourself. You will assume the stature and the status of the giant who is coiled up inside you like a tightly wound spring. You will ride the roller coaster that your life was designed to be. Don't sell yourself short."***

We all have the opportunity to weave the intent of giving what each situation requires into our value base. By trying to live it every day to the best of our ability, we can, in an incremental manner, mature towards our fullest potential as human beings.

Maturing to a leader

Mature people give more than they take, listen more than they speak and can subordinate their own agendas to those of others. Such people show humility, respect and courage.

The *Maturity Staircase*, with its message of unconditional generosity, has important general implications for everyone – but it has an even greater relevance for a person who wants to lead. In fact, developing into a true leader rests on setting an example of demonstrating the intent to unselfishly give what the situation requires.

A mature leader will be able to support others to mature. This means that subordinates would likely follow the leader's example of unconditional giving by giving more themselves.

When everyone is prepared to give more than what they demand in return, the team will be able to bake a bigger cake. In other words; people who are prepared to unconditionally give more, form a better team, with better collaboration. In this way the team produces more value for all its stakeholders.

The opposite, a group of people who want to get more than they are prepared to give, will produce a negative spiral of deteriorating collaboration. I assert that the Maturity Staircase provides three important conclusions from a leadership perspective:

1. **Accept the present maturity level – act from the here and now.**
Acknowledge that you and your subordinates are human beings who will continue to act selfishly sometimes. But do not accept an unwillingness to grow – neither your own nor someone else's. Guilt and shame rarely form a good platform for improvements, but unwillingness to try is even worse. Each small step that you or your subordinates take, here and now, counts.

2. **Set an example – your behavior inspires followers.**
If your subordinates believe that you work mainly in order to enrich yourself, they will most likely be inclined to do it too. If they see that you regularly take the credit for their efforts, they may even start to oppose you (albeit mostly secretly) whenever they can. And if they think you are nice to them only because you want something from them, they will probably imitate some of that selfishness.

However, if they perceive that you are trying to make a contribution to the greater good of all stakeholders, including themselves, they will likely follow your example.

3. **See and acknowledge your subordinates as they move up the staircase.**
Every time you make a choice, you either move up or down the Maturity Staircase. Each moment defines us. Every selfish act is a missed opportunity for growth. Etsko Schuitema describes it like this: "When we do not act correctly, we waste the moment."

It is in the moment of choice that subordinates show their attitude – their intent to contribute to the collaboration. This attitude is revealed by what is said, done or expressed in some other way. The leader has to *see the game* – in order to observe contributions, strengthen means and abilities, as well as to coach the individuals to grow their attitude.

It is your job as the leader to help every subordinate to climb the staircase towards becoming a master, especially those who got stuck in being dependent victims (which can be pictured as being at the bottom left of figure 28).

Remember that the person who chooses egoistically is not evil, just immature. By encouraging giving, and confronting their selfish acts, you help them to grow.

A good starting point for your maturation as a leader is hence the intent to give, by making better and better leader contributions. Mature leaders cultivate attitudes, starting with their own. This is a life-long challenge.

That there is a definite connection between unselfish humility and excellent leadership has been shown by Jim Collins' research team in the studies that led to the book *Good to Great*. The team found low profile and modest level 5 leaders who created sustainable outcomes, and they found big personalities on level 4 who reached for the limelight, but were only able to create short-term results.

Collins stresses that this was contrary to what they had expected: "Our discovery of level 5 leadership is counterintuitive. Indeed, it is counter-cultural. People generally assume that transforming companies from good to great requires larger-than-life leaders."

He continues by describing the humility that characterizes the level 5 leaders: "Indeed, throughout our interviews with such executives, we were struck by the way they talked about themselves – or rather, didn't talk about themselves. They'd go on and on about the company and the contributions of other executives, but they would instinctively deflect discussion about their own role. When pressed to talk about themselves, they'd say things like, 'I hope I'm not sounding like a big shot', or 'I don't think I can take much credit for what happened. We were blessed with marvelous people'. [...] By contrast, level 4 leaders often fail to set up the company for enduring success – after all, what better testament to your own personal greatness than that the place falls apart after you leave?"[79]

Collins and his research team also found that the level 5 leaders had confidence in their people. This is in line with what Robert Levering emphasizes in *A Great Place to Work*. His research of effective and appreciated workplaces highlights the importance of trust. The people studied were less focused on monetary remuneration and more on building bridges of mutual trust to one another.

It is easier to give unconditionally to others if it goes both ways and is reciprocal. If the other (especially if it is one's boss) receives and uses your contributions without giving anything in return, the trust disappears. And lost confidence takes a long time to build again.

Mature individuals, in a trusting environment, want to pass on the knowledge, experiences and care they themselves have received. They give with gratitude.

79. From the article *Level 5 leadership: The Triumph of Humility and Fierce Resolve.*

Generous leaders will grow themselves and their subordinates, creating a generous team culture. In turn, a team with generous members creates more value to share. Etsko Schuitema expresses this dual effect as: "The intent to serve others explains both organizational and personal excellence."

The conclusion that giving is a foundation for personal excellence is confirmed by the answers to the question that Schuitema consultants have asked numerous times: "Who do you admire the most?" The answer is usually a grandmother or some other close friend or relative who has shown humility and the intent to serve. Nelson Mandela is the public person that is mentioned most often in the answers. He has, on numerous occasions, shown humility and care, both in words and actions. A quote from his 1994 election victory speech gives an example of this:

> ***"I stand here before you filled with deep pride and joy – pride in the ordinary, humble people of this country. [...] I am your servant; I don't come to you as a leader, as one above others. We are a great team. [...] And I stand therefore before you, humbled by your courage, with a heart full of love for all of you."***

Even though most of us serve in a much more limited context than Mandela did, we all have the opportunity to give our best to the people around us. It is the sum of all those contributions that best can change the world.

10.4 At last – your ladder against your tree

Our welfare, to a great extent, relies on organizations – small and large, private and public. They depend on good leadership at all levels. The Leader's Ladder is a model for such good leadership, based upon the Collaboration Tree.

Figure 29 illustrates how the ladder steadily rests against the tree, in order for you to climb it and let team collaboration deliver the fruits (value) you have the potential to grow.

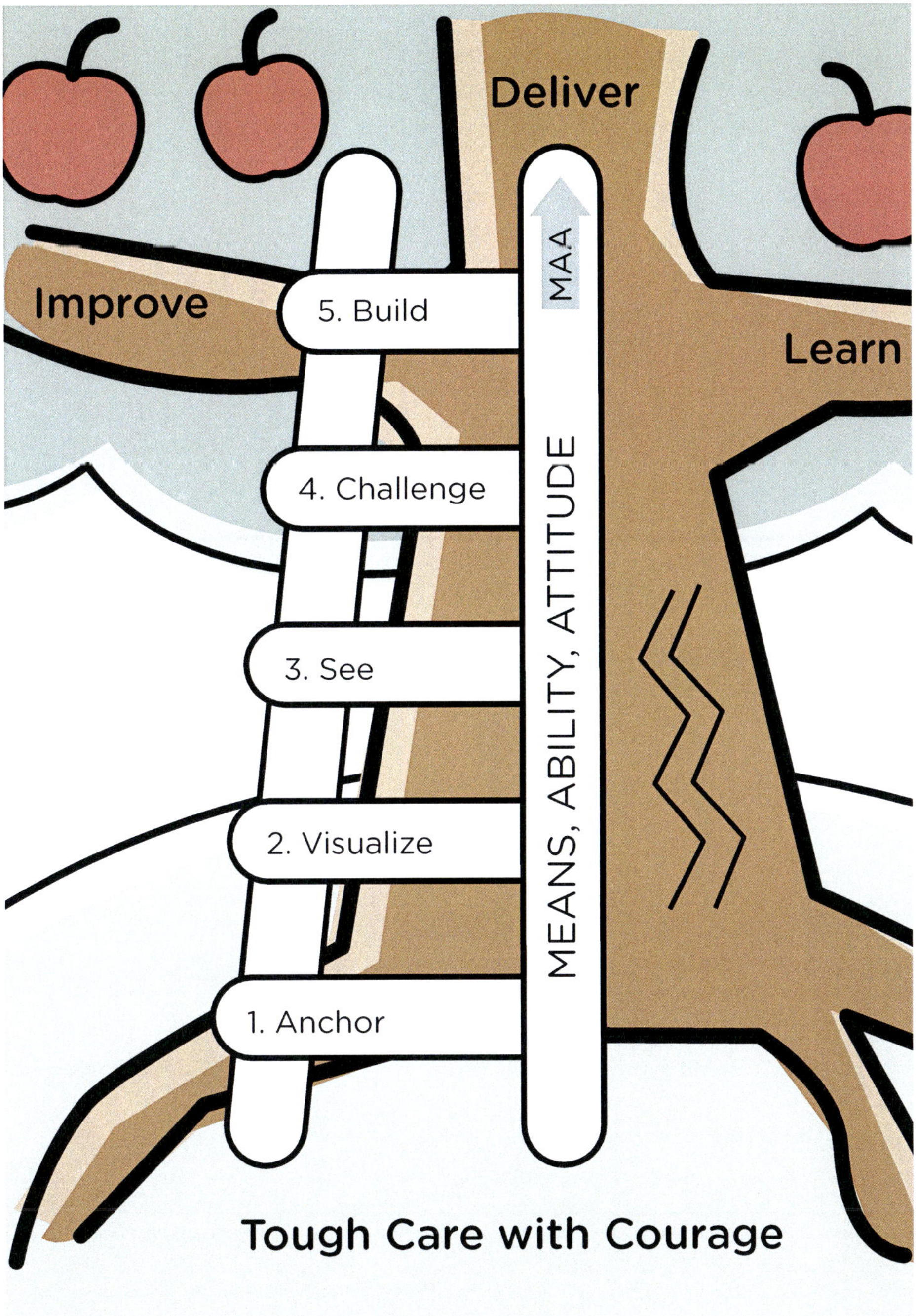

Figure 29 Reaching the fruits of great collaboration
The Leader's Ladder resting against the Collaboration Tree.

The tree shows why we need to collaborate – and to lead. The five steps of the ladder show how to do it.

No-one becomes a great leader overnight. The ladder, supported by the tool box in the appendices, provides many opportunities to learn from.

Choose what to start with based on your own current situation. Highlight what is most important in your own ladder for the near future. Or do it together with colleagues and create your common *leadership standard* inspired by the ladder.

Practice becoming a little braver with each important issue that demands your courage. Pick your battles and find comfort in the words by Reinhold Niebuhr: "... please grant me the serenity to accept the things I cannot change, the courage to change the things I can, and the wisdom to know the difference."

Do not underestimate your own potential, and be satisfied with every little step in the right direction. The world needs your better and better leadership!

Appendices
A Toolbox for The Leader's Ladder

The following three appendices contain tools that have the potential to support you in your leadership development. They are chosen to support all five of the steps of the Leader's Ladder. Together they form a leadership toolbox from which you can pick the tool you need and that is appropriate for the moment and for the tasks that you need to manage.

A leader tool is connected to a method in the same way as the *method* of sawing is dependent on the *tool* saw.

In the descriptions that follow, I sometimes only focus on the tool because the methods of how to use and apply it are implicitly understood. In other instances, when the ways one acts or uses it are vital, I focus on the method, pinpoint potential behavioral pitfalls and give tips that will help to increase the value creation.

It is a common mistake to dismiss a tool before its full potential is realized. I have seen good tools used half-heartedly and sometimes even for tasks that they were not intended for. Someone described this tendency as, "The person who is good with the hammer tends to look at everything as nails".

Thus, try to really understand the purpose of each tool, and try to understand how to use them better and more effectively. Most of the tools I describe here, not least the pulse meetings with visual control, will, if applied correctly, most certainly yield results right from the start. They will, however, prove much more effective and powerful in delivering more value once you and your team have practiced, learned and fine-tuned using them.

I have personally seen and experienced how well the tools I have chosen to describe here contribute to supporting leadership. Most of them, however, can also be used very effectively by your subordinates. In this manner, they become tools not only for leadership development, but also for subordinates' growth and of course for collaboration improvements, depending on which one of the three goals – *deliver, improve* or *learn* – the tool focuses on.

Look at the toolbox as a smorgasbord from which you can choose the tool you require the most at that moment. Try it, reflect on your experience, improve your handling of it and, when you can or need to, adjust the tool to your specific needs.

Appendix A
Leader tools to deliver

The tools described in this appendix are designed to help you and your coworkers to deliver better. They provide support for all five steps of the Leader's Ladder, even if they are, to a large extent, directed towards visualizing and acting on operational deviations – and to do that early, with high pulse. The tools are described under the headlines:

- **Pulse meetings with visual control**
- **Pulsed control in the line organization**
- **Pulsed control in projects**
- **Escalation and pulse rooms**
- **Leading pulse meetings**

A.1 Pulse meetings with visual control

Visual control techniques have the potential to improve your leadership by making important facts and relationships visible for better team understanding, better discussions, better decisions and a higher pulse.

Pulse meetings with visual control will support your leadership on two levels. On one hand, you create value from shared learning just by setting up visual control, deciding on the purpose, the data needed and the relationships to visualize. On the other hand, you create repetitive value each time you run the pulse meeting, creating a good discussion based on continuously updated facts.

Do not get stuck in trying to design the perfect visualization before starting with pulsed control. Make a draft version, test it and improve it together.

Make a clear connection between the design of the visuals on the board and the purpose of the meeting. Share the responsibility among the team members for updating the facts before and during the meeting.

Work-board or computer

You have the choice to visualize facts on a computer or on a work-board. A work-board is a physical space (a whiteboard, brown paper or something similar) on which the whole team can write and post notes. Using a whiteboard made from metal also makes it possible to use magnetic symbols and document fasteners.

Sometimes a computer is the best solution, for example if the team members work in different locations or if the meetings require huge amounts of data. However, be careful before you decide on a computer application for the visualization – you might risk preventing people from participating fully because they cannot access and understand all the important data and how it relates to other aspects.

Always see to it that your visualization design remains simple and understandable for all. In addition, try to ensure that facts remain visible between meetings and that everyone can add new facts, issues and actions between, before and during meetings.

It is precisely for these reasons that a physical work-board on the wall is often a better alternative. Such a board usually increases your ability to create understanding and dynamic interaction in the meetings – with everyone's active participation.

Work-board or display

The term "work-board" in itself already suggests that it should be used for working. Unfortunately, sometimes people misunderstand the essence of visual control, turning the board more into a display than a tool that really supports work. Such displays are often full of printed documents with nice-looking graphs that are rarely updated and seldom used for creating good discussions and actions.

A well-functioning work-board is dynamic and alive. Each team member is part of the process to update the facts and actions showed on the board, with the appropriate frequency decided according to the purpose of the meetings. Such a board might not look as neat and attractive as a display, for example being full of handwritten notes, but it is far more effective. Thus, focus your energy on creating dynamic work-boards instead of on nice-looking displays.

A signal system with colors

Boards for delivery-pulse meetings are often based on a signal system with colors signaling which issues need attention. A green indicator means that there is no need for new actions; red means that there is an immediate need to do something above and beyond what is normal or already planned.

The meaning of each color must be defined in relation to a base level (see section 4.3). Thus, green means we are maintaining our base level, while red means we have found a deviation that needs urgent attention. You can also use other colors, such as yellow indicators for highlighting risks for future reds or to show that an earlier red signal is now being taken care of through an action plan in order to turn it into green.

A generic definition of a three-color signal system for delivery-pulse meetings reads as follows:

● RED = ACT!

A problem/deviation with an immediate need for action

● YELLOW = WATCH

Risk for problem or ***A problem with a defined and realistic action plan***

● GREEN = OK

We are maintaining our base level

A delivery-pulse meeting must concentrate on the red indicators, that is, to catch and visualize problems in order to start immediate remedial action. Longer discussions on solutions must be referred to a special meeting in order to keep the pulse meetings short.

Hence, encourage participants to bring solution ideas to the meetings and lead the meetings so that all the red indicators can be handled swiftly, leaving some time for checking risks and action plans (yellow indicators).

It is important to be able to escalate the red indicators that you cannot solve yourself to the next level in the organization (or to an expert support function if appropriate). However, choose to escalate only the red issues that you need assistance to solve, and complement it by informing the next level above about other issues that they need to know about.

Delivery-pulse meetings require clear base levels. To achieve a balance between different targets, it is advisable to use base level measures that complement each other, such as with +QTE as described in section 3.3. Remember to be specific in defining each base-level measure. An example of such a specific definition of a three-color signal system with four complementing KPIs is shown in table 3.

Perspective	KPI measure	Green =base level	Yellow	Red
+ (SHE and learning)	**Number of near-accidents or signs of stress/ill health**	No near-accidents or signs of stress/ ill health	Minor near-accidents or signs of stress/ill health	Accidents or clear signs of stress/ill health
Q (Quality)	**Number of remarks**	0	≥ 1 with root cause action(s) initiated	≥ 1 with root cause unknown
T (Time)	**Present position related to schedule**	On time	Behind schedule with initiated recovery plan	Behind schedule without realistic recovery plan
E (Efficiency)	**Present position related to cost budget/estimate**	On budget	Above budget with initiated recovery plan	Above budget without realistic recovery plan

Table 3 Examples of color definitions for a delivery-pulse board

If there are only red indicators, it is normally a sign of serious under performance. It indicates insufficient work contributions caused by a lack of *means*, *abilities* and/or *attitude*. However, the reason might alternatively be that the base levels, for example defined as schedule and budget, are set unrealistically high or too difficult to reach.

Only green indicators are also a reason for concern. It indicates low expectations with no real challenge, that is, base levels that are set too low and are too easy to meet. This, in turn, might be an indication of a culture in which people are satisfied with the status quo, or even worse, a dishonest culture in which red signals are seen as something bad.

Use the SHE (safety, health and environment) and learning perspective wisely. Under that headline you can put KPIs that, for example, measure near-accidents, absenteeism, workload per person as well as realized improvements and learning opportunities. As a subjective complement, you can put up a *spirit meter* on which every individual can mark their current mood (e.g. with a symbolic happy or sad face). If used the right way, such a meter gives everyone the opportunity to explain personal circumstances, like troubles or stress, which in turn, creates the opportunity for collegial support.

Pulse control in different settings

Work can be more or less repetitive in nature. Production of services and goods, as well as support and administrative tasks, are often repetitive. These types of work are usually carried out in a line organization, that is, in a permanent hierarchical organization. Project work (a unique assignment with its own specific targets of outcome, budget and date of completion) however, requires a temporary project organization that secures the different skills needed for a limited time in order to meet the specific project targets.

However, all organizations need to be able to handle both repetitive tasks and once-off tasks. Take, for example, an industrial company with different functional departments. In the production, HR, finance and sourcing departments, repetitive work is normally dominant. Nevertheless, project work is also needed, such as for investigation, improvement and investment projects. Conversely, in the product development department, for instance, it is often the other way around, and project work is the dominant form of labor. But this does not mean, however, that they do not carry out repetitive work; there is still a lot of repetitive work done in such a department, both within and outside the scope of the projects.

Other types of organizations (such as hospitals, schools, municipalities, restaurants, etc.) should also be able to handle both mainly repetitive work (in the permanent line organization) and mainly unique work (in a temporary project organization).

The tools for visual and pulsed control differ depending on whether the work is predominantly repetitive or once-off. I will start by describing the tools for the former (pulsed control in the line organizations) before covering the latter (pulsed control in projects).

A.2 Pulsed control in the line organization

Repetitive work can, to a large extent, be prepared and standardized. An example of this is car production. In many ways, the automobile industry has been a forerunner in using visual tools for operational control. In their takted production lines, they visualize different base levels in order to see deviations from what is expected early (sometimes called the normal or standard state).

The early signaling of deviations is complemented with a so-called Andon System, with which the worker can easily get instant support from a team coordinator to fix a problem, and if necessary, stop the entire line to get more help.

The basic idea is to avoid hiding problems, but instead bring them to light so that they can be fixed immediately as well as to provide maximum support to the person doing the value-adding work.

Parallel with the visualization and quick fixes of deviations in the production line, repetitive pulse meetings are held to report statuses and determine the need for actions to learn and solve reoccurring problems for good. Scania, for example, has such pulse meetings (between the line manager and the team coordinators) every second hour to go through the operational deviations and incidents that have occurred in the past two hours.

Other private and public organizations have taken inspiration from the visual operational control now widely used in the automotive industry and started implementing similar tools. Pulse meetings that are held every day are often referred to as "daily control meetings" or just "dailies".

Visual daily control meetings have the purpose of making operational deviations visible before they turn into more serious problems. One such important deviation is if the team has failed to meet the due times prescribed by a delivery schedule.[80] The delivery schedule is one of many base levels that are easier to prepare with accuracy for repetitive work than for once-off work. In addition, efficiency targets and ways of working can be more easily fine-tuned when the work has been done many times before. However, irrespective of repetitiveness, the measures followed up at the daily meeting can be divided according to the +QTE[81] perspective (see section 3.3), even if the details of the visual boards would look different for project-pulse meetings compared to daily control meetings in a repetitive work environment.

A work-board for daily control can be formed around a deviations template with one field per day (in a week or in a month). Every morning you report if a certain measure has a deviation or not by filling in the corresponding field. One way of doing that is to add an actual value next to the expected one, as shown in figure 30.

Alternatively, you can use one template per measure, each with 31 fields, one for each day of the month.[82] By color-coding today's field on every form each morning, you can signal whether you are on track (green), or if you have a deviation to take care of (red).

80. Expected deliveries from repetitive work are often prescribed by a computer system, such as an ERP system, but can also be generated manually, e.g. by a so-called Kanban system, using cards for signaling the need for information, material or work. In many service businesses, the expected deliveries are set directly by the arrival of customers. The base level for deliveries is here decided by the expected maximum waiting time for each customer.
81. It is common to measure KPIs for the +, Q and T perspectives on a daily basis, but to measure financial KPIs more seldom, e.g. weekly.
82. Some organizations use four different templates, each with 31 fields, with the fields put together so that they form a "+", a "Q", a "T" and an "E" respectively.

DEVIATION CHART Expected value/actual value (negative deviation = red)						
	MEASURE	Monday	Tuesday	Wednesday	Thursday	Friday
+	Incident	0/0	0/0	0/0	0/1	0/
Q	% correct	100/100	100/100	100/95	100/100	100/
T	Delivered on time	20/20	20/20	20/19	22/23	22/
T	Longest lead time (hr)	11/9	11/7	11/8	11/6	9/
E	Expenses ($)	5/5	5/8	5/5	5/3	5/

Figure 30 One type of work-board for daily control
... updated after a Thursday morning meeting.

The black numbers in figure 30 show the base levels – the expected values – for five different KPI measures per day and are written on the board before the start of the week.

Each morning every base-level figure is complemented by filling in the actual status after the slash. If the actual value is within the acceptable range, it is written in green ink. If it is outside what is expected, it is written in red. Every red number should trigger one or more why-questions, followed by a decision on the necessary action to take the team back to base level performance.

After each week, the green and red figures are wiped out and if a base level needs to be adjusted in order to become more realistic or more challenging, the black figures are altered accordingly.

The example in figure 30 shows that the cost budget was not met on the Tuesday. On the Wednesday, the team failed to reach the quality and on-time delivery targets. At the latest meeting (Thursday morning), one safety incident was reported. Note the rise in the production-rate base level from 20 to 22 per day and the new expectations (valid as from Friday) on lead time, lowering the longest acceptable lead time to 9 hours.

The short morning meetings need to concentrate on new problems (red indicators) and the related quick fixes needed. The corrective actions decided upon need to be listed on an action list, coupled with the name of the person responsible and an expected completion date. The purpose of these quick actions should normally be to get performance back to the base level by the next day, or at least in the near future. It is wise to reserve the quick-action list for tasks that can be handled within a set time frame, for example within two days. If a quick-fix adjustment needs to be complemented by a solution directed at a root cause, you can refer that task to the next improvement-pulse meeting. In such a meeting, you can use PDCA tools for systematic problem-solving as described in appendix B.

A daily control meeting normally starts by looking back at what transpired since the last meeting, followed by looking forward to what is expected for the coming day, including any special challenges that need to be addressed. Thus, the visualization of deviations from yesterday might need to be complemented with showing the present status on the availability of persons, equipment, material, etcetera.

A.3 Pulsed control in projects

Pulse meetings for projects share many similarities with pulse meetings for the line organization. Both are based on frequent and short meetings focusing on fixing operational deviations early in order to deliver on time. They are also both aided with visual control techniques, for example with a whiteboard with color indicators, and a quick-action list beside it.

The main difference is that project-pulse meetings concentrate on the unique activities that need to be started, coordinated or finished in the near future (things that often are obvious in repetitive work). This normally calls for more agility in the planning and execution of the work.

Researchers have found that the use of pulsed project control, supported by visual control methods, have many positive effects. Users often report higher productivity and less stress. The reports also indicate other benefits, such as improved quality and on-time delivery performance, less bureaucracy and earlier problem detection. Maybe the most important effects, however, are improved commitment and collaboration. Researchers concluded that the use of visual techniques strengthened communication by increasing face-to-face interaction and providing more relevant data without risking information overload.[83]

You can create project-pulse control in different ways. One such way, based on Agile principles, is Scrum. It comprises an excellent set of principles and tools for managing projects that require adaptability to possible changes in needs and requirements. Another way is project VP, which is discussed in the following section.

Project VP

The project-VP method (or just VP in short[84]) is a variant of visual planning (VP). It is suitable for leading work where unique activities need to be divided and coordinated between individuals. Such work can include anything from large projects (such as product or operational development) to leading management team meetings (e.g. to visualize *leader contributions* in leader-pulse meetings as described in section 9.2).

Project VP has strengths and weaknesses compared to Scrum.[85] One of VP's major strengths is that it provides an overview of the whole project (when it is possible to define the project in an early stage). The major advantage of Scrum is that it provides support for an adaptive approach to project control (when requirements and other major inputs are likely to vary during the course of the project).

It is, however, possible to compensate for VP weaknesses in this area by adopting solutions from Scrum, such as introducing planning cycles (sprints) that trigger reflection sessions when the team stops for demonstrations, learning and adjustments.

Project VP is based on the principle that everyone contributes to both the

83. While studying visual project control in three industrial groups, Alfredsson and Söderberg (see Ludvig Lindlöf's dissertation *Visual Management: on Communication in Product Development Organizations* from 2014) found that the biggest advantages were increased communication and holistic understanding, as well as increased participation and focus on deliverables. They also found other positive effects, such as better prioritization of tasks, improved leveling of workload between individuals, greater involvement and an increased consensus around critical issues.

84. VP roots can be tracked to a method called KI-VP, short for Knowledge Innovation Visible Planning, from the Japanese company JMAC. It is easy to see that the board is used for planning. However, it is also used for learning. Thus, it is not only a planning tool – a simplified version of Microsoft Project. It is a tool for creating good discussions, quick responses and Agile rescheduling, as well as for creating improvement and learning opportunities.

85. VP gives a visible support for the breakdown of project targets into time-set activities. It also gives a clear overview of the workload per person that can be used for good discussions on work sharing between colleagues to keep a leveled load on each individual. Scrum, on the other hand, provides a set of very usable concepts, e.g. the *Product Owner* who inserts the customer's voice into the project, and the *Scrum Master*, who coordinates the team's work based on a *Backlog* of tasks. Scrum provides both a daily pulse and a *sprint* pulse (normally 2-4 weeks). In complex projects, a third level of pulse, with increments consisting of a number of sprints, might be needed to coordinate the different Scrum teams in order to reach a common goal.

coordination and execution of the common work. All team members are supposed to be active at the work-board, handling the post-it notes representing the tasks they have accepted accountability to perform.

To start using project VP, you need a board, some small post-it notes in different colors, and an empty wall for the board. The work-board is preferably constructed by combining large (A0 or A1) paper templates. A VP template is a matrix of columns representing time, and rows representing different persons or teams. Such a template can be adapted to different planning horizons as shown in figure 31.

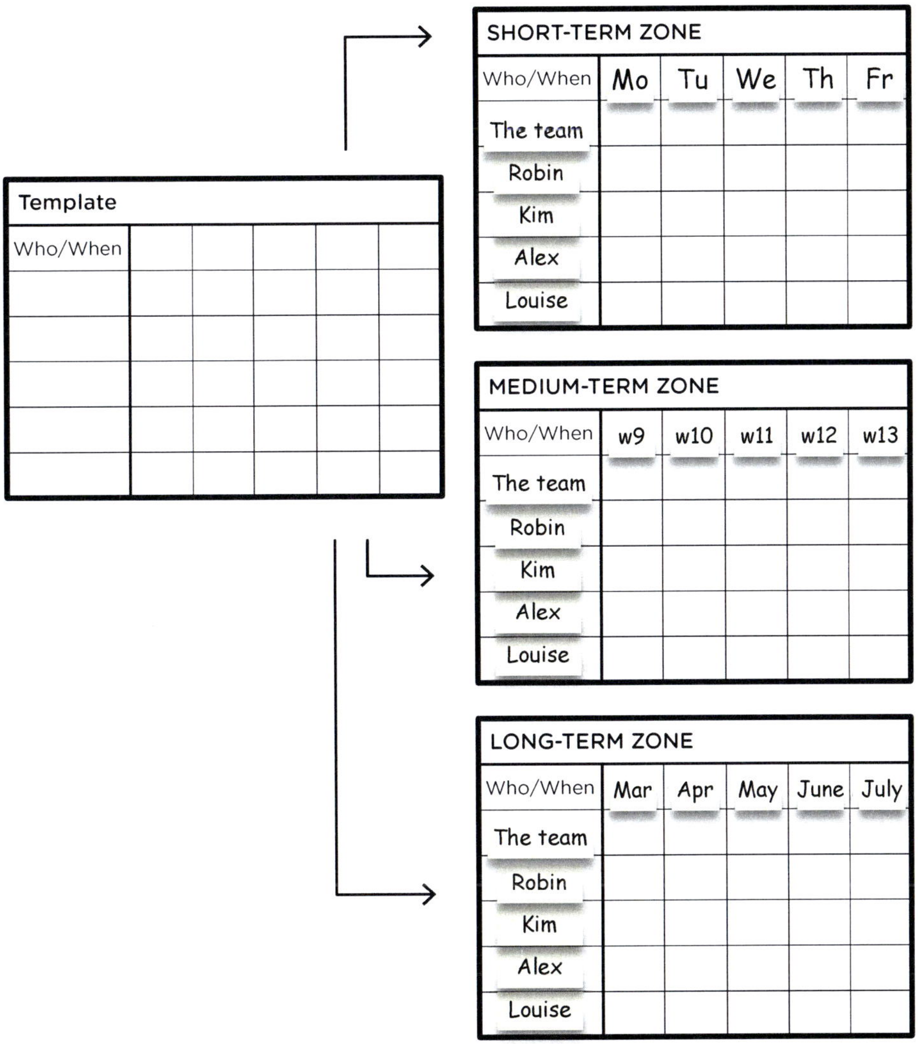

Figure 31 Using a VP template
Three planning horizon matrices with different time frames, created from the same template.

Put a suitable number of paper templates up on a wall (or foldable screen) and adjust the different planning horizons. The long-term zone matrix is there to give the overall view of the whole project, highlighting the expected end result and the most important deliveries and milestones on the way towards the target. The purpose of the short-term zone matrix is to provide a detailed plan for *who does what* in the upcoming days.

For a long project of many months, there might be a need for three horizon matrices, for example divided as (1) a *short-term zone* with daily planning for the coming two weeks, (2) a *medium-term zone* with weekly planning for 1-2 months and (3) a *long-term zone* with monthly planning until the end of the project. By using a generic base template and adding post-it notes on the time line as in figure 31, it is possible to define and adjust the length of the zones according to the specific needs of the project.

After defining the time frames of the work-board matrices, it is time to make all the team members' names visible through post-it notes in the left-most column, showing which line belongs to whom. The top row under the time line should be reserved for common activities and deliverables. The rest of the rows are normally allocated to one individual each, but when sub-projects need to be managed in a hierarchy, the boards for higher levels will, instead, show one responsible team per row.

When the matrices have been marked with both time-frame notes (top row) and responsibility notes (left column), it is ready for use. Now you need small post-it notes in different colors. Blue notes represent *what* should be achieved, such as the deliverables. Yellow notes represent *how* it will be achieved, for instance the activities to be done.

By breaking down the goal and the end deliverable(s) of the project into sub-deliverables and activities, you can realize one of the important benefits of VP – the involvement of all the team members in understanding what to do, and how to do it.

Start by writing the project goal and the associated deliverable(s) on the blue note(s). Put it in the time column that corresponds with when it is required. Continue by breaking it down to sub-deliverables and put each of these blue notes in the time column that indicates when it needs to be ready, and in the row representing who is mainly responsible for its delivery. Finally, every blue note should be broken down into the activities that need to be carried out. Hence, a blue note generates from one up to dozens of yellow notes to the left of the blue one, distributed between the responsibility rows of the people involved.

Avoid the common trap of breaking down only the known parts of the project into detailed schedules of yellow notes. Focus instead on the unknown parts of the project – the parts with the biggest risks. Take the time necessary to understand how to approach risks, uncertainties and other issues in order to find countermeasures at an early stage.[86] Translate your new understanding into additional yellow notes that describe the complementing activities that are needed to reach the target. The resulting VP-board will then include activity notes not only for the direct value-adding steps, but also for learning through experimenting, for removing obstacles and for reducing risks.

Every individual is responsible for their own row on the board. This rule is fundamental to VP because it is the base for everyone's commitment and accountability. It means that no-one should either put up a new note in someone else's row, or move an existing note without clear consent from the person involved. Not only is everyone therefore responsible for each blue and yellow note in their row, but also for ensuring that their total workload (illustrated by all the yellow notes in their row) is realistic to handle. Accepting a yellow note constitutes a commitment to a work contribution.

At the short (daily) meetings, all team members briefly report on deviations since the last meeting, things that affect the others or the next deliverable. Requests for help and other issues that need to be addressed should also be brought forward at the meeting.

The activities finalized according to plan do not need to be addressed at the meeting; they should just be marked with an "X" before the meeting starts.

86. There are different approaches to finding risks, uncertainties, obstacles and knowledge gaps in order to learn and decide on the proper actions, such as the Lichtenberg (based on the Successive Principle), Kata and Issue breakdown methods. It is possible to visualize both risks and obstacles that might prevent the team from reaching a deliverable (a blue note) and then define the sequence of countermeasure activities as yellow notes that can be put up on the VP-board, together with the parts of the project that have already been planned. Use the opportunity to do analyses of success factors, issues and countermeasures with the team in conjunction with the normal breakdown of project goals and deliverables.

The blue and yellow notes for deliverables and activities are complemented with three other types of notes, each with its unique color and meaning, see table 4.

Color	Meaning	To write on the note
	Deliverable	1. What is to be delivered 2. Name of responsible 3. Due date
	Activity	1. What is to be done 2. Name of responsible 3. Due date 4. Expected/actual execution time
	Absence	1. Reason for absence 2. Name 3. Expected date of return
	Input dependence	1. What is needed from others 2. Responsible for (external) delivery 3. Responsible to monitor in our team 4. Responsible (in our team) to monitor
	Issue	1. Problem, risk or obstacle 2. Name of issuer 3. Date when noted

Table 4 A common color standard for project VP

The notes of absence (orange) and input dependence (green) are put up by each team member in their own row. Issues (red notes) are, instead, put up in a separate area, either at the meeting or in-between meetings whenever a crucial concern is found.

There needs to be a special point on the meeting agenda for discussing these issue notes. Such a red note discussion normally results in someone taking on the responsibility to carry out or suggest a countermeasure, manifested by a corresponding yellow note put up on their row.

The area for posting the red issue notes should be prepared adjacent to the matrices, preferably in a place where other required information can also be posted, for example, meeting rules and an inbox for new tasks or deliverables.

You can build and expand further on this project-VP basis together with your team. By complementing the short daily meeting with longer ones, for example once a week, you can create learning opportunities around deviations in quality and time.

In order to create a basis for the latter, it is a good idea to note both the expected and the actual time spent on each activation note. The notes stating differences between the estimated and actual times can then form the base for a good discussion in the weekly meeting. In addition, a yellow note that has been postponed (marked by a dot every time it has been moved forward) is also a good base for a root-cause discussion at the next weekly meeting.

Lawn charts

A *lawn chart* can be used to complement the VP-board, or to replace it. Use it when you need to visualize the planning in more detail than the VP-board can support, for instance when there are many short activities per person, or several sub-projects that need to be controlled and coordinated.

The name of the chart comes from the metaphor that a lawn needs attention when it is becoming yellow or red. By coloring the cells of the chart in three colors (green, yellow or red) you can, over time, build up a very visual image of what needs attention.

Every team member has a responsibility to keep one or more rows updated with color indicators. Each cell in the row corresponds to a task in a work process, such as providing something to a customer, or finalizing a step in the procurement process of a certain part number. When a person has many such tasks per day (i.e. related to many customers or many part numbers) the lawn chart becomes a better tool than the VP-board.

Start creating the lawn chart by defining the process. This means listing the sequence of activities that are needed for each object (e.g. each customer served or each part number handled) and naming each column according to each activity. The next step is to name the rows in the chart with the names of the responsible persons as in figure 32, or with the objects that must be handled (e.g. customers or part numbers) as in figure 33.

Once that is done, you can start using the chart in pulse meetings. For every activity that has been completed, the responsible team member marks the corresponding cell in green before the meeting starts. If an activity is threatening quality, schedule or cost commitments, and it lacks a plan to recover, it is marked red. If it is late, but there is a plan to recover, the cell should be colored yellow.

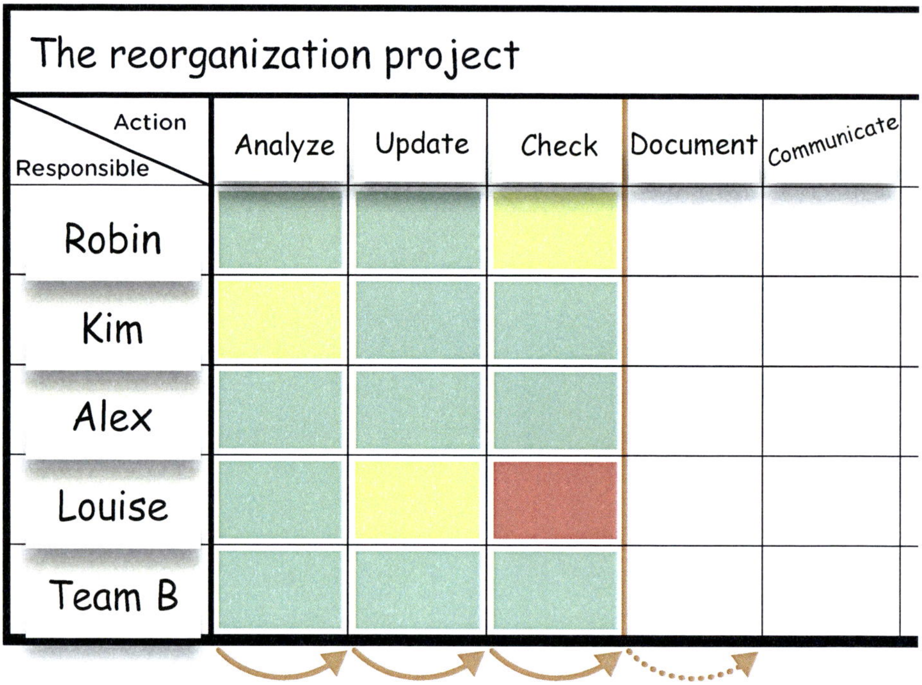

Figure 32 One type of lawn chart
... showing status per responsible person.

The example shown in figure 32 describes the process and status in a reorganization project. The "now line" in the chart (the brown vertical line between the "Check" and "Document" columns) shows that three activities were ready at the most-recent follow-up meeting. Two deviations were reported: Robin stated a problem with a recovery plan, while Louise reported a problem without a viable plan, that is, a call for support.

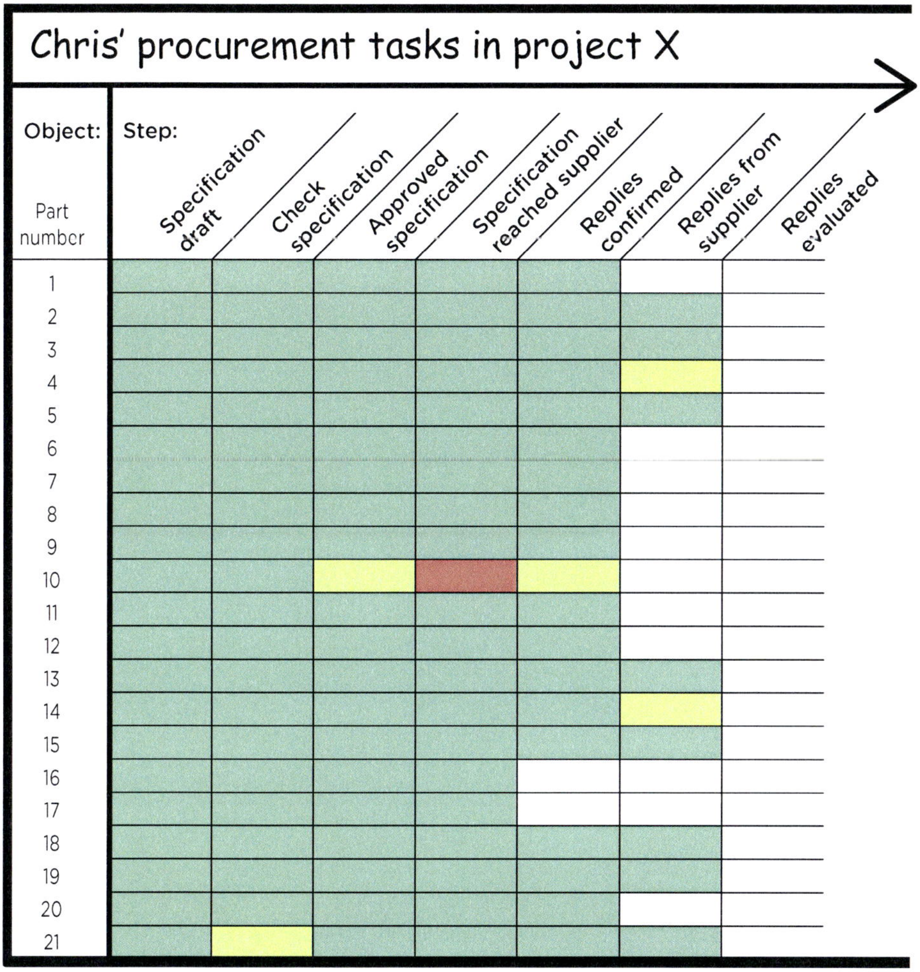

Figure 33 Another type of lawn chart

... showing status per object (here part numbers) and steps in the process.

Figure 33 illustrates another example of a lawn chart, where the whole chart is dedicated to one person's commitments or tasks. It shows Chris' work to deliver actions related to many different part numbers.

A lawn chart, like other good pulse-meeting tools, provides a very visual way to represent both expectations and status – highlighting deviations that require extra attention and support. Used the right way, they are powerful aids for creating good discussions that create consensus around who needs to do what.

The lawn chart also provides a very clear overview when handling a large number of tasks. Where the lawn turns yellow or red, extra care is needed (compare watering a real lawn). The excellent summary view it provides is of great help to keep pulse meetings short, frequent and productive.

Matrix-pulse meetings

In a matrix organization[87] another form of meeting is needed, the so-called matrix-pulse meeting.

A work-board for a *matrix-pulse meeting* aims at providing the overview needed for coordination of a multi-project environment, including securing extra resources for a project or to assign one project as a higher priority than another.

It is about synchronizing the work on the organization's project portfolio by involving the right people (both line managers and project leaders) around the right facts, and with the right frequency (the pulse) – that is, creating fruitful discussions. By handling all projects during one short meeting, it is possible to get the total picture in order take appropriate decisions on reinforcements, reallocations and prioritizations of skills, equipment, etcetera.

If handled in an optimal manner with effective meetings (normally less than half an hour), and with the right pulse (normally once a week), matrix-pulse meetings can become the hub for multi-project control.

On a matrix-pulse board, all projects are listed along one axis and all departments along the other. You can also add information on project status in parallel with the departments. In figure 34, this is done by adding four status columns, one for each of the four +QTE perspectives.

87. In such an organization several projects depend on getting their team members allocated from different departments in a line organization.

	Project status				Capability provided by line organization			
					Department			
Project	+ SHE	Q Quality	T On-time delivery	E Cost	1 Marie	2 Jaime	3 Rokhi	4 Martin
A Charlie	Green	Red	Yellow	Green	Yellow	Green	Green	Green
B Virginia	Green	Green	Yellow	Green	Green	Green	Green	Green
C Ali	Yellow	Yellow	Yellow	Yellow	Green	Red	Green	Green
D Signe	Green	Green	Green	Green	Green	Green	Green	Green
E Wilhelm	Green	Green	Green	Green	Green	Yellow	Green	Green
F Gustav	Green	Green	Green	Yellow	Green	Yellow	Green	Green

Green = OK (stays in line with base level)
Yellow = Recovery plan/Decided action to get back to base level
Red = Deviation without a recovery plan

Figure 34 An example of a matrix-pulse board
... showing project status per KPI and department dependence.

All project leaders should have updated their rows before the weekly matrix-pulse meeting, which typically happens on a Monday morning. To do that correctly, they need to have discussed current deviations with the line managers involved, so that they hopefully have the same understanding of both the deviation and the recovery plan.

In the example shown by figure 34 , Project A has a problem with meeting due dates, as shown by the yellow indicator in the intersection cell between the project A-row and the T-column. The project leader for Project A, Charlie, has been in contact with the manager for Department 1, Marie, before the meeting, and they have decided on a realistic recovery plan. This is why Charlie has chosen a yellow indicator in the T-column as well as in the Department-1-column.

Project A also has a quality problem, but the project team has not yet had the time to analyze the problem and decide on a suitable countermeasure (possibly with support from the line). Thus, Charlie has put a red indicator in the intersection cell between the project A-row and the Q-column.

Matrix-pulse meetings must be kept short and effective. Thus, the red indicators must be the focus. A meeting starts with each project leader going through their row and quickly describing new red indicators as well as new risks and circumstances that will affect the others. After that, it is the line managers' turn to give their quick views on new problems (red indicators), risks, and status of recovery plans/actions (yellow indicators).

All these very short presentations give you (and the others) numerous opportunities to give quick feedback, even if it is just as a "Well done!" to encourage continued good attitude, or as a comment on work contributions related to agreed principles and values, or as a tip of what else needs to be done.

But again, keep the meetings short. Encourage discussions between project and line managers to sort out problems and solutions before the meeting. If you have to shorten an interesting discussion, refer the completion of the discussion to a separate session after the pulse meeting. This is even more important if the discussion only involves a few of the people present, or if the input of people who are not present is needed.

A.4 Escalation and pulse rooms

Individual pulse meetings have the potential to create many positive effects, but it is when they are combined that they become really powerful.

The combination can be done both through communication between meetings (e.g. to provide for quick escalation of problems) and through assembling different types of work-boards in a common pulse room.

Communication between pulse meetings

You can speed up communication between both functions and hierarchical levels through connecting pulse meetings.

Connected pulse meetings provide the opportunity to catch all deviations in the working-level pulse meetings and relay the tricky or risky ones to other pulse meetings. This way, a deviation can reach the right receiving team within an hour or two. The appropriate receiver of a deviation is the person or team that has the capability to make a quick adjustment to get back to the base level. Some deviations must also be relayed to an improvement-pulse meeting in order to find the root cause and solve the problem for good. This means the issue can end up with another team that possesses the problem-solving ability themselves, or with a manager who has the authority to order external support.

It is important to try to catch the "buds of the problems", that is, signs of deviations that have not yet caused serious problems.

Based on a signaling system with colors that is shared and understood by all teams, deviations may, in this way, be caught early and can very rapidly be transferred to the right receiver on any level. This will significantly reduce the need for putting out fires. Use your feedback to praise proactive behavior that helps to shift the organizational culture from firefighting to problem prevention.

Allowing too much upward delegation can choke any management team. It also prevents the lower level from taking responsibility for problems that they can solve themselves, or learn to solve themselves. Thus, see to it that every problem is handled on the lowest possible level. Give training and mandates so that you can delegate even more decisions.

Pulse rooms

A *pulse room* is a place where you gather several boards for visual control to enhance motivation, understanding and effectiveness – by visualizing the system, targets, status and actions.[88]

A rightly used pulse room reduces "departmental silo thinking" by creating good discussions on important topics that stretch across functional borders. The different work-boards should complement each other to support holistic and fact-based debates in order to deliver, improve and learn.

The work-boards, with constantly updated information on status and actions, constitute the core of a pulse room. Each board has a different purpose. One type of board is directed towards deliveries – tracking targets, progress to date and +QTE issues, as well as the quick-fix countermeasures required. Such a delivery-pulse board needs to be complemented by improvement-pulse boards focusing on solving the root causes of problems. Strategy-pulse boards are the third type of board. Their purpose is to challenge the present base level and lift it up to a new, challenging target level. Yet a fourth type is directed to visualizing current and targeted ability levels in order to coordinate and grow the skills of the team members. Together these four types of work-boards support all three goals of collaboration: to *deliver*, *improve* and *learn*.

The *team information* you need to post in the room may, for example, be a presentation of the team members, the agreed team rules and the latest news.

The *goal information* you need in the pulse room may vary from mission and vision statements (or pictures) through key performance measures, long-term and short-term targets to customer surveys and owner requirements.

88. Pulse rooms are sometimes called Obeya, which comes from the Japanese word for "large room" or "war room".

The *system information* you might need includes organograms with responsibilities per department, role descriptions with responsibilities per role/person, collaboration principles, process graphs, as well as descriptions of the agreed best ways of working.

The reason for making the different work-boards and the above types of information visible in the same room, is to bring people and tasks together in a systematic and pulsed way. Not only are people dependent on each other when collaborating, but the tasks are also dependent on other tasks. Take, for instance, the task of improvement, which can be triggered by the task of catching and fixing deviations. The task of (re)planning is similarly dependent on the frequent updating of current positions and targets. By visualizing the facts in the same room, you create the base for better discussions and, ultimately, both better motivation and better decisions.

Takashi Tanaka expresses the purpose well: "All the pulse meetings tie together all the efforts from all the employees into one network."

A.5 Leading pulse meetings

Below I have listed the most important things to keep in mind when leading delivery-pulse meetings. They are valid irrespective of whether you decide to lead the meeting yourself or let a team member do it.

To remember

In a small team, you need to prepare a few things *before the very first pulse meeting* in order to be able to create good discussions:

- **Discuss and document the purpose of the meeting.**
- **Decide on attendees based on the purpose.**
- **Discuss and document the agenda and team rules.**
- **Discuss and document the facts needed and who is responsible for bringing them to the meeting.**
- **Design a first (draft) version of a work-board that will make the meeting's purpose and the related facts easy to understand.**

Don't over-do it. It is better to get going and make adjustments as you gain experience than to get stuck in trying to perfect the above.

To be able to keep the meetings short and effective, with everyone actively involved, it is advisable to have the meetings standing up. Post essential rules, together with the meeting's purpose and the agenda, in an area next to the board. See figure 35 for an example of this.

Figure 35 Pulse-meeting reminder
... with the aim, agenda and rules for a delivery-pulse meeting.

Before every meeting, the leader needs to check that:

- **Everyone has done their respective committed updates of facts on the board.**
- **New tasks, issues and ideas have been noted.**

During the meeting, the leader needs to:

- **Keep the meeting short by maintaining discipline related to the agenda and rules.**
- **Trigger good discussions about deviations (new reds).**
- **Interrupt long discussions, referring the continuations to a later time, if needed.**
- **Invite everyone to participate and give their view on actions and improvement opportunities – interrupting dominant attendees when necessary.**
- **Involve everyone to be part of the actions decided upon, making commitments and putting up notes to prove it.**
- **Discuss/repeat vague conclusions until they are clear and understood.**
- **Remind attendees to keep the level of detail good enough for catching buds of problems early and coordinating the work in the best way.**
- **Ask follow-up questions on details to find root causes and knowledge gaps.**
- **Set an example of an attitude of respect, openness and care.**
- **Set an example by listening, looking for facts and opportunities, being brief and clear, as well as by recognizing good work contributions.**
- **Confront obvious and deliberate demonstrations of bad attitude, e.g. disrespect of others.**

After every meeting, the leader needs to:

- **Go and see root causes of reported deviations (preferably straight after the meeting).**
- **Reflect on what can be improved before the next meeting.**

Involve everyone to speak

Involve everyone to participate and get a turn to speak. We learn both from listening and speaking. Not only is it beneficial for the team if new ideas and perspectives are raised, but it is also good for the individuals who speak because they learn through translating their ideas and thoughts to spoken words.

Researchers Johnson and Johnson from the University of Michigan have, for instance, found that understanding is enhanced when thoughts and ideas are formulated into words. This is because we organize information in a different way when we need to express it to someone else, compared to when we try to understand it internally by ourselves. This information restructuring before speaking can provoke valuable new insights. Invite your team members to try it.

Furthermore, encourage everyone to question and disagree. One-sided perspectives often lead to bad decisions. There is some truth to the saying that new insights cannot dawn on a mind that is already made up. Thus, refrain from expressing dead certain positions yourself and try to keep others from doing it too, especially the dominant team members. Encourage the quiet ones to express their views and see disagreement as a starting point for good discussion. However, do not let arguing continue after a well-founded decision has been taken.[89]

Endurance and celebrations

Delivery-pulse meetings are directed at spotting and fixing deviations – day after day, year after year. It requires you to be consistent and persistent. Do not let a deviation pass just because it is Friday afternoon. If you are low on energy yourself, let someone else help you to keep a consistent and positive approach in maintaining the agreed base level you have set together.

See to it that the number of red indicators do not become either too many or too few. The right number of deviations, challenges and ideas are energizing. Too many will wear you out. Keep the improvement pulse balanced so that it doesn't tip over into too much negative stress.

Tough Care means combining clear expectations with authentic care for everyone. It is your job as the leader to find each individual's ideal balance of workload and challenges in order for everyone to contribute their best, and at the same time enjoy coming to work.

89. A good discussion based on respectful listening and arguing leads to a better decision, but not necessarily as a compromise. I once heard a manager at Toyota comment on this by quoting his CEO, Katsuaki Watanabe: "Pick a friendly fight – otherwise it might end with a compromise."

Realistic individual workloads, combined with team spirit, encouragement and support, prepare the ground for endurance and sustainability.

You can encourage people in many ways. One is to celebrate achieved targets, for example that the project milestone X has been accomplished, that the customers have been completely satisfied for Y days or that the number of realized improvement ideas has reached Z. The celebration can be something like inviting the team to a common lunch or a field trip to another organization.

Put up a *celebration chart* on the wall that visualizes the targets and the current status. Figure 36 shows an example of such a chart where every blue note corresponds to a finished task. There is one more task to complete before the first celebration target (of 12 deliveries) is reached.

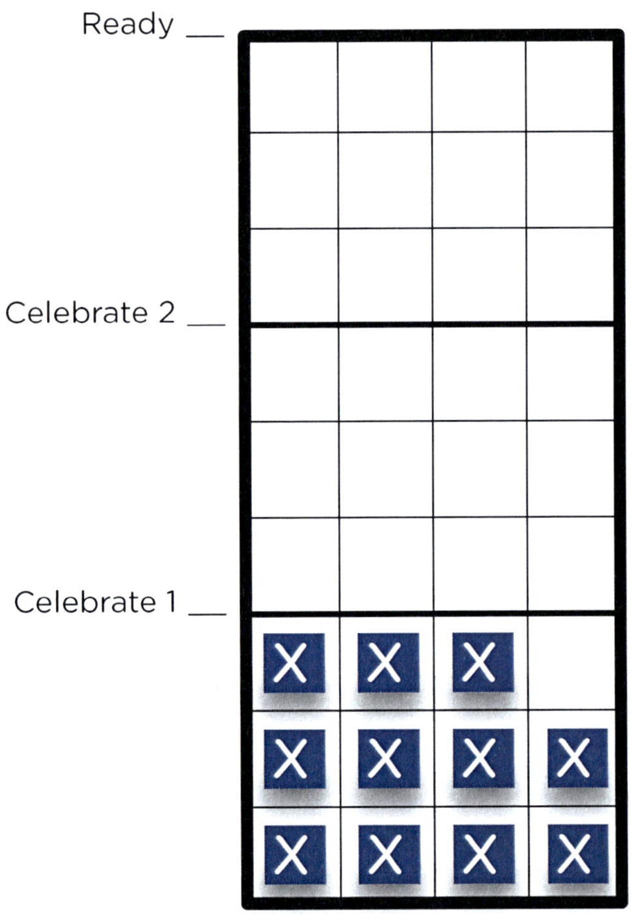

Figure 36 An example of a celebration chart
... with one delivery left before the first celebration.

Appendix B
Leader tools to improve

The tools described in this appendix are designed to support you and your coworkers in making better improvements. They provide support for all five steps of the Leader's Ladder, but most of them are focused on anchoring in goals, finding root causes and building systematic improvements based on PDCA. The tools are distributed under the headlines:

- **Prioritizing tools**
- **Tools for Leading by Objectives**
- **PDCA tools**
- **Root-cause analysis**
- **Leadership diagnostics**

B.1 Prioritizing tools

Your diary

Your diary is the simplest and most powerful tool you have. Use it to prioritize your time for making *leader contributions*. Be extra careful in scheduling time for:

- ***Seeing the game*** **and everyone's work contributions.**
- ***Go and look*** **for root causes to both positive and negative deviations.**
- ***Reflecting*** **on your new experiences from both a collaboration and a leadership perspective.**

Try to make your own *daily leader contribution schedule* with a go-and-look period straight after every delivery-pulse meeting. Complement with slots for seeing the game and reflection. Safeguard your schedule from competing tasks that may look urgent, but are less important.

Leader Contribution Study

You need to be aware of your leader contributions – how much of your time you spend on them and the effects they have on your team's work contributions. From that you can decide whether you need to spend more time on making leader contributions and how to maximize their effects.

A good start is to map out how you spend your time during a normal workweek. This is one simple way of conducting such a *Leader Contribution Study*:

- **Book 15 minutes for reflection at the end of each day in the week to come, with an extra 15 minutes on Friday afternoon.**
- **At the end of each day, allocate one of the following six codes to every task you have done during that day: (1) Leader contribution for securing/improving *means*, (2) Leader contribution for securing/improving *abilities*, (3) Leader contribution for securing/improving *attitudes*, (4) Administration, (5) Miscellaneous, (6) Waste. Write down the time spent on each task. Choose an adequate resolution, e.g. cut a long meeting short, and assign different task codes to different parts of the meeting. Add comments about your view of the quality/effectiveness of the leader contributions you have made.**

- **At the end of the week: Add up the time spent on each of the six categories and transfer the six sums to a bar chart.**

Study the height of the bars together with the comments you have been writing during the week. Reflect on what long-term improvements you can make and decide what you should try to do differently for the coming week.

Perform Leader Contribution Studies regularly by yourself. However, also try to involve colleagues to meet and discuss everyone's conclusions from their respective analyses.

Work Contribution Study

A *Work Contribution Study* focuses on work contributions, that is, how your subordinates contribute to delivery, improvement and learning. A simple way of doing the study is based on the template in table 5.

Start time	Task/activity	Color code	Ideas for improvements in means, abilities or attitudes	Comments

Table 5 A Work Contribution Study template[90]

90. In a very repetitive work environment it is advisable to change the "Task/activity" headline to "Disturbance/issue".

Give the template to one or two of your team members and ask them to fill it in the following day, guided by these instructions:

Running during the day

- **Note time and task in the two left columns every time a new activity is started. Differentiate between the core task and other tasks needed for preparing and checking/administrating the core tasks.**

At the end of the day

- **Color code each task in the third column based on the estimated level of value added as seen from the customer's perspective:**[91]
  1. Task with effective customer value added [DARK GREEN]
  2. Task with only partly effective value added [LIGHT GREEN]
  3. Task for preparing or finishing value-adding task(s) [YELLOW]
  4. Quality checks and administration [ORANGE]
  5. Pure waste of time [RED]
- **Make your suggestions for improvements in the fourth column. All tasks, except the dark-green ones, have potential for improvement. Remember that removing unnecessary activities is also a type of improvement. Question waiting times, interruptions, obstacles and conflicts. Try to relate all of these issues to possible improvements in means, abilities and/or attitudes. Suggest possible solutions or experiments.**
- **Use the fifth column for comments. Put an "E" for the tasks that can be improved easily. Put an "I" for tasks that are important but difficult to improve. Put a "?" when the actions needed are unclear.**

Ask the team member(s) who has done the study to present it to you and to the rest of the team. Discuss the findings and decide what to prioritize by using the idea-selection matrix described later in this section. Use the PDCA tools (described in the next section) to support the implementation of the actions decided upon.

It is often a good idea to complement this type of Work Contribution Study with a deeper analysis of the means and abilities needed to perform each task in the best possible way.

91. Normally this is done by taking a present customer perspective. However, tasks with the aim to improve and learn for the future can be distinguished by using a separate color, e.g. blue, complementing the green.

Use a *competency matrix*, in which the needed abilities are mapped to each individual, in order to visualize both the status and the targets. The matrix becomes the base for individual training plans and development discussions as described later in this appendix.

Use a *means list* in order to visualize all the means necessary for the different tasks. Such a list should include all means required to do a good job, including tools, work descriptions and other support documents, computer applications and available expert support. After listing the ideal set of means required for the specific task, go through the list and mark each item by ticking two out of four columns: (1) is adequate, (2) is lacking or can be improved, (3) is used in the best way, and (4) is not used or can be used in a better way.

If you find that descriptions of the best ways of working are not used, ask "why". Is the reason a matter of lack of training or lack of attitude? Or is it a matter of poorly updated base levels – standards that do not cover the best-known ways of working or are too limiting, given the variation of personal or situational circumstances? In any event, address the root cause and find suitable countermeasures, using the tools in the coming sections.

Matrices for creating good discussions and decisions

Very simple matrices can provide an excellent basis for stimulating good discussions. By picking two interesting and contrasting variables of a decision, and comparing the actual situation to them, you can trigger debate, learning and action.

The main aim is to make a good decision, in other words, selecting the best alternative. That is why I call them *selection matrices*. Here I will describe four examples of pairs of contrasting variables, but you may create your own depending on the challenges you face.

The four different tools depicted here are: (1) the *idea-selection matrix* for selecting from ideas with the two variables *effect* and *implementation effort*, (2) the *strategy-selection matrix* for selecting from strategies with the two variables *importance* and *relative market position*, (3) the *Eisenhower principle* for selecting from tasks with the two variables *criticality* and *perceived urgency*, and (4) the *risk-priority matrix* for selecting risk mitigation actions with the two variables *probability* and *effect*.

Idea-selection matrices

An *idea-selection matrix* supports the selection of ideas based on different levels of effect and different levels of implementation effort. The matrix becomes an excellent support for creating good discussions in your team for picking which ideas, deviations or challenges you need to address next.

The *effect* of implementing an idea can be estimated in different ways, such as the short-term financial return or, more widely, how it affects all the aspects of +QTE. I suggest you use the latter, but complement it with a detailed financial estimate when needed. Thus, the scale will go from "Large effect on +QTE" to "Small effect on +QTE".

The *implementation effort* can also be judged in different ways, for example as the estimate of hours multiplied by the hourly cost, or more comprehensively, taking into account the available people who possess the abilities necessary to implement the idea. I summarize this reasoning in the scale from "Easy and inexpensive" to "Difficult and expensive".

These two scales create a matrix, as shown in the example in figure 37.

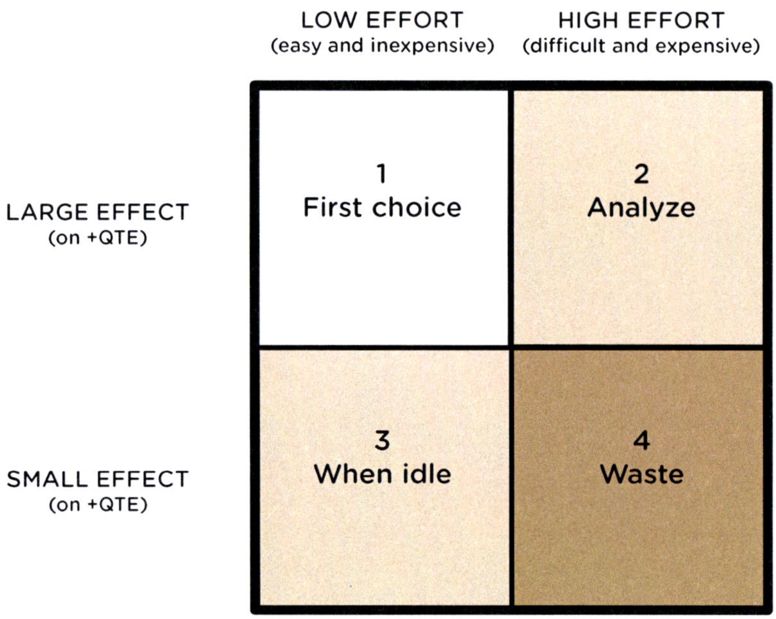

Figure 37 An idea-selection matrix
... for prioritizing tasks.

Encourage everybody's contribution in identifying ideas, deviations and challenges. In-between pulse meetings everyone should be asked to write post-it notes and put them in an in-basket for the improvement-pulse meeting. At the meeting, the notes are taken from the basket one at a time. A note's effects, and the implementation effort required, are discussed before the note is placed on the agreed spot on the matrix.

A note placed in quadrant 1 (the top left position of the matrix) has the highest priority – it has a potentially large effect on +, Q, T or E and an estimated low cost to implement (including able people available). If the note describes a concrete action with no negative side effects it should be considered a "low-hanging fruit" and should be implemented straight away. It might be impossible to estimate the implementation effort for a note describing a vague solution to an important problem. In these situations, if the effect from solving the problem is judged to be large, the note needs to be chosen – not for implementation straight away, but for further investigation of the best solution supported by PDCA tools (e.g. the A3 described in section B3).

A note placed in quadrant 2 needs additional estimates before it can be approved because it drives cost and/or it requires the allocation of scarce skills. These notes are the only ones that require proper financial estimates.

Notes in quadrant 3 are not very important due to their limited effects on +QTE, but on the other hand, they cost very little money and effort to do. Thus, decide to do them as soon as you have the required time available.

The notes in quadrant 4 should not be implemented. Take care to ensure that the person who suggested something that ends up in the bottom right of the matrix understands why the effect is too small compared to the effort. If you do that, you get an added advantage from the idea-selection matrix, namely that a person who may have been whining for months about "Why don't we just do this?" can leave the subject and move on.

The idea-selection matrix provides a tool for prioritizing, but it will also give you the opportunity to increase involvement and motivation.

Except in cases where you are in command of a very dysfunctional team where there have been widespread attitude problems, trust the team! If a note has been placed in quadrant 1, it should be taken care of in the near future – without the need for wasteful paperwork applying for the financing of a few hours – just do it. Be generous in the interpretation of the effect if a note is placed between quadrant 1 and 3 – the positive impact it will have on motivation compensates for the small cost, even if the other effects of the idea is limited.

Decide when formal estimates will be needed by using an added vertical line in quadrant 2 of the matrix. Notes placed to the right of that line will require a financial estimate to be done, while those to the left are okay to do as soon as the able persons have available time.

Start using the matrix for boosting your continuous improvement work. It helps you to control the influx to the improvement-pulse meetings as described in section 7.4, figure 19. Thus, it is an excellent complement to the PDCA tools (e.g. the improvement board) described in the following section.

Strategy-selection matrices

A *strategy-selection matrix* supports the selection of improvement strategies based on different levels of strategic importance and relative market position. The matrix supports the stimulation of good discussion in order to choose which improvement strategy to embrace.

Strategic importance can be defined in different ways, but it is commonly connected to what the customers view as important. Thus, a suggested scale starts with "Important (to our customers)" and ends with "Less important (to our customers)".

The *relative position* in the market is naturally defined in terms of a comparison to the present (and estimated future) performance of competitors. Thus, the scale on the other axis goes from "We are behind (our competitors)" to "We are ahead (of our competitors)".

These two scales create a matrix as shown in figure 38.

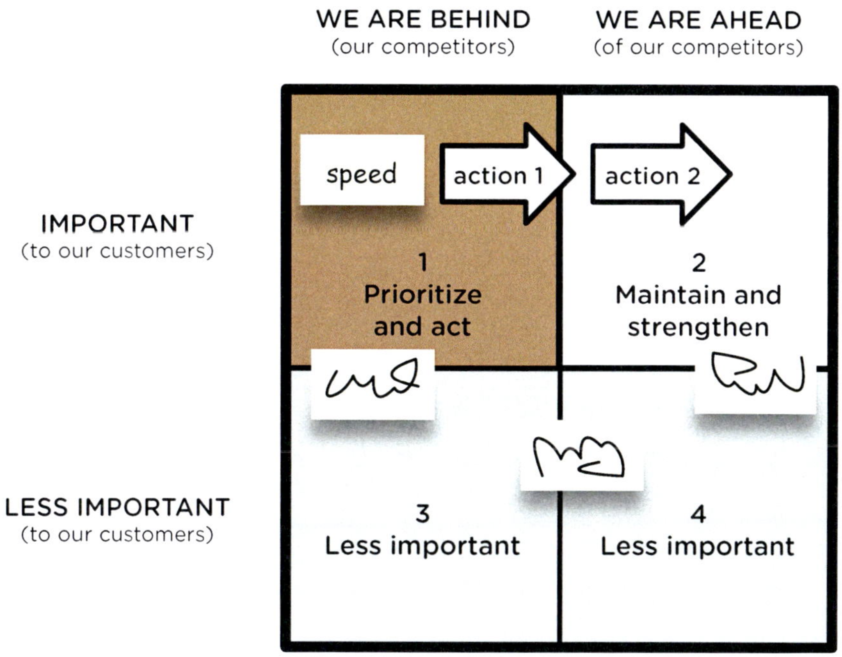

Figure 38 A strategy-selection matrix

... for developing strategies.

The strategy-selection matrix makes your strengths and weaknesses very visual relative to what is needed. Use it to discuss what would strategically be the best way forward, but also to trigger analysis of what the customers value the most, as well as how competitors perform now and will likely be able to perform in the future. Market research is an important part of the preparation – without reliable facts based on environmental scanning, the discussion will more closely resemble mere guesswork rather than fact-based clever reasoning.

When using the matrix, you need to gather the right people around it, bringing in facts and insights from different areas. Start with collecting facts and opinions about which areas are considered most important by present and future customers. Write the areas on post-it notes. Take one note at the time and place it on the matrix after comparing your present performance with that of your competitors. After placing all the notes, start to focus on how to improve the ones in quadrant 1 and how to defend positions in quadrant 2.

In the example shown in figure 38, four areas have been identified and put up on the matrix. The note "speed" has been judged to be the most important to the customers (placed at the top of the matrix). At the same time, it is judged to be a very weak area compared to the competitors' performance (placed in the far left of the matrix). Thus, it is the natural choice for deciding on an improvement strategy. The question becomes: How can we long term become better than our competitors in delivering our goods and/or services faster?

The conclusion from answering that question has been translated to a strategy in two steps, illustrated in the figure as the two arrows. The plan called "action 1" will bring the performance in line with that of the competitors, while "action 2" will move the speed of the organization past the best competitors' performance.

Because the strategy-selection matrix supports the identification of strategically important areas, it is a natural starting point for formulating strategic goals and tactics. Thus, the tool is a great complement to the tools for Leading by Objectives (LBO), described in the next section.

The Eisenhower principle

> ***"I have two kinds of problems: the urgent and the important. The urgent are not important, and the important are never urgent."***
> ***– Dr. J. Roscoe Miller***

In 1954, former U.S. President Dwight D. Eisenhower quoted Dr. Miller, president of Northwestern University, in a speech to the Second Assembly of the World Council of Churches. The above quote has subsequently been referred to as *Eisenhower's Urgent/Important Principle.*

The principle forms the basis for another way to use two variables; this time around urgency and importance, in order make better decisions. In addition to what previously was described as idea selection and strategy selection, these variables might be used for task selection.

The Eisenhower principle can be translated into a matrix in which "seemingly very urgent" and "seemingly not urgent" form the extremes on one axis, and "critical" and "unimportant" on the other. However, the principle can also be turned into a simple priority list, a list that can help you to remove some of your time stressors:

1. **Critical and seemingly very urgent.**
2. **Critical, but seemingly less urgent.**
3. **Unimportant, but seemingly very urgent.**
4. **Unimportant and seemingly not urgent.**

The most interesting insight from Eisenhower's principle is that we have a natural tendency of making number 3-tasks more important than number 2-tasks. As a leader, you have to be aware of this and avoid it rigorously.

It has relevance for the tasks done by your team, but also for your own tasks. The reason for this being that a lot of your important leader-contribution actions will be found in number 2 and they must not be allowed to be down-prioritized by less important number 3-tasks. If we continue to give preference to the less important, we will end up having no time left for critical leader contributions.

This is about being effective as a leader, not only efficient.

The reason we all have a tendency to prioritize the seemingly very urgent even when it is not critical, is that the demands come from others (often from above) and that the consequences of not handling them might be both immediate and unpleasant. In other words, you often have to show courage to say no to number 3-tasks in order to do more of the number 2-tasks.

Hence, schedule your tasks based on criticality, not on how urgent it seems to be. Test yourself once in a while. Assign the appropriate number from 1 to 4 according to the Eisenhower-principle priority list to every task you have done during the day. Ask yourself: "Have I been able to free enough time to spend more quality time on leader contributions? Am I really choosing number 2s before number 3s? Can I do more to delegate or remove the number 3s and 4s? Do I need to remove stressors by freeing some time in my diary to handle number 1s that come in on short notice – or can I even proactively reduce the occurrence of unnecessary number 1s?"

You can also form the habit of classifying each potential new task with a number 1 to 4 as soon as you become aware of it. Thus, the Eisenhower principle supports you to quickly choose the critical tasks, the ones with long-term importance, and avoid or delegate the others.

Reflect regularly on your choices and priorities. Do it alone, but also with colleagues in order to learn together.

Risk-priority matrices

The fourth two-variable tool I want to emphasize here is also about selecting tasks, but this time related to risks and opportunities. Such a risk-priority matrix supports the selection of tasks in order to mitigate risks and promote opportunities based on different levels of probability and effect. This matrix becomes an excellent support to stimulate good discussions about what is worthwhile doing, given the estimated probability, and the effects, of something happening.

The risk-priority matrix can be drawn as a two-by-two matrix creating four quadrants. The probability axis of such a matrix may consist of the states “Very unlikely” and “Very probable”, while the two states on the effect axis can be labeled as “Insignificant effects” and “Revolutionary effects”.

Use the risk-priority matrix at the end of an environmental scanning effort in order to turn new facts into actions. Complement facts with a brainstorming session to create a set of post-it notes, each with one possible happening that would affect the collaboration if it were to materialize. Take one note at a time and discuss the probability of it occurring and the possible effect if it does occur. Put the note up on the corresponding place on the matrix.

The notes ending up in the quadrant with high probability and large effect need to be addressed first. If such a note implies a negative effect (a risk) you need to ask: “What do we need to do to be more prepared if this should happen?”

If the note implies a positive effect (an opportunity) you need to ask: “What do we need to do in order to trigger this to happen?” The resulting list of answers can provide valuable input for your next improvement-pulse meeting.

B.2 Tools for Leading by Objectives

Both the risk-priority matrix and the strategy-selection matrix can provide you with excellent input for formulating appropriate goals. However, there are several other tools you can use to improve your success in *Leading by Objectives* (LBO) as described in section 3.3. I will explain five of them, namely LBO process descriptions, the ITA technique, goal graphs, strategy maps and strategy pulse meetings.

LBO process descriptions

A good *LBO process description* visualizes the holistic aspects of LBO and, at the same time, serves as a reminder of important details that are easily forgotten.

By using graphs you can make the process easier to understand. A complete LBO process description visualizes the important activities needed in order to go from environmental scanning and strategic goals formulation, all the way to implementing jointly agreed and concrete targets for each team and individual.

Your LBO process description needs to include all the seven main activities (or subprocesses) presented in section 3.3. That includes describing *how* you intend to:

- **Gather environmental market information, e.g. on trends in customer expectation and competitors' performance.**
- **Put together a balanced set of key performance indicators (KPIs), e.g. through using +QTE.**
- **Break down long-term goals to concrete and agreed-upon targets, level by level.**
- **Regularly work to measure gaps, and find and implement activities in order to reach the targets, in all teams.**

An LBO process description (as all process descriptions) can be mapped using different formats, for example in the form of a role-activity diagram as described in section 7.1.

Remember that a process document has no value in itself. It is when you use it for remembering important aspects and for improving the flow of activities that it will create value through good discussion, learning and better decisions. Use the following tools to support you in that.

The ITA technique

The *ITA technique* (ITA is short for "Individuals-To-All") is a very simple way to involve people in mirroring a message or responding to a question. The aim is to create a good discussion in which all participate. It starts by letting everyone individually reflect on a message, question or issue. It continues with one or two steps of discussion before ending with a summary and conclusions.

The reason for starting with individual reflection is that it forces everybody to formulate their own perspectives before listening to the others. To make it easier for the more introverted participants to air their views, you can let everyone talk in small groups before bringing the discussion into the larger group. As a result, you are then more likely to have a balanced discussion, with less domination by a few very verbal individuals.

The ITA technique consists of six steps:

1. **The facilitator (e.g. you as the leader) explains the aims (create a good discussion, increase understanding and decide on actions) and everyone's tasks (to write down opinions and questions and then contribute to the discussion).**
2. **Someone (e.g. the leader) presents a message or a question.**
3. **Everyone gets a few minutes to reflect and write down their comments or questions.**
4. **The comments and questions are discussed and summarized in small groups.**
5. **Each small group presents its conclusions to the whole group.**
6. **The facilitator leads a discussion and summarizes important conclusions and actions.**

This method works well in very large groups. In a very small group, or in a group where everyone is comfortable with expressing their honest opinions in a larger group, you can skip step 4 and 5.

It is possible to use ITA for very different situations. You can prepare carefully for using it for a very important issue, inviting a large group for the specific occasion. However, you can also use the technique spontaneously in a meeting (by using steps 2, 3 and 6) whenever you see the need for involving everyone in a discussion.

If you want everybody to understand the rationale behind a decision around a major change that will seriously affect many of the people, you can use ITA to mirror your message. By being open with facts, and opening up for questions and opinions, you will increase everybody's understanding of the reasons and logic behind it, including your own. It may also result in adjustments of the decision.

However, ITA fits even better in situations before a decision is taken. Using it wisely, you may get many perspectives on a question or issue.[92]

In the LBO process, there are many questions (e.g. related to cause and effect) that you can try it on. Not the least, use ITA for goal sharing (i.e. understanding top-level goals and breaking them down to concrete targets) by mirroring goals coming from the level above, and getting support through ITA in answering the question: "How do we translate this goal into concrete targets on our level?"

Goal graphs

A *goal graph* is a tool for visualizing and understanding the connections and causal relationships between goals. This, in turn, can be the base for good discussions on what is required to do in order to reach them.

The means-goals relationships created resemble the cause-and-effect relationships described in section 5.3. However, the former is created by repeatedly using how-questions starting with the wanted position, instead of why-questions starting with a problem.

Start from a really important long-term goal and answer the how-questions. These answers will give you a set of sub-goals that constitute the means to reach the main goal. Continue asking "how" from each sub-goal to a build a network of goals, with some of them being the means to reach other goals, see figure 39.

92. Three questions related to risk analysis are: "What risks can we foresee?", "What are the most probable and serious consequences of each risk?" and "What can we do to mitigate the risks?" By running each question through the ITA sequence, you will get many perspectives on risks, consequences and solutions. The risk-priority matrix from the previous section can be used for illustrating the answers to the second question.

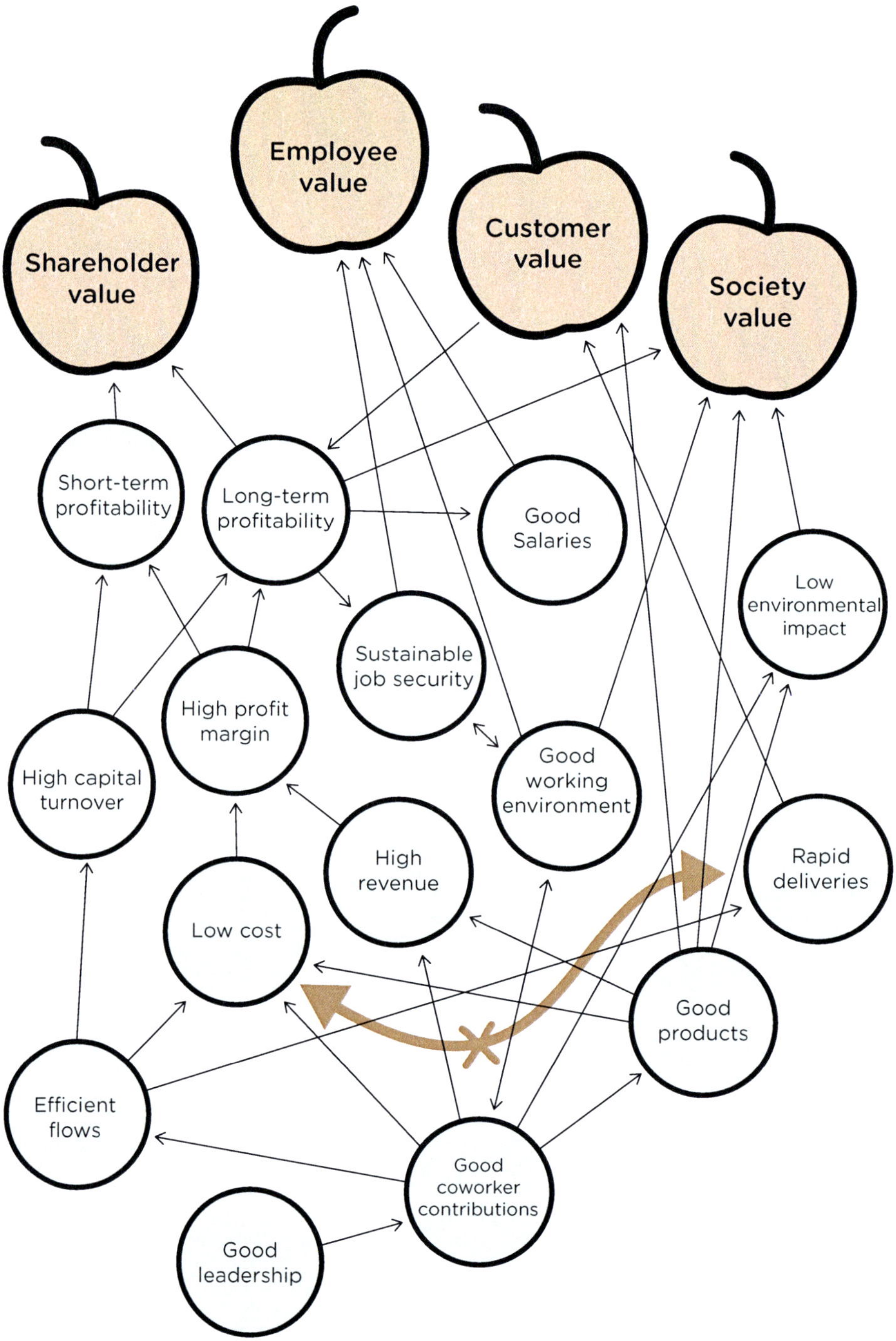

Figure 39 An example of a goal graph
... showing cause-effect relationships.

The figure shows a goal graph starting from the overall goals of creating stakeholder value for shareholders, employees, customers and society. Every black arrow in the figure should be read as "are needed for". The directions of the arrows are not always obvious, and can be used as a topic for good discussions.

The brown arrow with a cross illustrates a perceived conflict of interest between the two goals of low cost and rapid deliveries.[93] Such an interpreted conflict is extra important to debate around questions like: "Is there really a conflict?", and if it is, "How can we reach the best compromise?"

It is not necessary to start the goal graph all the way up from the stakeholder values. If you start from one of the sub-goals, for example rapid delivery, you can use the how-questions to dig down to very concrete short-term targets and actions.

Thus, the goal graph can be a good tool, not only for increasing everyone's understanding of the relationships and conflicts between goals, but also for having very concrete discussions on how to reach the different goals. Furthermore, the graph can also be a trigger to debate how the best balanced set of measures (e.g. KPIs divided into +QTE) should be set up. By relating your present or suggested measures to the graph, you can decide on a set of complementing KPIs without unnecessary overlaps.

Strategy maps

A *strategy map* is an illustration of how decided strategic actions, in the different strategic areas, together lead towards the vision. See Figure 40 for an example of this:

93. There are ways (e.g. by using Lean tools) to achieve both speed and low cost.

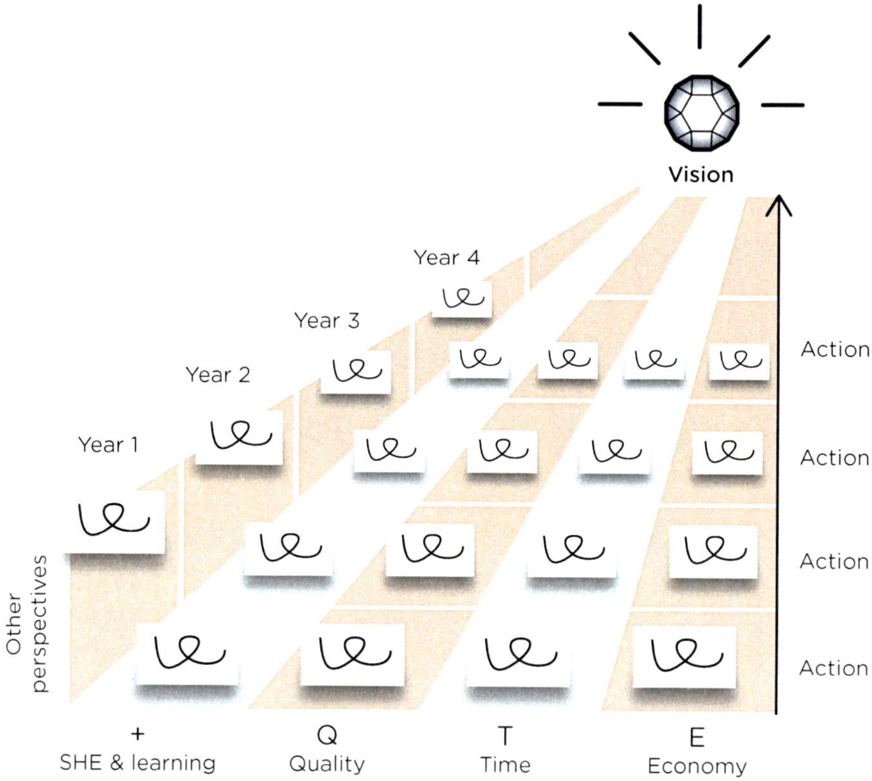

Figure 40 A strategy map
... showing major actions to reach the vision.

Strategy-pulse meetings

In *strategy-pulse meetings* you turn targets into actions, that is, strategy realization. It corresponds to the last two activities in the LBO process, where PDCA is used to plan and execute actions to reach the targets as described in section 3.3.

With the support of visual control, you can make the target levels, the actual performance from measurements and the status of started activities very clear. That clarity makes it possible to create more effective meetings, and increase the pulse.

A work-board for strategy-pulse meetings needs to present your strategic goals together with your current performance compared to short-term targets – supplemented by an action list showing the current execution status. It should be very easy to see the trends and gaps in performance (with color indicators), but also where improvement activities deviate from the plan.

Complement the board with supporting documents describing, for example, the mission, vision, principles and a strategy map.

Many organizations perform this type of *challenge-driven improvement* with such a low frequency that you can barely call it a pulse. However, by using visual control, you can speed up the pulse.

At Saab's radar facility in Gothenburg they decided to introduce a weekly strategy pulse. They formulated the aim as creating "continuous work to reach our strategic goals in which everyone feels responsible and participates". The method was based on the yearly goals (with measurement and target levels) that had been decided upon using the four +QTE perspectives. The management team started to meet once a week for 15-30 minutes, standing up in front of a work-board. Every meeting was dedicated to one perspective, which meant that all four perspectives (+QTE) were covered after four weeks.

This strategy-pulse method can be summarized as:

- **The meeting starts at the work-board with a short discussion on the last four weeks' performance as measured against the targets for this week's perspective – with special attention given to the KPIs with red indicators. The last four-week plan is then gone through and the corresponding activity notes are removed from the monthly plan.**
- **New monthly targets are derived from the yearly goals, taking the last month's performance into account. The new targets are then translated into new activities, possibly complemented by input from new ideas gathered in an inbox.**
- **Every action is noted on a post-it note with a specific color per perspective (in order to make the +QTE balance visible), assigned to a responsible member of the management team, and given a planned completion date.**
- **Every note is put up on the short-term planning board (similar to the VP-board described in appendix A, with a one-month horizon) in the intersection between the row belonging to the responsible person and the column representing the week of the coming month that it is due.**
- **Towards the end of the meeting, the participants check that the balance between the +QTE perspectives are maintained and that all the team members have become responsible for at least one new action.**

Strategy-pulse meetings can help you change your actions from being mostly reactive to being more proactive, and move from a culture of merely putting out fires towards a more challenge-driven one.

B.3 PDCA tools

All seven of the steps in PDCA, described in section 7.4, are very important for continuous improvement. The following two tools support you not only to remember them all, but also to carry them out.

The first one is the *improvement board*, which provides a structure to keep many improvement tasks going. The other one is the *A3* for systematic improvement, which helps you to handle one task thoroughly.

Improvement boards

The purpose of an *improvement board* is to support PDCA work for the bulk of improvement tasks. The really small and obvious tasks (the quick fixes that can often be done from day to day) can be handled outside the board on a "quick-action list" put up next to it. The really big issues need to be handled by an A3 team (with a reference note on the board), or if it is even more challenging, through an improvement project.

The board provides an overview of how far along the PDCA wheel a task has come, from the inbox, through the seven PDCA steps, until the verification of a solution is completed.

Each task is written on a post-it note. Sometimes a note carries a lot of information about the task (e.g. under preprinted headlines for names, due dates, target conditions, etc.) and at other times serves merely as a reference to a *problem-solving A3* that conveys the PDCA summary.

A note is first placed in the inbox, see figure 41, while waiting for the next improvement-pulse meeting. At the meeting, each task will be prioritized in the idea-selection matrix before following the other six steps of PDCA.

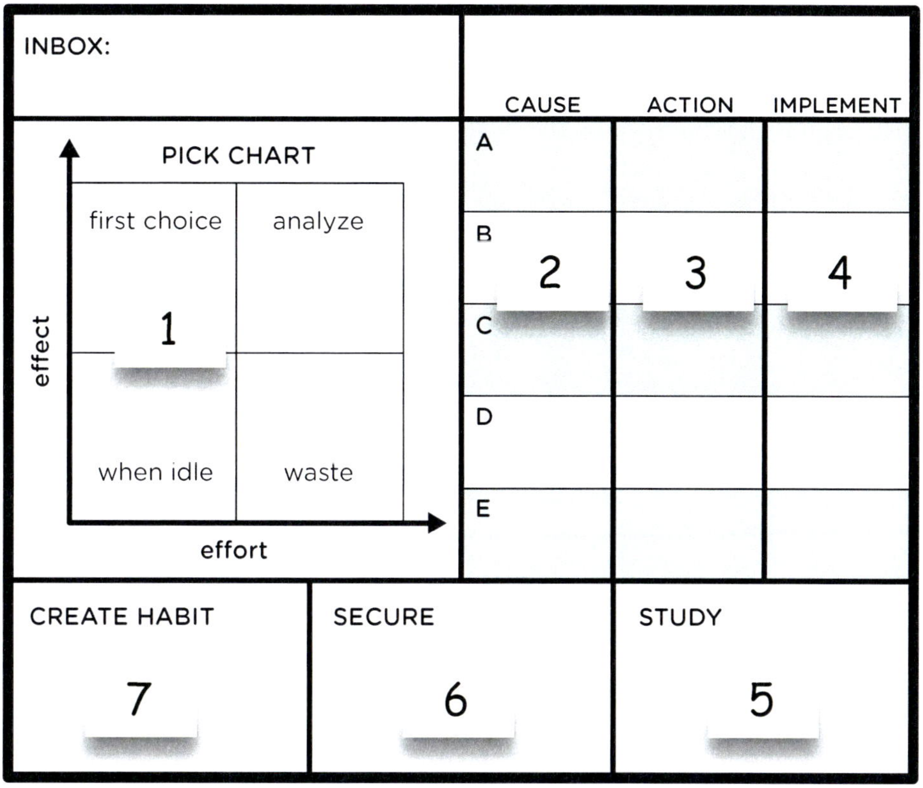

Figure 41 An improvement board
... supporting continuous improvement through PDCA. Every note, each describing one task, is moved from the inbox, through the positions 1 to 7 (corresponding to the seven PDCA steps according to section 7.4).

When leading an improvement-pulse meeting, you need to start with the tasks that have progressed the furthest. This means that you start by seeing if any notes at step 7 are ready to be moved, then go to step 6 and so on until your reach the notes in the column for root-cause analysis (step 2). When that is done, take new notes from the inbox and prioritize them, together with the ones already in the idea-selection matrix (step 1).

A3s for systematic improvement

An *A3* is so named because it is a story written on an A3-paper. One purpose of A3s is supporting systematic improvements. Such an A3 is sometimes called a problem-solving A3. A template for such an A3 will summarize each of the seven PDCA steps. Not only does it guide you through the PDCA, it also forces you to summarize the key issues in the problem-solving process. Thus, the A3 is a very powerful tool to coach your subordinates to advance their abilities to do continuous improvement.

Even if the A3 only provides summaries of the steps, it contains more information about the assignment than the post-it note on the improvement board. Thus, it is a good idea to use the board for getting an overview of the many smaller tasks and use the A3 for handling the details of bigger tasks. However, some organizations have chosen to skip the board and only use A3s, complemented by an idea-selection matrix and a quick-action list. Others, such as medical giant Astra Zeneca, introduced variants of the A3 – one for a very quick analysis of a deviation and another for a more thorough one.

You need to assign someone to lead a new A3 task as soon as the root cause of a problem is considered important and not obvious. This person becomes responsible to form a small team (that secures the necessary knowledge and perspectives to support the analysis), to summarize the conclusions on the A3 and to report progress, for example in weekly improvement-pulse meetings.

A problem-solving A3 template[94] typically contains the following fields to cover the whole story from problem identification and chosen countermeasures, to eventual learning:

- **Name of the problem and the affected process.**
- **Name of the person responsible (for problem-solving task) and the date started.**
- **Description of the real problem, relating it to a target (e.g. the current base level) and measures of success.**
- **Immediate containment and quick fixes needed.**
- **Root-cause analysis, choosing the most important root cause to solve.**
- **Chosen countermeasures to the chosen root cause, with an implementation plan.**
- **Dates for follow-up and verification of the corrective actions.**
- **Results and learning.**

Do not routinely write down the first symptom or apparent cause of a problem. Analyze instead what the real problem is, referring to an already defined base level or a new target description.

94. "Problem-solving" here means taking the performance back to a defined or agreed base level. A template for challenge-driven improvements, i.e. to raise the base level to a challenging new target condition, will contain very similar fields (as the aims are similar to finding a solution to close a gap). However, it would use some different terminology, e.g. "challenge with obstacles" instead of "real problem with causes", "new target condition" instead of "present base level", and "improvement/experiment plan" instead of "root-cause countermeasure".

Once you are satisfied that you got to the core of the problem, write up a summary on the A3, outlining where the symptom was spotted and what is considered to be the *real* problem.

Be as careful with the root-cause analysis and avoid groundless guessing. Use the *5-whys* and challenge the answers (see next the section). At the back of the A3 template, you can include the outline of a fish-bone diagram to support the root-cause analysis.

Remember to spread the learning from each finished A3 task and also to recognize the team members for good contributions. See section 7.4 for more information on the seven PDCA steps.

Used the right way, the A3 offers great support to come up with and implement improvements – and to learn. However, no tools in the world can replace the genuine will to improve.

Lack of attitude cannot be compensated for by structure, but it can be fought with it!

Takted improvement

Takted improvement means moving each PDCA task one step at a time, in a predetermined takt time and by letting new tasks in at that same pulse. You need to adapt the takt time and the number of simultaneous tasks to the team's improvement ability. A weekly takt time, coordinated with weekly improvement-pulse meetings, is probably a good start.

The improvement board in figure 41 can be used for takted improvement by using the five rows (marked with A through E) as limiting lanes for the number of tasks allowed to be worked on simultaneously. If you need to start cautiously, you might even close some lanes, for example using three lanes and allow only one note per lane. Little by little, you might open it up, and possibly reach the point when your team has the ability and capacity to keep all five lanes open. This allows for one note in each cell, resulting in 15 simultaneous tasks at the top right part of the board (in the PDCA steps 2-4, from root-cause analysis to implementation).

By preventing one task from passing another, you will be forced to pay closer attention to the issues that cause stoppages.

It is a good idea to let simple tasks with obvious solutions go straight to implementation. You can do that by creating a fast lane on the board, but an alternative solution is to handle these tasks separately in a quick-action list.

Lack of time or lack of ideas

Remember that it is possible to control the inflow of tasks to the improvement board as shown in figure 19 in section 7.4. You can set both your base levels and your target levels (as shown in figure 10) so that an appropriate number of new notes (with deviations, challenges or ideas) are gathered in the inbox of the board. As time goes by, and you build up your systematic improvement capacity, you can lift both your base and target levels in order to match the influx with your capability.

It happens too often that improvement boards are empty of notes. This happens for a variety of reasons, the worst of which is no will to make improvements, especially from the side of managers. Two other explanations, however, seem to predominate (at least officially), namely lack of time or lack of ideas.

Lack of time is a very natural excuse for not improving. It takes time to invest in a structure that provides for aligning of direction, coordinating work, addressing opportunities, and solving problems. Not taking that time can cause serious trouble – see figure 42.

Many managers argue that in order to reach the financial targets, work time needs to be exclusively directed towards delivering. Using expensive labor time to learn and improve is seen as waste. In the long term, however, quite the contrary is true, and an investment in systematic improvement may very well become the difference between success and failure.

By systematically learning and improving, you can free up time that can be used to make more improvements and, ultimately, to expand the business. To be able to trigger such a positive spiral, you must start somewhere. However, it is like most investments – it will start with a dip in cash flow before it pays back.

In other words, lack of time might very well be a relevant excuse for a limited period of time, but in the long run, it is not an acceptable reason for not allocating time for improvements.

Figure 42 Get going with systematic improvement
Above, dysfunctional efforts. Lack of leadership, neglecting improvement ideas (the compass, the bucket and the megaphone), has ruined the collaboration.
Below, excellent teamwork. Three implemented ideas have resulted in a lighter boat (using the bucket), coordinated rowing (using the megaphone) and the right course (using the compass).

Along the same lines, a lack of ideas is often a bad excuse for not improving. If you really want to become better there are always ways, or as Jeffrey Liker writes in *The Toyota Way to Lean Leadership*: "No matter how many improvements have been made, every process is still full of waste and rife with opportunity to improve." If the authentic will to improve is in place, there are lots of ways to stimulate idea generation. Most often it is done best by creating good discussions. Try to involve the whole team, and to bring people in from the outside, who can offer new perspectives.

There are several ways to trigger good discussions. You can, for instance, center them around: (1) deviations and challenges caught in delivery-pulse meetings and strategy-pulse meetings, (2) lessons learned and reflection sessions, (3) benchmarks and dialogues with customers, (4) risk analyses, and (5) external and internal audits or self-assessments.

Another powerful trigger for generating improvement ideas is workflow analysis.

Simple workflow analysis

Workflow, or *value stream*, *analysis* is a rich source of improvement ideas. Such an analysis starts by visualizing the workflow and ends with a prioritized list of improvement activities. Involve people representing the whole process under review. Perform the study through good discussions about present and future states. The fundamental questions are: "How is the value creation performed today?", "Where are the issues, waste and bottlenecks?" and "What do we need to improve and how?"

There are several tools for workflow analysis (WFA), but most of them share the same basic method:

1. ***Map* the real flow in the current state.**
2. ***Analyze* the current state of value creation for improvement areas.**
3. ***Decide* and prioritize actions needed to reach the wanted future state.**

In the following, I describe a very easy way of performing a WFA that I call *simple WFA*. It may be used with very short notice, and can be completed in less than half a day if the process you're studying is reasonable in size.

1. ***Prepare***
   - Invite people representing the entire flow that you want to analyze. Start by preparing a room with a big whiteboard or sheet of brown paper, post-it notes in five different colors and pens.[95]
2. ***Map* the real current flow**
   - Begin with a rough mapping of the flow and detail the parts with the greatest uncertainties/issues.
   - Use yellow notes for activities, blue for deliverables and green for external inputs needed.

95. If you choose a large piece of brown paper taped to a wall, you get the advantage of being able to re-roll it and save it for continued work. You may, of course, also draw the flow in a computer application, but be careful not to lose the visibility and interaction that the post-it note set-up provides.

- Start from the right by putting up the blue output notes (the value delivered from the process). Continue by adding the yellow notes with main activities, from right to left, until you reach the first activity and the trigger that starts it.
- Make the necessary adjustments so that the flow (from trigger, through activities, to deliverables) becomes clear and understandable.
- Complement the flow by adding yellow and green notes. Add arrows between activities to clarify the order.
- Mark activities that include critical decisions with an X.

3. ***Analyze* the current state of value creation for improvement areas**
   - Remind attendees of the importance of openness and a no-blame approach in creating a good discussion.
   - Include all participants in the validation of the map during the process of summarizing of the flow.
   - Include everyone to identify the parts of the process that involve the biggest disturbances in the flow, for example bottlenecks or quality problems, and the parts that involve waste, that is, non-value-adding tasks. Write all disturbances and other forms of waste on orange notes and put them on the map where they occur.
4. ***Decide* and prioritize actions needed to reach the desired future state**
   - Decide on a preliminary appropriate action for each orange note. Write the action on a white note and attach it to the corresponding orange note.
   - When all orange notes have been handled, take a step back and scrutinize the complete picture with the flow, problems and proposed actions. Ask the question: "Is it better to totally redesign the process rather than to do the suggested actions?"
   - If the answer is "yes" invite attendees to a redesign meeting in which you can start with a blank paper in order to create the best possible future-state process. The method for such a meeting is similar in the sense that it starts with the wanted deliverables (considering the customers' real needs) and is also mapped out from right to left. At the end, the effect and the effort required to create a completely new process must be compared to fixing the problems in the existing workflow (the orange and white notes on the map from the previous session).

- If the answer is "no", it is time to prioritize the actions, either directly in a idea-selection matrix or by referring all the tasks to the next improvement-pulse meeting by putting each orange note (with its white accompaniment) in the inbox of the improvement board. By using the board, you secure the proper PDCA handling from verifying the real problem to verifying the implemented solution.

If the scope of the analysis and the number of people involved are limited, you can perform a simple WFA in a few hours. There are more ambitious methods that will take considerably longer. They come in different versions and with different names, for example Kaizen Event or Rapid Improvement Workshop. These often encompass much more than mapping and analyzing – such as vision formulation and the concrete realization of the quick-fix activities possible to achieve in the allocated time (often 3-5 days).

B.4 Root-cause analysis

The visible is often caused by the invisible. In section 5.3, I emphasized the importance of uncovering the real causes of both failures and successes. Not understanding these real reasons behind the quality of the collaboration is a threat to your leadership.

To find a root cause, you have to start with something visible. Even a seemingly tiny problem can be used to reveal a serious root cause.

Root-cause analysis is the work to find the origin of a deviation, starting with what is visible. There are several tools supporting this type of work.

Fishbone diagrams

A *Fishbone*, or *Ishikawa, diagram* supports you to find and illustrate a network of reasons.[96] It is so named because the cause-and-effect relationships are illustrated as the skeleton of a fish, with the effect under study (often a reoccurring problem) as the spine and the different levels of causes as the bones leading to it, as shown in figure 43.[97]

96. It might be anything from easy to impossible to find cause-and-effect relationships. According to the Cynefin framework, systems might be simple, complicated, complex or chaotic. In simple systems the relationships are obvious and you can develop a best practice. In chaotic systems, they are virtually impossible to see. When system relationships are complicated or complex, it is not advisable to hammer out cause-and-effect relationships without gathering enough facts – the fishbone risks becoming a wishbone, derived from prejudice and exaggerated expectations of simple relationships.

97. A less visual, but easier to edit, alternative to a graph is to do the breakdown from effects to causes in a text document with an extra indent for every new level of answers to a why-question.

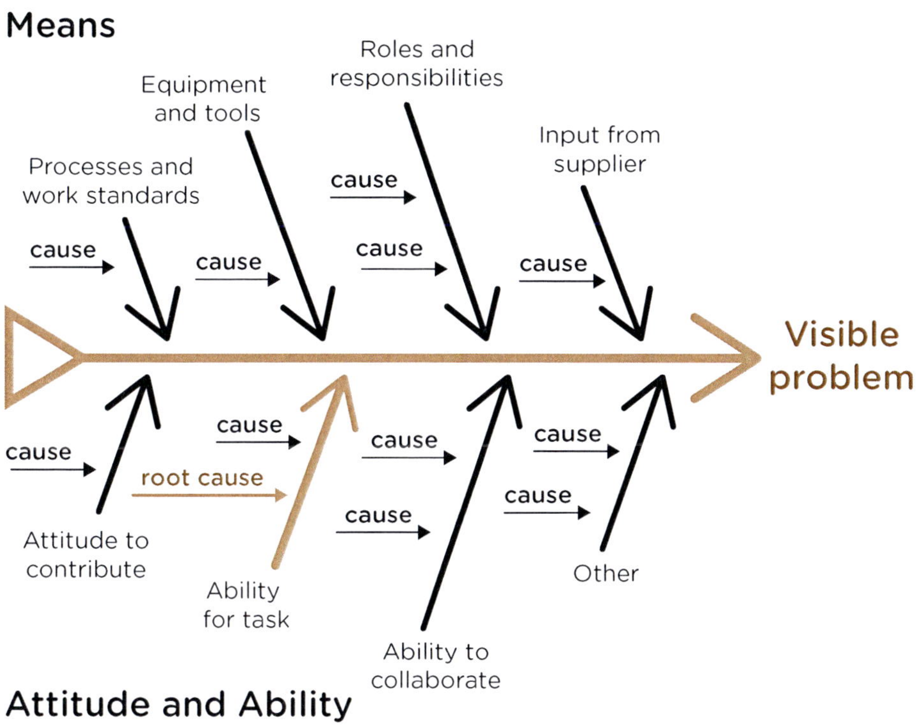

Figure 43 A fishbone diagram template
... showing cause-effect relations from a visible effect, via eight main cause areas (divided between MAA), to the root cause(s).

The method associated with the diagram guides you from the visible problem (or unexpected positive effect) to the causes leading to it. With consecutive why-questions from the problem, via main branches (cause areas), you dig deeper until you reach one (or more) root cause(s) that had the biggest impact on the visible effect under review.

If all key people with insight into the work are involved in the analysis, it increases your capability to go beyond the obvious and find the really important root cause. In order not to forget any important aspects, it is advisable to introduce main cause areas covering the three conditions for collaboration, MAA. "Equipment and tools", "Attitude to contribute" and "Ability for task" are examples of main cause areas that might explain good or poor outcome. These three, plus five other, areas are illustrated in figure 43.

The method is built around three stages:

1. Clarify the problem or other effect[98]

Write down a short description of the experienced effect you want to study, here called the main problem. Take care to make it very specific and concrete. Do not choose a problem definition of the type "we have quality problems", or not even "the number of customer complaints have increased by 50%". Rather choose a description like "we scrapped unit X yesterday afternoon" or "customer Y complained about service Z".

Complement the problem definition with a short explanation of why it is important to solve the problem so that it will never occur again.

2. Identify the root cause

Start with a go-and-look exercise at the place where the main problem appeared. Ask the questions "what", "when", "where" and "who" to understand the situation. Continue by repeatedly asking why-questions to every person involved. Do it several times, even when the answer might seem obvious.

Question old truths. Try to see another perspective than just what the people you are talking to bring up. Evaluate each answer and ask for more facts when necessary. Be careful not to miss any reasons by specifically asking about all cause areas, representing all MAA conditions.

This way, you will gather several reasons and possible cause-and-effect relationships that can form the base for a first version of a fishbone diagram. Adjust and validate the diagram together with everybody engaged in what has happened. Discuss which causes are the most important and decide on the one that you need to address. Ask the following question when choosing: "To what extent will the main problem be solved if we eliminate this cause?" Watch out for biased, circular arguments like:

- "We lost the game because of the lousy referee!"
- "How do you know the referee was lousy?"
- "He was lousy because we lost the game."

3. Choose a cause and a countermeasure

Gather key people with different kinds of expertise to discuss possible countermeasures to the chosen root cause. Ask several how-questions in order to see different perspectives and find details and obstacles that are not obvious. Decide on the most suitable countermeasure and write down the associated actions, each with a person who will be responsible for its execution. Use the steps 4-7 in the PDCA wheel to support the implementation, for example by adding action notes to an improvement board.

98. I assume here that the analyzed effect is a problem. However, I would recommend you to sometimes try the method on something that has gone surprisingly well. This can help you to spread and strengthen good behavior, as well as offer you the opportunity to give plenty of positive feedback. You may also try the method on a major risk in order to find its possible causes that, in turn, can be addressed by risk-mitigation actions for reducing probabilities and/or effects.

B.5 Leadership diagnostics

A root cause to a deviation is always an MAA issue, that is, it may be a *means*, an *ability*, or an *attitude* issue. Most often, the chosen root cause is a means issue, for example lack of a proper tool or lack of a proper method. Lack of ability, often stated as a lack of training on the working level, is also a commonly occurring root cause.

The absence of proper attitude or proper leadership is seldom put on the list of root causes. However unusual it might be in your organization, it is important not to overlook root causes related to attitude or leadership ability. If you choose not to see and act on these root causes, you will miss the biggest leverage to improvements in collaboration. In the long term, it is more important to address lacking attitude and leadership ability than it is to address the common means and ability issues.

Leadership diagnostics is a tool that helps you to do just this, to analyze and address all types of root causes, including deficiencies in attitude and leadership. The aim is to aid leaders in their growth by first taking an honest look at their leadership behavior before and after an important deviation (positive or negative) has taken place.

As with a standard root-cause analysis, you have to start from a very concrete incident or effect that you are curious to investigate the causes to. The starting point may be an unexpectedly good or bad result, but it also may be a sign of defective collaboration such as if something was performed the wrong way, or not at all.

A leadership diagnostic points out the causes as one or more of the three necessary conditions for good collaboration, MAA. The logic is that if anything turns out better or worse than expected, its origins lie in means, abilities or attitudes.

The leadership diagnostic can be applied on all levels in all types of organizations. You may use the diagnostic tool by yourself, but it becomes much more powerful if used together in a management team.

Thus, if you are the leader of leaders, the team can use it repeatedly in order to systematically learn from situations. However, it is extremely important to see it as a tool for leadership improvement and discussion – *not* for fault-finding and blaming. Everyone must be in agreement that the purpose is for everyone to grow, also upper management. After all, the end goal is better collaboration through better leader contributions.

Method for MAA Leadership Diagnostics

The following method is based on leadership diagnostics presented by Etsko Schuitema in *Leadership: The Care and Growth Model*, but with a new template and a terminology that fits the Leader's Ladder. The method has five stages, the first two of which are similar to what was described in the previous section about a traditional root-cause analysis.

1. *EFFECT:* Concretize the main problem (or other effect)

Write a short description of the experienced effect you want to diagnose. If it is a specific problem connected to a clearly identified event, you can skip the second stage.

2. *CAUSING EVENT:* Decide on a root-cause event to start from

Sometimes the problem is too wide to diagnose in one go and needs to be broken down to a well-defined starting point. If the main problem is reoccurring, you need to choose one occasion, preferably the latest. If the main problem is complex, you need to first do a rough root-cause analysis in order to pick one important event leading to the fundamental problem.

3. *WORK CONTRIBUTION:* Choose one person's behavior that impacted the causing event

Reformulate the chosen event to a particular action performed by a specific person. Again, be precise. For example, reformulate "someone scratched the products with a ring (which led to us scrapping unit X yesterday afternoon)" to "Chris did not put on protective gloves as stipulated." Or, using another example, make an issue, such as "customer Y complained about service Z", more specific; "Robin's response made customer Y feel disrespected".

4. *DIAGNOSE:* Analyze the individual contributions, level-by-level

Do the diagnosis for each hierarchical level involved, starting on the working level and follow the line of command upwards. Include upper managers and other persons whenever their actions (including lack of action) affected the event – directly or indirectly.

Interview everyone involved in the event in order to really understand the work contributions under review. Ask people, one by one, about what was done, said or expressed in other ways. Continue by asking about the expected or ideal behavior. When there is a difference between real and expected, ask the individuals about their view about whether it was caused by means, ability or attitude. Ask "why" several times in order to gather different explanations of what caused the difference.

Draw your own conclusion on which gaps in means, abilities and/or attitudes affected the event the most. Finally, translate your MAA-gap conclusions into learning and actions for the leadership on each level: "What could the leader in question have done before, during and after the event?" "What do we need to do now in order to improve leadership?"

5. ***DISCUSS, LEARN and ACT:* Give feedback and plan from the conclusions made**

Discuss the conclusions from the diagnosis (based on a template as the one shown in figure 44) with the leaders involved. If you managed to create a no-blame culture, you can, preferably, undertake the discussion openly with the whole management team. If, however, there seems to be a severe lack of attitude shown by a manager involved, you need to address it privately.

Set an example by openly questioning what you could have done better yourself, and what you need to do or remember for the future. Ask each manager involved what they can learn from the diagnosis, and discuss it without blaming.[99]

Let every manager involved commit to what they need to do, both immediately and more long term. Decide if the whole team must do something together, for example updating the common *leadership standard* or adjusting the related leadership targets.

Using the diagnostic template

You can use a template, as the one in figure 44, in order to guide you through the diagnosis.

99. The reason for some of the leadership behavior deviations found might be interpreted as being in the border area between ability and attitude. It is advisable to be generous the first time a deviation appears and treat it as an ability issue. That gives the leader in question (including yourself) a chance to learn and improve. If the same deviation keeps coming back, it is time to question if it is related to attitude. This rule is also valid when addressing deviations caused on the working level.

	Prepare	
1	EFFECT Main problem or other effect	
2	CAUSING EVENT that led to the effect (only needed when effects are too comprehensive)	
3	WORK CONTRIBUTION to study (a behavior contributing to the event)	
	Diagnose	
4a	**WORKING LEVEL**	
	NAME of the person responsible (partially/wholly) for the event	
	REAL ACTION What did the person do?	
	EXPECTED ACTION (What would ideal/expected behavior have been?)	
	EXPLANATIONS OF THE DIFFERENCES between real and expected (note different explanations if stated)	
	MAA-GAP CONCLUSIONS (What M, A or A gaps are involved?)	
4b	**MGMT tier 1**	
	NAME of the leader	
	REAL ACTION What did the person do?	
	EXPECTED ACTION (What would ideal/expected behavior have been?)	
	EXPLANATIONS OF THE DIFFERENCES between real and expected (note different explanations if stated)	
	LEADERSHIP MAA CONCLUSIONS (What could have been or needs to be done regarding leadership MAA?)	
4c	**MGMT tier 2**	
	NAME of the leader	
	REAL ACTION What did the person do?	
	EXPECTED ACTION (What would ideal/expected behavior have been?)	
	EXPLANATIONS OF THE DIFFERENCES between real and expected (note different explanations if stated)	
	LEADERSHIP MAA CONCLUSIONS (What could have been or needs to be done regarding leadership MAA?)	

Figure 44 An MAA Leadership Diagnostics template
... for supporting the analysis of a deviation.

Let's go through how you can use the template by returning to the harbor example in section 6.4. If you had done a traditional root-cause analysis of the event at the harbor, you would probably have ended with the conclusion that a main cause to what had happened was the lack of a collision alarm in Pocket #1. Another main cause that perhaps would have been highlighted is that the maintenance manager did not know the risks of using a bigger line wheel on Crane #1. In other words, you would likely have identified one *means* issue and one *ability* issue. The natural countermeasures to those causes are to invest in an alarm system and to train the manager. However, are these actions a reasonable solution to a problem like this?

Let's see what an *MAA Leadership Diagnostic* will reveal by following the described 5-stage method. (The resulting filled-in template is shown as figure 23 in section 9.2.)

1-3. Preparation

EFFECT: The harbor manager decides to do an MAA Leadership Diagnostic on the collision that had risked people's health and resulted in a long standstill of the harbor with serious effects on both customers and finance. Thus, in the top cell of the template, describing the effect, he writes: *Collision between Pocket #1 and Crane #1 on Monday xx-xx-xx.*

CAUSING EVENT: After a root-cause investigation, the causing event was found to have been the mounting of a too-large line wheel on the crane. Thus, in the second cell of the template, he writes: *The new line wheel mounted on Crane #1 was too large, causing it to collide with the pocket.*

WORK CONTRIBUTION: The harbor manager concludes that the most interesting behavior to start the diagnosis from is the action of the mechanic. Thus, he writes: *The mechanic NN did not tell the maintenance manager about the risk of collision when he was asked to change to a larger wheel size even though he knew what would happen.*

4a. Diagnosis of the working level

After a discussion with the mechanic (NN), the harbor manager concludes that he obviously knew what was going to happen and that his explanation is irrelevant. He summarizes his conclusions in the template as:

REAL ACTION: *NN changed the wheel without warning his manager about the risk. Instead, he told his colleagues that an accident was going to happen.*

EXPECTED ACTION: *NN ought to have to have warned his manager of the risk when he was asked to change the wheel.*

EXPLANATIONS OF THE DIFFERENCES: *NN blames the system for not requiring him to warn anyone in a situation like this. It seems that NN's intent*

was to discredit his manager for not knowing that the collision would happen.
MAA-GAP CONCLUSIONS: *NN had the means and the abilities required to do the right thing, but did not do it. NN showed a severe lack in attitude by not wanting to do the best for the collaboration. Thus, NN needs to be censured.*

4b. Diagnosis of the first management level

After a discussion with the maintenance manager (MM), the harbor manager concludes that MM was acting in good faith for the best of the harbor, interacting respectfully with NN. The harbor manager therefore concludes that MM lacks ability, not attitude. He summarizes this in the template:
REAL ACTION: *MM decided that the wheel size should be altered in order to save costs. He took part in the investigation of the collision, but did not do anything besides supporting the repair of the crane and the pocket.*
EXPECTED ACTION: *MM ought to have censured NN for behaving in an unacceptable manner.*
EXPLANATIONS OF THE DIFFERENCES: *MM was wrong when he decided to change wheel size, but he took and communicated the decision with good attitude. However, he did not reprimand NN, which amounts to an insufficient leader contribution.*
LEADERSHIP MAA CONCLUSIONS: *MM obviously did not possess the ability to handle challenging behavior from subordinates. He needs feedback and leadership training to be able to handle similar situations in the future.*

4c. Diagnosis of the second management level

The harbor manager finally analyzes his own behavior. He tries to be honest when reflecting on his actions both before and after the event. He summarizes his conclusions in the diagnosis template:
REAL ACTION: *I have given MM feedback and started coaching him in handling bad attitude.*
EXPECTED ACTION: = *See "REAL ACTION" above.*
EXPLANATIONS OF THE DIFFERENCES: *N.A. (no major difference).*
LEADERSHIP MAA CONCLUSIONS: *I have so far given sufficient leader contributions related to this particular event. However, I have underestimated the lack of attitude, here shown by NN and others. Thus, I have shown weakness in my ability to see and act proactively. I should become more active in seeing the game as well as in allowing time for reflection. I also need to be clearer with all employees of my expectations regarding attitude, e.g. by updating and communicating our policy (a means), highlighting requirements for safety, openness and honesty, as well as for everyone's accountability for contributing their best to the greater good of the collaboration.*

In summary, the diagnosis shows that the mechanic had the means and ability needed, but he lacked the *attitude*. Hence, he deserves being censured.

The maintenance manager has not shown any lack of attitude in this case, but he needs better leadership *ability* to handle discipline issues and he also needs support in supplementing some *means* (e.g. in the form of a clearer policy). Hence, he deserves training.

The harbor manager needs to strengthen his *ability* to see the buds of problems in order to support his subordinated manager earlier, before a big problem like this manifests.[100]

Diagnosing tips

When deciding on using MAA Leadership Diagnostics, always pick the most recent, concrete event. Do not always start from a negative effect, but try it also on things that have turned out unexpectedly well.

If you are a first-line manager, you may use the tool for all major deviations in your area of responsibility. If your position is higher up in the hierarchy, you must choose more carefully. Rather concentrate on the really big deviations, especially the ones affecting more than one part of your organization.

Be careful with the finding of facts. Go to look for them, and talk to everyone involved. Explain why you are curious. Ask "why" and "how" until you have seen the event from several different perspectives. After doing this, you can start drawing conclusions about whether there are gaps in means, abilities and/or attitudes.

If you suspect that someone is trying to hide the truth, you must sharpen your questions even more. Try to see through smoke screens, for example if someone blames a lack in means or ability in order to mask bad attitude.

Applied the right way, MAA Leadership Diagnostics is an excellent tool for leadership development. It is best applied as a team tool rather than as an individual tool. Thus, use it consistently together with colleagues, and do it for both positive and negative deviations.

When it has become a habit, all members of the management team can diagnose events naturally and rapidly – some events might still take hours to diagnose, while others can be done in minutes.

If you all take turns in sharing your conclusions in regular leader-pulse meetings (see section 9.2), the diagnoses can become the main triggers for good discussions in the management team. Such discussions should focus on

100. Because both managers were relatively new on their jobs, previous management has to bear the accountability for creating such a miserable culture. However, ideally the harbor manager should have been able to spot and act on signs of bad attitude earlier, e.g. by seeing the game, clarifying rules and expectations, as well as by training his subordinates in contribution management and in attitude-changing techniques, as described in the last appendix.

appropriate leader contributions, given different type of work contributions and MAA gaps. The discussions will make you anchor in a common value base (e.g. Tough Care with Courage). They will also give you a joint, and more mature, view of appropriate leadership behavior in different work situations. However, I must again stress the importance of an open and caring atmosphere when doing the diagnosis and the sharing of conclusions. If you allow it to become a blame game, it can do more harm than good. The higher up you are in the hierarchy, the more important it is for you to understand this. If the people providing facts and analysis cannot feel safe in trusting that diagnosis results will be used to help themselves and others to grow, the diagnosis will not be true, and the discussions will not be good.

Remember to set an example by openly showing your own willingness to improve.

Appendix C
Leader tools to learn

The tools in the previous appendix are directed at improving our ways to collaborate, but they also have the spin-off effect of providing opportunities for individual learning. The tools in this appendix are aimed more directly at learning, and specifically at the fourth step of the Leader's Ladder, challenging the individual.

These tools support you to systematically introduce learning opportunities. The tools are distributed under the headlines:

- **The Contribution Spiral**
- **Knowledge and innovation management**
- **Attitude-improving dialogues**

C.1 The Contribution Spiral

Contribution management is a way to help individuals to grow. When you manage in this manner, you are concentrating on the right input (contributions), trusting that the right output (result) will follow.

The basics are simple; each person must be challenged and rewarded for their contribution to common deliveries, improvements and learning. If everyone contributes their best to these three goals, the results will improve and the organization will prosper. Individuals cannot be held accountable for insufficient contributions unless they had the required *means* and *abilities* available. In other words, they can only be held accountable when they lack the *attitude* to contribute. You can read more about these fundamental principles behind contribution management in the sections 3.2 and 6.4.

The Contribution Spiral is a tool for creating a structure for contribution management. The aim is to support individual learning in order for everyone to grow their ability to handle both present and future tasks.[101] Each turn of the Spiral consists of four phases:

1. ***Challenge* to a clear contribution.**
2. ***Make arrangements* to ensure that the required means and abilities are available. Let the individual confirm with a commitment as soon as the means and abilities are in place.**
3. ***See the game* and give continuous feedback based on the real work contributions shown.**
4. ***Summarize feedback* on all contributions in a regular development discussion. Return to phase 1 and challenge to the next turn of the Spiral.**

By repeating the four phases you will help the individual to move in a positive spiral, as shown in figure 45.

101. This direct aim of *individual learning* is different from the common PDCA aim of improvements and *organizational learning*. However, using PDCA will, of course, be an important base for the individual's learning, as the Spiral also highlights.

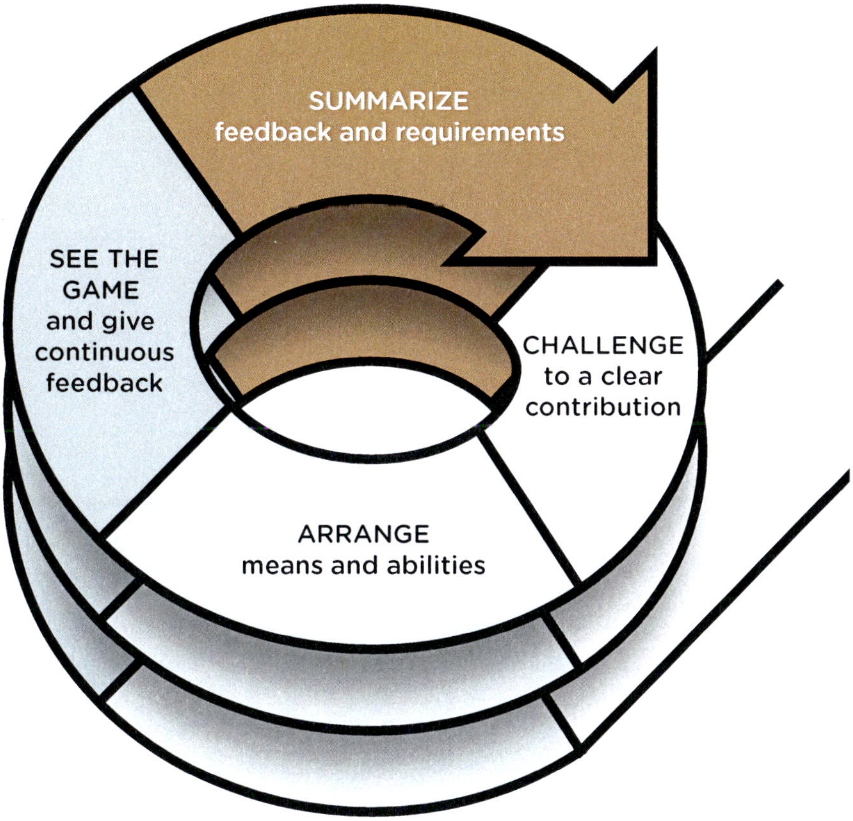

Figure 45 The Contribution Spiral
A model for supporting individual growth and empowerment through contribution management.

1. *Challenge* to a clear work contribution

Expectations of work contributions must be made very clear. It is a leadership responsibility, but it has to be done in a dialogue. Describe your expectations of the other person's contributions, both connected to present and new tasks. Remember to relate them to organizational and team targets, as well as to the individual's potential. Discuss if you see the needs and targets differently. When you think you have understood one another, ask the other to summarize the new work challenge they need to take on.

Challenges must be adopted both to the individual and to what needs to be achieved. The expectations can be formulated in a number of different ways – anything from clarifying a target and trusting the person to find the way, to giving very detailed instructions on how to contribute.

If the will to contribute is absent, you have the right to put up very detailed demands on that person. However, many attitude problems stem from previous bad management. Thus, try involvement, trust and frame management before resorting to detailed control.

You normally don't have to spell out the need to follow already communicated rules and regulations. This is often especially true related to what the team has agreed on, for example team rules and common ways of working. The team spirit, or group pressure, will keep most individuals in line with what has been decided. However, this should not prevent experimenting, if it's done openly and with the attitude to contribute.

Clear expectations form part of the means required to do the job. Thus, you cannot hold people accountable for something if the expected *work contribution* is unclear to them. It works exactly the same way as if any other means (or abilities) are missing.

2. *Make arrangements* to ensure availability of means and abilities

For the person to be able to meet the expectations agreed upon (under phase 1), all the necessary means and abilities need to be in place. It is the joint responsibility of the leader and the subordinate (supported by others) to ensure that they become available. However, because the means are part of the common system, the main responsibility for ensuring them rests with the leader. On the other hand, because the ability to perform the tasks is strictly connected to each individual, it becomes obvious that the subordinate bears a big part of the responsibility to acquire the skills needed – with the support of the leader and others.

Be clear when deciding who is responsible for what. If what is needed is not obvious from the start, try to iterate in order to build the knowledge about which means and abilities are required. In order for the work contributions to meet the expectations, you need to arrange sufficient means (e.g. time, budget, specifications, formal authority, tools, etc.), and you need to arrange for the necessary training.

An agreement that the required means and abilities are in place is like a *handshake* between you and your subordinate. It means that both of you agree that the means are sufficient, as is the ability to meet the expectations. Their handshake is also a *commitment* to a work contribution based not only on the means and abilities, but also on attitude (their willingness to contribute their best).

In extreme cases, you might need a detailed and signed written agreement as the handshake. On the other extreme, the handshake can be replaced by a nod, implying, "We understand each other".

3. *See the game* and give continuous feedback
If you plan regular time slots to *see the game*, you give yourself lots of opportunities to give feedback on *how* each subordinate contributes. If you spot contributions or results that do not meet expectations, you can use the *5-whys* in order to understand the reasons behind it. Remember that by being curious, you are showing respect for the other's work. Besides that, you are also setting a good example by demonstrating your own willingness to learn.

Acknowledge contributions to standards and praise unselfishness, for example in the form of helpful, generous and courageous acts. Make a note of the feedback you have given so that you can summarize it later.

4. *Summarize feedback* in a development discussion
At regular intervals, invite every subordinate to a development discussion meeting. See to it that you can meet uninterrupted. Start by letting your subordinate summarize their view of the period since the last meeting, focusing on the work contributions they had committed to give the last time you met. Then, summarize your view of their contributions based on the notes you have made while seeing the game (under phase 3). The second half of the growth dialogue should be about what needs to be done next, that is, challenges in accordance with phase 1.

Regular development discussions are an important part of the Contribution Spiral. Try to make them as natural as possible, maybe shorter and more frequently than you do today.

Use a template based on the Spiral to guide you through the meeting. The template should, for example, include space for feedback on work contributions decided at the last meeting – preferably divided into delivery, improvement and learning (phase 4). It also needs to cover space for specifying "next steps" in the form of new agreed contribution targets (phase 1) as well as the associated required means and abilities (preparing for phase 2).

Base your summarized feedback primarily on the notes from what you have seen (phase 3), and only secondarily on results and rumors. In other words, rather praise the contributions than the results.

The next development step could be something your subordinate is already doing, but can be done better or more specialized. It could also be a completely new task that will increase the organization's capacity, robustness and/or flexibility. A third option for the next step is for you to delegate one of your own tasks (see "other tasks" in figures 4 and 22) in order for you to free more of your time for more *leader contributions*. These tasks could include anything from gathering and presenting data, to leading meetings or performing root-cause analyses for problem-solving.

Contribution management, done turn after turn in the Spiral, and based on continuous scanning of both business needs and individual factors, is a way to create *systematic empowerment*. This means systematically building better ability, and at the same time, granting authority to and expecting accountability from each individual.

The method for systematic empowerment follows the Contribution Spiral. Remember that the aim is both to improve organizational performance and to let individuals grow towards their full potential. The phases in the Spiral support the process of broadening and deepening both ability and accountability. However, avoid training a person for a task you (or someone else) cannot offer them. Instead, try to be specific with which new business needs are required and fit the challenges to it. It motivates to train for an ability that you know is important and will be needed.

The more each team member grows, the more you have succeeded as a leader, and the less you need to control their daily work. You are then building an autonomous team.

A *feedback list* such as the one in figure 46 is a simple visual tool that helps you to remember to give everyone feedback (phase 3) and to recall what you have discussed when it is time for the summary (phase 4). The list can be on paper in the top drawer of your desk or on your laptop. The important part is that it is easy for you to use and that it gives you a reminder of whom you need to see next.

Feedback list for month: January					
	Week 1	Week 2	Week 3	Week 4	Notes
Maria	III	III	III		[illegible]
Ali	I	III	I		[illegible]
Charlie	III	II	II		[illegible]
Robin	III	II	II		[illegible]
Chris	I	II	II		[illegible]

Figure 46 A simple feedback list
... showing number of interactions per person and week.

C.2 Knowledge and innovation management

The Contribution Spiral illustrates your learning interaction with each individual. However, it is not enough to work with each individual's learning in order to maximize the common learning. So let us also look at learning from an organizational perspective.

Organizations create value from repetitive and/or once-off value-creation processes. In order to utilize the learning opportunities inherent in these processes, you need to design them consciously to provide and take care of learning. The resulting process design should support the creation and sharing of knowledge (e.g. by experimenting) as well as the capturing and storing of information.

This is valid for all value-creation processes, but maybe most obvious in research and product development (R&D). The *Golden Arrow* or *Knowledge Value Stream Model* (based on Kennedy, Harmon and Minnock's *Ready, Set, Dominate*) is a valuable illustration for learning in an R&D context. However, the model can be extended to all parts of an organization in order to build a supporting learning structure for all departments and processes.

Figure 47 illustrates such a generic model for systematic knowledge and innovation management.

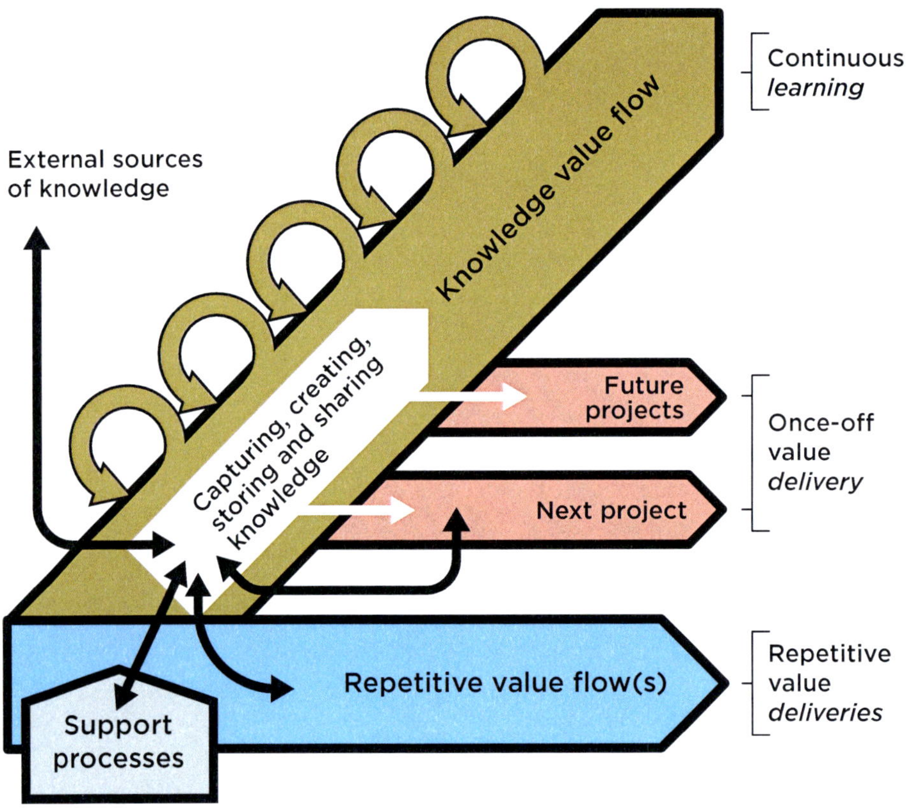

Figure 47 Systematic knowledge and innovation management
The knowledge value flow needs to be fed from four different types of sources/processes.

The figure illustrates an organization with four types of processes:

1. **Repetitive value flows that regularly creates customer value (sales).**
2. **Project value flows that create new or improved products/business/ways of working.**
3. **Support value flows that provide necessary input and support to the other processes.**
4. **Learning/knowledge value flows for creating and sharing knowledge.**

The first three types, together with external sources, provide important inputs for learning. All four types need to be designed and improved for better learning.

Figure 47 has a clear connection to figure 16 in section 7.3 in that *continuous improvement*, with the related learning, should take place in all processes while *improvement projects* are handled separately (illustrated by the red arrows in figure 47). In this context, a project can be about creating a new product or redesigning ways of working. Before a project can be started, enough knowledge must have been built up in the knowledge value flow (illustrated by the golden arrow). This work covers the early stages of innovation – anything from incremental learning and gathering of facts, to breakthrough innovation from combining completely new ideas and diverse solutions.

Building systematic knowledge and innovation requires coordination and leadership. Make learning your priority, or as Mary Poppendieck puts it in *Lean Software Development: An Agile Toolkit*: "A mature organization focuses on learning effectively and empowers the people who do the work to make decisions."

C.3 Attitude-improving dialogues

Intent refers to what we want to achieve. We have a conflict when two people have contradictory intentions, or in other words, when one party needs the other party to sacrifice what they want to achieve.

However, every one of us has the power over what we strive for – our intent. We can all choose to give up trying to get, and instead start to give – or at least reach a win-win goal in dialogue with the other.

Getting everyone involved in a conflict to compromise their short-term egoistic intent for the greater good, is the fundament for conflict resolution and thus for good collaboration.

Conflict resolution starts with understanding both sides' agendas, that is, all the intentions involved. This understanding offers an opportunity for one or both sides to adjust their respective agendas. Thus, by anchoring in the bigger picture and understanding the other side better, it is often possible to find concrete actions to resolve the conflict. This implies an about-turn from *demanding to get to offering to give.*

You can use this insight to turn a lack of attitude into a willingness to contribute. One technique for doing this is called the *attitude-improving dialogue.* It aims at changing an attitude from taking to giving, from griping to acting.

When using the attitude-improving dialogue, you start from a concrete situation that you believe is hurting the collaboration. The dialogue process I describe here is inspired by Schuitema's *gripe-to-goal* as well as Bodaken and Fritz's *managerial moment of truth* (MMOT).

The process implies that, after some preparations (1), you let the subordinate formulate their view of the problem (2), the root cause (3), the goal (4), the solution (5) and a commitment to act (6). It also includes your follow-up of, and the feedback on the committed actions (7).

1. **Address the problem as soon as possible...**

... once you have evaluated the situation. Arrange a one-to-one meeting opportunity. The earlier you take on an attitude problem the better. However, sometimes it requires some fact-finding before you can start. Use the following checklist questions:

- The actions: "Do I have sufficient trustworthy information about what really happened?"
- The person: "Do I know the subordinate well enough regarding their sensitivity, the history leading up to the current situation and their relationships with the other parties involved?"
- Myself: "Am I objective enough to have the dialogue straight away without falling victim to overly emotional behavior and/or preconceived ideas?"

If you are an experienced leader, and you know your people well, you will often be in the position to answer these questions with "yes" in a few seconds. If not, you need to postpone the conversation. In very difficult and serious matters, seek support from your superior and HR.

When you decide to start, you need to create enough undisturbed time so that you can be fully present. If you need to talk to several persons involved in the matter, start by talking to them one at a time.[102]

Remember that the dialogue should start purely based on the other's opinion of what has happened and why. Also, remember that an attitude problem is not only a problem for the collaboration, but also for the particular individual. If you can help to turn a bad attitude to a good one, you are doing the person a big favor – you are helping them to grow.

2. Reveal the core of the perceived problem ...

... by asking the subordinate to describe the situation and what caused it. Listen carefully. Validate what you hear by repeating, for example, "So, you mean that ..." or "So, you feel that ...". Write down your conclusions.

3. Sort out the perceived root cause(s) ...

... by asking the person "why" several times. Listen attentively in order to catch the root cause(s) of the concluded problem. Complement the "whys" with "when", "where", "what" and "how" to get a clearer and shared picture of the reasons. Watch out for the buddy trap, that is, to agree on seemingly wrong facts only to remain friends. However, also avoid questioning your subordinate's perceptions and feelings. Discuss facts and whether the related reactions are well grounded or not. Close the meeting and set a new time to continue later if more facts need to be collected – or if anyone becomes too defensive to continue in a productive manner.

Be understanding of what they say as long as the person doesn't deliberately lie or make disrespectful comments about others. They are entitled to their own views, even when that view is about you. Be prepared to accept relevant criticism of your own actions.

Summarize what you have heard by formulating your conclusions, for example, "So, you mean that the root cause is ... ?" Document the root causes you have found.

4. Let the other restate the problem as a goal ...

... by letting them formulate a statement like "For me, it is a problem that ... Thus, it is my goal to ..." Trigger it by asking "But what would you want it to be like?"

This reformulation might look trivial, but it has the potential to break a negative thought pattern. The step from "I have a problem with Chris!" to "I want to have a good relationship with Chris!" may look small when put into words, but it is great in mindset. It is about changing from a griping victim to an acting professional.

102. If the problem is a conflict with a colleague, work with both separately before you bring them together in order to understand each other's views and to offer their own contributions to a win-win solution.

The goal should not be formulated as a solution. To say, "My goal is to talk to Chris every morning" is to become too specific too early. By doing this, your subordinate might not only make the mistake of excluding better solutions, but may also forget what the real goal is – in this case it is to have a good relationship and not just only to talk regularly. Write the goal down together.

5. Find solutions to reach the stated goal ...
... by compiling a list of ideas together. Allow the list to become long. Let the other start and complement with new perspectives when needed. Reason out whether the solution will have a permanent effect on the root cause, or if it is just a step on the way. Book another meeting if you need more time to think.

Conclude by making the list shorter. Try to prioritize the actions that your subordinate can be fully responsible for him/herself.

6. Let the other commit to the actions ...
... by asking if they are prepared to do their part of the action list. If the answer is "no", your subordinate is accountable for not doing their part of the problem-solving. You need to make that clear to the person and also to document it for future reference.

However, the answer will most likely be "yes". After all, the person has been the main contributor to the process, from setting the goal to creating the action list. Agree on when the first of their actions should commence. Make the same commitment yourself on the things you need to do, for example supporting activities and activities needing your authority, such as addressing means issues and issues connected to other persons' attitudes.

7. Follow up and give feedback ...
... by regularly asking for progress and encouraging all signs of better attitude. Breaking commitments without a good reason is not acceptable. However, give generous acknowledgement if your subordinate actively strives in the right direction.

Going through the process 1-7 has, by now, given you a good understanding of the situation and the persons involved. Thus, you can stand steady in your leadership. Be braver when it is necessary, and trust your own ability to make good leader contributions.

Do what each situation requires for the benefit of all the stakeholders, not the least the subordinate you are trying to help grow.